READING RESEARCH

Advances in Theory and Practice

Volume 4

READING
RESEARCH

Advances in Theory and Practice

Volume 4

G. E. MACKINNON
Department of Psychology
University of Waterloo
Waterloo, Ontario, Canada

T. GARY WALLER
Department of Psychology
University of Waterloo
Waterloo, Ontario, Canada

ACADEMIC PRESS, INC. 1985
(Harcourt Brace Jovanovich, Publishers)

Orlando   San Diego   New York   London
Toronto   Montreal   Sydney   Tokyo

ACADEMIC PRESS, INC.
Orlando, Florida 32887

United Kingdom Edition published by
ACADEMIC PRESS INC. (LONDON) LTD.
24–28 Oval Road, London NW1 7DX

ISSN 0191-0914

ISBN 0-12-572304-0

PRINTED IN THE UNITED STATES OF AMERICA

85 86 87 88   9 8 7 6 5 4 3 2 1

CONTENTS

INDIVIDUAL AND DEVELOPMENTAL DIFFERENCES IN READING DISABILITY
Richard K. Olson, Reinhold Kliegl, Brian J. Davidson, and Gregory Foltz

LONGITUDINAL STUDIES OF READING AND READING DIFFICULTIES IN SWEDEN
Ingvar Lundberg

LEARNING TO READ: A LONGITUDINAL STUDY OF WORD SKILL DEVELOPMENT IN TWO CURRICULA
Alan Lesgold, Lauren B. Resnick, and Kathleen Hammond

INFORMATION PROCESSING IN SKILLED READERS
Geoffrey Underwood

RAPID READING PROCESSES AND SKILLS
Michael E. J. Masson

ACQUIRED DYSLEXIA: IMPLICATIONS FOR MODELS OF READING
Eleanor M. Saffran

CONTRIBUTORS

Numbers in parentheses indicate the pages on which the authors' contributions begin.

BRIAN J. DAVIDSON (1), *AT&T Information Systems, Lincroft, New Jersey 07738*

GREGORY FOLTZ (1), *Department of Psychology, University of Colorado, Boulder, Colorado 80309*

KATHLEEN HAMMOND (107), *Learning Research and Development Center, University of Pittsburgh, Pittsburgh, Pennsylvania 15260*

REINHOLD KLIEGL (1), *Max-Planck Institute for Human Development and Education, D-1000 Berlin 33, Federal Republic of Germany*

ALAN LESGOLD (107), *Learning Research and Development Center, University of Pittsburgh, Pittsburgh, Pennsylvania 15260*

INGVAR LUNDBERG (65), *Department of Psychology, University of Umeå, S-902 47 Umeå, Sweden*

MICHAEL E. J. MASSON (183), *Department of Psychology, University of Victoria, Victoria, British Columbia V8W 2Y2, Canada*

RICHARD K. OLSON (1), *Department of Psychology, University of Colorado, Boulder, Colorado 80309*

LAUREN B. RESNICK (107), *Learning Research and Development Center, University of Pittsburgh, Pittsburgh, Pennsylvania 15260*

ELEANOR M. SAFFRAN (231), *Department of Neurology, Temple University School of Medicine, Philadelphia, Pennsylvania 19140*

GEOFFREY UNDERWOOD (139), *Department of Psychology, University of Nottingham, Nottingham NG7 2RD, England*

PREFACE

This is the fourth volume in a serial publication devoted to original invited papers on reading. Our intention with the series has been to provide an outlet for systematic and substantive reviews, both empirical and theoretical, and for extended integrative reports of programmatic research. Our view is that such papers might in a modest way facilitate communication among the diverse groups concerned with research on reading and might make it easier for researchers, whether basic or applied, students, and consumers of reading research to keep abreast of developments in the field.

We are aware that any subdivision of the field of reading might well be at best contrived. Nevertheless, we have planned each volume in the series around a general theme. In doing so, it is not our purpose to present a unified perspective in each volume. Nor is it our purpose that each volume cover any particular topic comprehensively. Rather it has been our hope that the general framework provided in each volume will help to bring into sharper focus the issues that require the attention of both researchers and practitioners alike. In doing so, of course, we knowingly run the risk of presenting viewpoints with which not everyone will agree. But that is, we are convinced, as it should be.

The articles in the present volume focus on the nature of *varieties of skill* in reading and their implications for both theory and practice. The book begins with a report by R. K. Olson, R. Kliegl, B. J. Davidson, and G. Foltz on an extensive long-term study carried out in Boulder, Colorado on the nature of individual differences in reading disability. In Chapter 2, I. Lundberg reports on the current status of an on-going longitudinal investigation in Sweden on the development of reading skills and reading disability. The issue of identifying specific subtypes of reading disabled children is a major focus of both the Olson *et al.* and Lundberg chapters. In Chapter 3 the important question of the extent to which differences in instruction may contribute to the development of differences in reading skill is addressed by A. Lesgold, L. B. Resnick, and K. Hammond. G. Underwood in Chapter 4 surveys the basic research and theoretical literature on the nature of the skill possessed by the skilled reader. In Chapter 5, M. E. J. Masson discusses the processes involved in rapid reading and the nature of the skill in speed readers. Finally, in Chapter 6, E. M. Saffran describes what happens to reading skill following brain damage and discusses the implications of studies on individuals so disabled for models of the reading process.

The Editors thank the editorial consultants for this volume, Rod Barron, Derek Besner, Meredith Daneman, Maureen Lovett, and Ed Ware for their advice and support.

G. E. MacKinnon
T. Gary Waller

INDIVIDUAL AND DEVELOPMENTAL DIFFERENCES IN READING DISABILITY

RICHARD K. OLSON,* REINHOLD KLIEGL,†
BRIAN J. DAVIDSON,‡
AND GREGORY FOLTZ*

*Department of Psychology
University of Colorado
Boulder, Colorado

†Max-Planck Institut for Human Development and Education
Berlin, Federal Republic of Germany

and

‡AT&T Information Systems
Lincroft, New Jersey

1

I. INTRODUCTION

Some children and adults have abnormal difficulties in reading, although their IQ, quality of schooling, and emotional adjustment are normal (Benton & Pearl, 1978). These poor readers are often referred to as specifically disabled or dyslexic to distinguish them from poor readers whose disability is associated with generally low IQ, poor schooling, or emotional problems. There is an impressive amount of evidence showing that groups of normal and disabled readers differ primarily or most strongly in verbal skills (see Perfetti, 1984a; Vellutino, 1979, for reviews). We support and extend this basic finding in the present research. However, a number of recent studies have suggested that group comparisons between disabled and normal readers may conceal important individual differences (Boder, 1973; Denkla, 1977; Doehring, Trites, Patel & Fiedorowicz, 1981; Fisk & Rourke, 1983; Lyon & Watson, 1981; Malatesha & Aaron, 1982; Mattis, French, & Rapin, 1975; Mitterer, 1982; Satz & Morris, 1981). These studies have reported a variety of distinct subtypes within the reading-disabled population. In contrast to the consensus regarding group differences between disabled and normal readers in verbal processes, there has been much less agreement about how to characterize within-group differences among disabled readers or whether significant within-group differences exist (see the debate in Fletcher, Satz, & Vellutino, 1979). If there are major individual differences within the reading-disabled population, these different reading disabilities could have different genetic or environmental etiologies and require different remediation programs (Johnson, 1978; Lyon, 1983). Thus, a thorough description of individual differences among disabled readers is important for both theoretical and practical reasons.

The study reported in this article evaluates the nature and distribution of different reading disabilities for 140 children between 8.5 and 16.9 years of age. These children were referred from schools in the Boulder, Colorado area. A matched normal control sample was also tested for the purpose of group comparisons.

A. Theoretical Framework and Selection of Tests

The development of the test battery was based on the assumption that reading is a complex skill involving several component processes, and several basic cognitive and perceptual resources must be marshaled to effectively learn and integrate these component processes. Failure in reading may be due to deficits in one or more of the component processes and related cognitive resources. Therefore, we adopted a "component skills analysis" (cf. Carr, 1981; Frederiksen, 1980; Singer & Crouse, 1981) that seeks to identify the patterns of component skills distinguishing disabled and normal groups as well as within-group individual differences in reading disabilities.

The tests fell into two general categories. First, there were tests of component processes in reading and spelling that indicated each subject's use and general efficiency in phonological and direct visual access to the lexicon. The selection of these tasks was motivated by a theory of reading that postulates two different ways in which readers can identify words (cf. Coltheart, 1978; Huey, 1908; LaBerge & Samuels, 1974). Readers may analyze the sounds of letter patterns in words and see if the derived sound codes correspond to known words in their oral vocabulary. This approach is represented by the upper route in Fig. 1 that passes from visual memory for letter patterns through auditory memory for the sound of the letter patterns and finally to semantic memory. There is still a great amount of debate about the importance of this path in skilled reading (cf. Andrews, 1982; Humphreys, Evett, & Taylor, 1982; McCusker, Hillinger, & Bias, 1981; Singer, 1980; Parkin & Underwood, 1983; Treiman, Freyd, & Baron, 1983), but it is generally agreed that it must play an important role in the initial encounters with printed words as the child is learning to read. We will use the conventional term "phonological" to refer to this mediated path to the lexicon.

Alternatively, or in addition, readers may identify words directly by their unique letter patterns, without the mediation of phonological memory, as represented by the lower path in Fig. 1. Singer (1980) has argued that the direct route is of primary importance in reading for normal adults, and others have suggested that it may play an important role even in early reading development after only a few exposures to a word (Ehri & Wilce, 1979; Ehri, 1980; Reitsma, 1983a,b). The direct route will be referred to as the "orthographic" path to indicate its dependence on the specific patterns of abstract letter identities associated with different words. Although the operation of this path has often been assumed to depend upon the overall shape of a word, recent research in a variety of paradigms has indicated that letter identities are the primary basis for word recognition (see for reviews, Allport, 1977; Barron, 1980; Henderson, 1982).

The model in Fig. 1 is a much simplified representation of the alternate pathways in reading. The data will suggest that some elaboration of this model is needed to account for individual differences in reading processes associated with different types of phonological paths, and bidirectional interactions between visual, phonological, and semantic memory.

Two tests were designed to evaluate the subjects' skill in using the phonological and orthographic paths to the lexicon. Several other tasks evaluated the relation of phonological and orthographic coding to differences in reading regular and exception words, spelling error patterns, and eye movements in text. These different tests provided the convergent perspective needed to isolate important dimensions of individual differences among disabled readers. In addition, there were standardized tests for reading comprehension, spelling, and word recognition from the Peabody Individual Achievement Test (PIAT).

The second general category of tests included measures of visual and verbal skills in nonreading tasks. The Weschler Intelligence Scale for Children—Revised (WISC-R) included several relevant subtests. In addition, the children were tested for their speed in generating names for common pictures, their use of phonological codes in memory, and their eye movements in a visual tracking task. These tests allowed for comparisons of the subjects' component reading processes with their pattern of basic cognitive and perceptual skills in nonreading tasks.

B. Related Studies of Reading Disability Subtypes

Although individual differences in reading disabilities were noted as early as Bronner (1917), a theoretical interpretation did not emerge until Johnson and Myklebust (1967) proposed that reading-disabled children could be distinguished by having either an auditory or visual processing deficit. Related distinctions have been made by Ingram, Mason, and Blackburn (1970), Boder (1971, 1973), Bakker (1979), and Pirozzolo (1979, 1983). Boder's classification system has been the most influential over the past decade and it is related to several of the present tests for reading and spelling. Boder proposed that the majority of disabled readers have difficulty in phono-

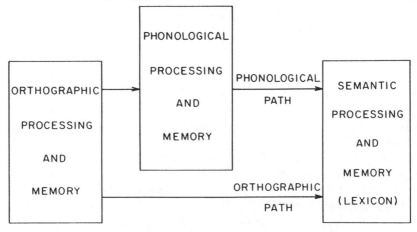

Fig. 1. Two of the possible paths to the lexicon in reading.

logically decoding words, and she labeled them "dysphonetic." In addition, a smaller subgroup was described whose phonological skills were relatively good, but their ability to recognize the visual gestalts of whole words was limited. This second subtype was labeled "dyseidetic." A more detailed description of Boder's subtypes will be presented later. What made Boder's approach unique was her reliance on distinctive reading and spelling patterns for the diagnosis of these two subtypes. In addition, she speculated that the two different reading and spelling styles were caused by different patterns of deficit in basic visual and verbal cognitive resources.

Our approach to the study of individual differences in reading disability was also stimulated by Baron and Strawson's (1976) distinction between "Phonecian" and "Chinese" reading styles among normal college students. Within the framework of a reading model that included phonological and direct visual paths to the lexicon, Baron and Strawson reported that subjects with strong phonological and weak orthographic coding seemed to rely more on the phonological path in reading (Phonecians), while subjects with weak phonological and strong orthographic coding relied more on the visual path (Chinese). Baron and other researchers have made similar distinctions among both normal and poor reading children (Baron, 1979; Mitterer, 1982; Treiman, 1984). Baron's reading styles seem similar to those described by Boder (1973), but he hypothesized that the different styles were due to "phonic" and "sight-reading" approaches to teaching reading (Baron, 1979).

C. Overview of Specific Questions and Article Outline

A number of specific issues in reading disability are addressed in this article and their complete introduction will be deferred to later sections. A brief overview is presented here to help orient the reader to the major questions and conclusions. In Section II, selection criteria and psychometric test results are presented for the disabled and normal groups.

The third section presents group comparisons between disabled and normal readers for phonological coding, nonreading linguistic skills, orthographic coding, and sensitivity to orthographic structure in regular and exception words. Consistent with previous research, the disabled readers are uniquely deficient in phonological coding and the nonreading linguistic tasks. The deficit in phonological coding is emphasized by comparing older disabled subjects with younger normal subjects matched in reading ability. The disabled subjects are still significantly worse in the phonological coding task. In contrast, the reading matched normal and disabled subjects are not significantly different in orthographic coding or in their response to orthographic structure when reading regular and exception words.

The fourth section examines individual differences in reading processes, independent from reading ability, within the disabled group. Reading style differences are inferred from tests of phonological and orthographic coding, regular and exception word reading, and spelling errors. Individual differences on these measures support a reading style dimension based on the subjects' differential use of the orthographic and phonological paths in lexical access and spelling. Analyses within younger and older age groups suggest that decoding processes change qualitatively with age, and some of the reading style differences observed among the younger disabled readers are diminished in the older subjects. Although the developmental comparisons are cross-sectional, the older subjects were identified as reading disabled in a previous study at about the same age as the younger subjects in the present study (DeFries & Decker, 1982).

The fifth section presents a "plodder–explorer" dimension of reading style defined by the subjects' eye movements when reading short stories aloud and silently. This dimension provides a base for the integration of individual differences in coding and spelling described in the fourth section. In addition, it reveals a strong link between individual differences in reading style and verbal intelligence within the disabled group. A separate test of disabled and normal readers' eye movements in a nonreading tracking task indicates that group and within-group differences in reading eye movements are not related to general differences in oculomotor control.

Finally, the sixth section considers the distribution and causes of individual differences in reading disability. Most researchers have argued that reading disabilities fall into a few distinct subtypes. However, the reading style and component skill differences observed in the present study fall on normally distributed dimensions. The implications of these distributions for the etiology of different reading disabilities are discussed. The question of etiology is also addressed by comparing individual differences in reading processes with patterns of cognitive skill in nonreading tasks. No significant relations are observed with perceptual skills and there is no evidence for a "visual–spatial" subtype that is related to differences in reading skill or style. However, the higher level verbal skills measured by the WISC-R are strongly related to individual differences in reading style among the disabled readers.

II. SELECTION CRITERIA AND PERFORMANCE ON STANDARDIZED MEASURES

Normal and disabled readers were matched on sex and age within 6 months. There were 111 males and 29 females in each group. This sex ratio is typical of many previous studies that have reported a three- or four-to-one ratio of male to female disabled readers (cf. Critchley, 1970). The subjects ranged in age from 8.5 to 16.9 years.

The exclusionary criteria for selecting normal and disabled readers were consistent with the majority of studies in the literature. The children were all from English speaking families, had at least normal educational opportunity to learn to read, and normal range IQ (at least 90 on the WISC-R verbal or performance subscales). In addition, the children could not have shown any direct evidence of neurological damage, emotional problems, or sensory deficits.

The schools were requested to refer children for the reading-disabled group who were reading at less than half of their expected grade level, and to refer normal children who were reading at or above their expected grade level. A proportional reading level criterion was used because the children ranged from the third grade to the eleventh grade. The actual deficits shown by the reading disabled children when evaluated against national norms for the Peabody Individual Achievement Test (PIAT) are generally less severe than the requested half-grade-level criterion (see Table I). The disabled group's average proportional achievement of the national grade-level norms for their PIAT word recognition is 72% (grade level would be 100%). Their PIAT spelling is slightly lower (63%) while their PIAT reading comprehension is slightly higher (76%). However, when the disabled group is compared with the normal group, the disabled readers' average deficit appears much more severe. The normal readers average 132, 114, and 128%, respectively, of the national norms for their expected grade level on the PIAT recognition, spelling, and comprehension tests. This level of performance is close to the average in the Boulder area. From this viewpoint, it is not surprising that a teacher might identify a few children as reading disabled even when they are performing near the national norm on the PIAT recognition test, since the national norm is substantially below the mean for most children in the local schools. The disabled readers averaged only slightly more than half of the normal control reading grade level.

Some of the disabled readers in the present sample are more skilled than the commonly used criteria of 2 years below grade level on the national norms, even though they are substantially below their normal controls. These children certainly fit into the common "poor" reader category used by many studies but it is arguable whether their deficit is severe enough to be identified as reading disability or "dyslexia." Certainly the half of the sample who are below 70% of their expected grade level on the PIAT would meet the reading deficit criterion used in most studies of reading disability. For example, a recent study by Finucci, Isaacs, Whitehouse, and Childs (1983) used a criterion that would be roughly equivalent to 80% of expected grade level as an upper limit for reading disability. Although most of the analyses reported in this article used the entire sample of disabled readers, separate analyses were also performed with the half of the sample below 70% of their expected grade level on word recognition. Some of these analyses are presented in the fifth section. In general, the results of the group comparisons and the within-group individual differences analyses for those subjects below the 70% criterion are similar to those for the entire sample.

A final issue in subject selection is that beyond the minimum criterion of at least 90 on either the WISC-R verbal or performance scales, there was no attempt to match normal and disabled readers on IQ, and there are significant group differences for both verbal and performance IQ (see Table I). There were two major reasons for this strategy. First, the disabled readers fall around the normal IQ range and would therefore be expected to read normally, as do most children from this IQ range in the Boulder area. Second, the primary focus of this research was on the within-group differences among disabled readers who meet the minimum 90 IQ criterion, rather than on comparisons with IQ matched normal readers. However, it can be clearly demonstrated that the group differences in reading ability are not simply based on IQ differences. Comparisons are presented in the right half of Table I for a subset of disabled and normal readers who were matched on mean verbal IQ by deleting all disabled readers below 100 full-scale IQ and all normal readers above 120 full-scale IQ. Matching on verbal IQ is a conservative approach. Most studies match on performance IQ, since reading deficits may actually cause a depression in verbal IQ. It can be seen in Table I that substantial and significant differences in reading ability are still present. (The significance criterion for all statistical analyses in this chapter is $p < .05$, two-tailed.) In fact, matching on verbal IQ results in diminished differences from the whole sample of only 11% for PIAT recognition, 13% for PIAT spelling, and 19% for PIAT comprehension. It is clear from these comparisons that the disabled group presents a specific deficit in reading, and the IQ differences between the complete samples do not make a substantial contribution to the group differences in reading ability. It may seem surprising that after reducing the verbal IQ difference for the selected groups by 13 points, there is only an 11% decrease in the substantial group difference in word recognition. This result emphasizes the relative independence in this reading-disabled sample between reading ability and the higher level verbal skills measured by the WISC-R verbal subscale.

A number of studies that have used the WISC-R have noted that disabled readers are more deficient on some of the subtests than others. About two-thirds are lower on the verbal subscale than on the performance subscale (Gordon, 1983). Two specific subtests often show the greatest discrepancy: Disabled readers matched in full scale IQ with normal readers are usually above normal in block design and substantially below normal in digit span

TABLE I

WISC-R Full Scale IQ (FSIQ), Verbal IQ (VIQ), Performance IQ (PIQ), and PIAT Reading Recognition (REC), Comprehension (COMP), and Spelling (SPELL) Grade Equivalents for Disabled and Normal Readers

	All subjects		IQ matched groups	
	Disabled ($n = 140$)	Normal ($n = 140$)	Disabled ($n = 74$)	Normal ($n = 92$)
FSIQ	102	113[a]	109	108
VIQ	100	114[a]	107	108
PIQ	104	112[a]	110	106[a]
REC	5.0	9.4[a]	5.2	9.1[a]
COMP	5.4	9.1[a]	5.7	8.7[a]
SPELL	4.3	8.1[a]	4.3	7.6[a]
Age	12.8	12.8	12.7	12.9

[a] $p > .01$, for the difference between groups.

(Gordon, 1983; Naidoo, 1972). This pattern is also present for our disabled and normal readers when they are equated on full-scale IQ. The digit-span deficit has been the focus of many studies and it is one of the more reliable findings in the literature (see Jorm, 1983, for a review). Moore, Kagan, Sahl, and Grant (1982) have also found large memory span deficits for a variety of other stimuli besides digits. Cohen and Netley (1981) reported that the memory deficit is present independent from group differences in rehearsal strategies. Katz, Shankweiler, and Liberman (1981) found that the deficit was specific to stimuli that could be labeled, which suggests that the underlying deficit is in phonetic memory. The first experiment to be described in the following section evaluated group and age differences in the use of phonetic memory codes for words.

III. GROUP DIFFERENCES BETWEEN DISABLED AND NORMAL READERS

In this section, group differences between disabled and normal readers are reported for three sets of experiments. The first set includes two tasks that evaluated the subjects' use of phonetic codes in memory and their speed of name code retrieval for pictures. Through these tests we hoped to identify basic language skills that might be related to group differences in reading ability as well as within-group differences in reading style. The second set of tests evaluated the subjects skill in using the phonological and orthographic paths in lexical access. In the third set of tests, subjects read regular and exception words, which were intended to evaluate their relative use of phonological and orthographic coding when reading.

A. Phonetic Memory

Many studies have shown that disabled readers, as a group, are deficient in their ability to deal analytically with the sounds of language. These deficits include the ability to segment spoken words into phonemes (Liberman, Shankweiler, Fisher, & Carter, 1974), and the ability to make rhyming judgments for reviews (see Gleitman & Rozin, 1977; Frith, 1981). In addition, Shankweiler, Liberman, Mark, Fowler, and Fisher (1980) found that young normal readers used phonetic codes in memory for lists of letters, but young disabled readers did not. This group difference was present regardless of whether the stimuli were presented in the visual or auditory modalities. Similar group differences have been reported for words and sentences as well as letters (Mann, Liberman, & Shankweiler, 1980), and in recognition memory as well as recall (Byrne & Shea, 1979; Mark, Shankweiler, Liberman, & Fowler, 1977).

It seemed from the above studies that a test of phonetic memory would provide a measure of individual differences in a basic language skill that was related to reading ability, and perhaps also to within-group differences in reading style and phonological skill. The present test of phonetic memory was based on the study by Mark et al. (1977). They found that second-grade normal readers were more likely than second-grade poor readers to recognize words falsely that were phonetically similar to words from a list they had read previously. This indicated that for normal readers but not disabled readers, the words previously seen had been stored in memory using a phonetic code.

The youngest disabled and normal readers in the present study are nearly the same age as the Mark et al. subjects. These younger subjects replicate the Mark et al. results, but our older disabled and normal readers do not (see Olson, Davidson, Kliegl, & Davies, 1984, for further details). Two other studies have failed to find phonetic memory confusion differences between disabled and normal readers around twelve years of age (Johnston, 1982; Siegel & Linden, 1984). Also, Hall, Wilson, Humphreys, Tinzmann, and Bowyer (1983) failed to replicate Shankweiler et al. (1980) with good and poor readers in the second grade. Hall et al. argued from their null result that there are no phonetic memory deficits in disabled readers. In contrast, we argue from our pattern of results that older disabled readers may use phonetic codes in memory for words, but their phonetic codes are less precise than those of normal readers. The primary basis for this argument is that the older disabled readers in the present study actually show a larger rhyming confusion effect than the older normal readers. Unfortunately, since rhyming confusion may not be linearly related to phonetic memory and the measure is somewhat unreliable, it is not suitable for comparison with the other measures of reading processes. The following task provides a measure of basic language skills that is more interpretable across the age range.

B. Picture-Naming Speed and Automatic Responses to Print

If disabled readers are generally deficient in their linguistic production abilities, then they might be deficient not only in reading words but also in naming pictures. In fact, several studies have found that disabled readers as a group are both slower and less accurate than normal readers in naming pictures of familiar objects (Denkla & Rudel, 1976; Jansky & de Hirsch, 1972; Katz, 1982; Wolf, 1981). Furthermore, Katz (1982) and Wolf (1981) have shown that the deficit is due to linguistic rather than perceptual factors.

In the present test, pictures of common objects were used so that the subjects would recognize all of them and be highly familiar with their names. Thus, errors in naming were infrequent, and the dependent variable was voice-onset time. Slower naming times could be associated with individual differences in the speed of access to the phonological code and/or speed in activating the articulatory codes (Perfetti, 1984b). In either case, slower picture naming could indicate a basic deficit in language skills outside of the reading process.

The picture-naming task was also designed to evaluate the subjects' automatic and involuntary reading of random consonants, pronounceable nonwords, and words that were superimposed on the pictures (see Fig. 2). Several studies have examined automatic reading processes by monitoring the interference and facilitation effects on picture naming that result from superimposing letters and words on a picture (Golinkoff & Rosinski, 1976; Guttentag & Haith, 1978; Posnansky & Rayner, 1977). If the subjects' response to print on a picture is activated automatically and involuntarily (the subjects are told to ignore the print), the resulting phonological and semantic codes will interact with the naming response to the picture. Unless the print generates phonological codes that are similar to the picture name, the subject's naming response to the picture will be slowed. We hypothesized that the disabled readers would be less automatic in their responses to print as indicated by the interference effects of superimposed letters and words on picture naming. Also, following Guttentag and Haith (1978), we

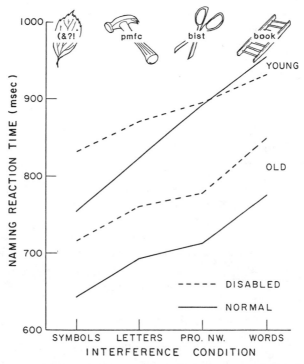

Fig. 2. Picture-naming latencies for younger and older groups of normal and disabled readers.

hypothesized that the disabled readers would show proportionally less interference from the pronounceable nonwords because of their deficiency in phonological decoding.

The major experimental conditions and important results of this study may be summarized briefly. The children named 130 pictures of common objects with four different superimposed stimuli; nonverbal symbols (e.g., =%+) that served as a measure of basic picture naming speed without linguistic interference, random consonants (e.g., *sbkw*) that would indicate automatic responses to letters, pronounceable nonwords (e.g., *dake*) that presumably would indicate the additional interference caused by the automatic generation of phonological codes, and words, that would cause additional interference from their familiar orthographic images and semantic processing (see Fig. 2).

Developmental comparisons of the naming latencies were made by separating subjects into groups above and below the median age of 12.8 years. In addition to differences in automatic responses to print associated with group differences in reading ability, there might also be independent age effects within the normal and disabled groups.

1. Basic Picture-Naming Speed

As can be seen in Fig. 2, the disabled readers are significantly slower than the normal readers in naming pictures with the nonverbal symbols. The slower naming times of the disabled readers may indicate a fundamental language deficit outside of the reading process (Denkla & Rudel, 1976). However, the size of this deficit is not very large in the present study, and naming latency is not a very powerful discriminator of group membership. The larger differences reported by Denkla and Rudel may have resulted from the rapid sequencing of naming required for a series of pictures on a page in their study.

2. Linguistically Based Interference from Print

There is a significant crossover interaction for the younger subjects between reading ability and the different linguistic interference conditions (see Fig. 2). Using naming times for the pictures with abstract symbols as a control condition, the young disabled readers show significantly less interference than the young normal readers for all of the different linguistic interference conditions. This result suggests that young disabled readers are less automatic in their processing of linguistic symbols ranging from random consonants to words. However, the interaction is not significant for the older subjects. The older disabled and normal readers show similar levels of interference from the different print conditions. This result is consistent with other studies that compared older disabled and normal readers and found no group differences in print interference (Briggs & Underwood, 1982; Golinkoff & Rosinsky, 1976). Apparently, reader ability differences in the subjects' automatic responses to print are only present for younger groups that are substantially different in reading skill.

It should be emphasized that the similar interference effects for the older groups does not necessarily imply their similarity in the type of automaticity described by LaBerge and Samuels (1974), who emphasized the importance of speed, efficiency, and a lack of demand on central processing resources in good readers' word decoding. It can be clearly seen in Fig. 2 that the older disabled readers are significantly slower in all conditions. Thus, their linguistic responses to both pictures and print may be generally less "automatic" in LaBerge and Samuels' use of the term.

The final hypothesis was that since disabled readers are uniquely deficient in phonological coding (see the following experiment), they would show proportionally less interference from pronounceable nonwords (Guttentag & Haith, 1978). However, Fig. 2 shows that the interference patterns for the different print conditions are nearly identical for the two groups. Although the interference from pronounceable nonwords was intended to be an index of automatic phonological coding processes, it is possible that the subjects' involuntary responses to pronounceable nonwords may have been based on direct lexical coding processes associated with the pronounceable nonwords' orthographic similarity to words.

Although there was no significant evidence of a qualitative group difference in the interference effects from pronounceable nonwords, phonological coding of the nonwords was not explicitly required in the picture-naming task. The following experiment will show that when phonological coding of nonwords is explicitly required, the disabled readers show a substantial deficit.

C. Phonological and Orthographic Skill

The dual encoding model provided the rationale for the next two tests of component processes in reading. Recall from the introduction that lexical access in reading single words may employ two basically different processes. Phonological coding involves the internal generation of an abstract sound-based code from the letter string that is used to access the lexicon. Orthographic coding involves accessing the lexicon directly based on the sequence of abstract letter codes (Besner, Coltheart, & Davelaar, 1984), without relying on the prior generation of a sound-based phonological code.

1. Phonological Skill

The test of phonological skill was a modification of the nonword-lexical-decision task used by Baron and Strawson (1976) and Saffran and Marin (1977). In our version of this test, the subjects viewed two pronounceable letter strings presented side by side on a television monitor (e.g., *caik dake*) and they pushed a button in their left or right hand to designate the pseudohomophone letter string that sounded like a common word (e.g., *caik*). All of the appropriate lexical entries for the pseudohomophone targets were common words from the reading vocabularies of the average second grader (Harris & Jacobson, 1972). The complete set of stimuli is listed in Table II. Eight practice and 40 experimental pairs were presented, and the subjects received error and latency feedback on each trial (see Davidson, Olson, & Kliegl, 1983, for further details). The phonological task required first that the subject generate the internal sound codes for the nonwords. (Because there was no oral response, variability in articulatory skills should not have had any direct influence on performance in this task.) Second, the task also required the subject to match the sound code for the nonword (e.g., caik) to a word (e.g., *cake*) in his/her lexicon.

A second test of phonological skill was added for the younger subjects. Fifty-nine disabled readers (mean age = 10.8) and 63 normal readers (mean age = 10.8) were given the above stimuli a second time and were asked to pronounce aloud the sound of the letter string they thought was a word. There was no time pressure in this task, latencies were not monitored, and the subjects were not given feedback on the accuracy of their responses. This second test of phonological skill was added for the younger subjects because the error rates for the disabled readers were quite high in the forced-choice-lexical-decision task, and we were not sure that they always understood the instructions. Although subjects were not explicitly required to use their phonological codes to access the lexicon in this task, it will be shown that the lexical-decision and oral-nonword-reading tasks seemed to be measuring the same underlying phonological skill.

2. Orthographic Skill

The test of direct orthographic access to the lexicon required subjects to distinguish words from nonword letter strings that would be identical in sound if pronounced (e.g., *rain rane*). The complete stimulus set is presented in Table II. The subjects pushed a button with their left or right hand to designate the letter string that was a word. This task requires subjects to match the orthographic patterns on the screen to a word in their lexicon. Although it does not preclude the generation of sound-based phonological codes during lexical access, and we will see that some subjects may have inappropriately used this path, phonological codes could not be used to make a correct decision between the two letter strings, since both sound the same. A correct decision had to be based exclusively on the word's orthographic code. The orthographic coding task had the same number of trials and followed the same basic procedure as the phonological task. The words were drawn from the second-grade reading vocabulary (Harris & Jacobson, 1972).

3. Results

Response times and errors for the orthographic and phonological forced-choice tasks for the complete sample are presented in the top half of Table III. There are clear main effects of task and reading ability, and there is a significant interaction wherein the response time and error differences between disabled and normal readers are greater in the phonological task.

The phonological task was substantially more difficult for both groups, and the interaction with performance in the orthographic task does not cross over. Since scaling problems may limit the interpretation of interactions that do not cross over (Loftus, 1978), it is not certain from this analysis that the disabled readers are uniquely more deficient than normal readers

TABLE II

Orthographic condition

room	rume	bowl	boal
young	yung	clown	cloun
turtle	tertle	circus	sircus
snow	snoe	wrote	wroat
take	taik	word	wurd
goat	gote	coat	cote
please	pleese	rain	rane
sleep	sleap	store	stoar
street	streat	wagon	wagun
answer	anser	believe	beleav
between	betwean	choose	chooze
deep	deap	dream	dreem
easy	eazy	every	evry
face	fase	few	fue
heavy	hevvy	hole	hoal
hurt	hert	keep	keap
lake	laik	learn	lurn
need	nead	nice	nise
roar	rore	scare	scair
sheep	sheap	skate	skait
smoke	smoak	stream	streem
tape	taip	thumb	thum
toward	toard	true	trew
wait	wate	wise	wize

Phonological condition

baik	bape	fead	feem
lait	lote	fense	felce
braive	broave	thair	theer
bloe	blog	fether	fither
kake	dake	bote	boaf
trane	traif	bair	beal
broun	broan	caim	pame
fite	fipe	naim	nade
ferst	filst	gaim	gome
ait	afe	kard	carn
klass	cliss	craul	crail
derty	dorty	docter	doftor
eer	eap	fearce	fairce
flote	floap	floar	ploor
hawl	harl	hoap	hote
joak	jope	leeve	meave
neer	nerr	reech	reash
plaice	plice	saif	saip
seet	seaf	shaip	shate
shurt	shart	strate	strale
teech	neach	thurd	thord
thrue	threp	tracter	trastor
tirn	turt	werld	warld

in the phonological task. To provide an opportunity for a more interpretable cross-over interaction and to see how disabled and normal readers similar in reading ability would perform, we compared the performance of the 50 disabled readers who were older than 14.1 years (mean age = 15.4 years) with that of the 50 normal readers who were younger than 11.5 years (mean age = 10.1 years). The mean PIAT recognition grade-levels for the older disabled (6.7) and younger normal (7.3) readers were not significantly different.

Response times and errors for the older disabled and younger normal subjects are presented in the bottom half of Table III. The response times for the two groups are not significantly different within the phonological and orthographic tasks, but there is a significant cross-over interaction for the errors. On the orthographic task, the older disabled readers make slightly but not significantly fewer errors than the younger normals (12.45 vs 12.95%), but on the phonological task they make significantly more errors than the normals (30.05 vs 17.75%, chance performance in this task is 50% errors). This result provides strong support for the hypothesis that disabled readers, as a group, are uniquely deficient in phonological skill (Bradley & Bryant, 1978; Firth, 1972; Golinkoff & Rosinski, 1976; Kochnower, Richardson & DiBenedetto, 1983; Snowling, 1981; Perfetti & Hogaboam, 1975). In addition, Bradley and Bryant (1981) reported that disabled readers matched to younger normals in reading ability were deficient in a task that involved the detection of rhyme and alliteration. This suggests that phonological skill and related language skills may play an important causal role for individual differences in reading ability.

TABLE III

Mean Response Time and Percentage Errors in the Orthographic and Phonological Tasks[a]

	Orthographic		Phonological	
	Latency (msec)	Errors (%)	Latency (msec)	Errors (%)
Disabled (all)	1397	18.1	2718	32.8
Normal (all)	900	10.8	1568	17.0
Difference	497	7.3	1150	15.8
Old disabled	1107	12.4	2041	30.1
Young Normal	1005	12.9	1901	17.8
Difference	102	−.5	140	12.3

[a]There were 50 subjects in each of the old disabled and young normal groups and their mean ages were 15.3 and 10.2 years. Means for all subjects are presented in the upper half and means for reading-matched groups are in the lower half.

Developmental analyses of the phonological forced-choice error percentages indicate that while the normal readers show only a slight and nonsignificant improvement with age in their phonological coding accuracy, the disabled readers' deficit in phonological skill is significantly larger for the youngest third of the subjects below 11.5 years (39 vs 18% errors) than for subjects between 11.5 and 14.5 years (30 vs 17% errors) and the oldest third of the subjects above 14.5 years (30 vs 16% errors). The older disabled readers seem to have reached an asymptote in their weak phonological skill, with no improvement in accuracy from the middle to the older age groups. Rudel (1981) has reported that deficits in phonological skill persist even in "remediated" adult dyslexics whose word recognition has reached or exceeded normal levels (see also, Johnson, 1980).

Results from the oral nonword reading task that was given to the younger subjects also reveal a substantial deficit in phonological skill for disabled readers. The percentage-correct responses are 58% ($SD = 24\%$) for disabled readers and 89% ($SD = 13\%$) for normal readers. Thus, in both the silent-phonological-lexical-decision task and the oral-nonword-reading task, the disabled group is substantially deficient in phonological skill.

A deficiency in phonological skill could contribute to reading difficulties in two different ways. First, from the perspective of the dual encoding model, having two efficient paths to the lexicon may confer an advantage in reading regular words. Some studies with normal readers have found that they read regular words faster than exception words. The regular words are presumed to be processed by both the phonological and orthographic paths, while the exception words are confined to the orthographic path. In this model, disabled readers should show a smaller regular word advantage because their phonological coding is uniquely deficient. Barron (1980) has provided some support for this prediction. It is tested with the present subjects in the following study of regular and exception word reading.

A different view of how a deficit in phonological skill could contribute to reading problems has been presented by Venezky and Massaro (1979). They suggest that phonological skill helps orient the beginning reader to the orthographic structure for words that may later be employed independently from phonological coding in lexical access. Thus, any weakness in phonological coding would hinder the development of word recognition abilities, as it apparently did for our disabled readers, whether or not phonological coding actually played a major role in lexical access for familiar words. From this point of view, one might not expect a regular word advantage for familiar words in either the normal or disabled groups, since both types of words would be read primarily through the orthographic path. The results of the following experiment will support this view. However, a second test of the regularity effect will show that there is a substantial regular word advantage for less familiar words in both the normal and disabled groups.

D. Easy Regular and Exception Word Reading

In the first test of the regularity effect, subjects read 36 regular (e.g., *maid*) and 36 exception (e.g., *said*) words. The complete set of stimuli is presented in Table IV. All words were "inconsistent" in Glushko's (1979) analysis, e.g., the same letter patterns had different pronunciations in different words. All stimuli were easy, common words from the second grade reading vocabulary (Harris and Jacobson, 1972). The exception words were slightly but not significantly higher in average frequency than the regular words (1320 vs 1053, respectively; Kucera & Francis, 1967). The exception and regular words were presented in a mixed list, one word at a time, on a television monitor. The subject's vocalization latency was timed with a voice key and errors were recorded by the experimenter (see Davidson *et al.*, 1983, for further details).

The percentage errors and mean voice-onset times (for correct responses) are presented in Table V for three age groups. The mean ages and number of subjects for the three disabled reader groups are 9.9 years, $n = 46$; 12.8 years, $n = 45$; 15.4 years, $n = 50$. Respective values for the normal readers

TABLE IV
Regular-Exception Word-Naming Task

Regular	Exception	Regular	Exception
here	were	over	oven
note	done	gas	was
had	what	afraid	again
seen	been	open	woman
did	fruit	not	from
eat	break	cut	put
spoke	glove	more	move
sing	sure	mean	great
woke	some	later	water
stone	one	make	have
mail	said	no	who
but	buy	after	listen
shout	soup	that	want
blue	build	poor	door
call	calf	nose	none
twin	two	care	are
home	come	go	do
bone	gone	ride	give

TABLE V

Mean Response Time and Percentage Errors
for Easy Exception and Regular Words

Mean age (years)	Regular words		Exception Words	
	Disabled	Normal	Disabled	Normal
	Latency (msec)			
10.1	1136	601	1137	593
12.8	725	551	715	549
15.4	675	508	670	504
	Percentage errors			
10.1	22.8	3.5	30.3	3.4
12.8	8.3	1.6	9.6	3.5
15.4	5.1	1.7	5.7	2.1

are 10.1 years, $n = 50$; 12.8 years, $n = 45$; 15.4 years, $n = 45$. These are the same age groupings used in the previous comparisons of older disabled and younger normal subjects' orthographic and phonological skill, and they will also be used for the within-group analyses in the third and fourth sections. The ranges for the three age groups are 8.5 to 11.4, 11.5 to 14, and 14.1 to 16.9 years.

An analysis of variance revealed that there are significant effects of age and reading ability in the response times, but there is no significant main effect or interaction with the regular and exception word conditions. Within each group, the time taken to read regular and exception words is remarkably similar. Error rates for exception and regular words also are not significantly different within the groups, with the possible exception of the youngest disabled readers discussed below. Within the framework of the dual encoding model, and considering evidence from the previous study that disabled readers are uniquely deficient in the phonological path to the lexicon, it would appear that both groups rely on the direct path to the lexicon for these common words.

Our results are inconsistent with Barron's (1980) report that normal readers were faster in making lexical decisions for regular than exception words while disabled readers were not. It is hard to know what to make of our different results. Barron's words were less frequent than ours, his response latencies were generally longer, and his response was lexical decision rather than vocalization. Barron concluded that the latency results supported his hypothesis that normal readers used the phonological path in lexical decision and disabled readers did not. However, as we find in the following study, Barron found an equivalent regularity effect in errors for both his disabled and normal groups, apparently contradicting his hypothesis.

Perhaps regularity effects may be more readily observed for the present subjects with less familiar words. There is some limited support for this in the present study for the youngest disabled readers. Although the difference is not significant in the overall analysis of variance, the younger disabled readers made 22.8% errors on regular words and 30.3% errors on exception words. Clearly these were not "easy" words for these subjects. Perhaps the use of more difficult words adjusted for reading ability could reveal a more substantial regularity effect for all subjects and allow for a more comparable analysis of the effect for the disabled and normal readers. The following study tests this hypothesis by using regular and exception words that were selected for difficulty level according to each subject's general level of word recognition.

E. Difficult Regular and Exception Words

Differences in reading difficult regular and exception words were assessed using the word recognition portion of the Camp and McCabe test (1977). This consisted of a 20-word list that was selected for difficulty level so that the subjects read about 65% of the words correctly within a 10 second time limit for each word. Half of the words in each list were regular and half were exception words. They were roughly balanced in frequency, although one or two words were excluded from the analyses for some of the lists to achieve a better balance. Also, the definition of regularity was not as carefully controlled as in the previous study where both exception and regular words had inconsistently pronounced letter patterns such as m*aid* and s*aid* (Glushko, 1979). The basis for selection of regular and exception words is described in detail by Camp and McCabe (1977). Their selection procedure resulted in relatively more "inconsistent" exception words than regular words.

The list was shown to the subjects one word at a time and responses were scored as correct or incorrect by the experimenter. Latency data were collected with a voice key, but there were too few correct trials to yield reliable latency estimates for the regular and exception words. Only the error data will be reported.

In contrast to the results obtained with easy words, when words are selected to be difficult relative to the subject's reading level, a substantial regular-exception word difference is observed. Normal readers score 81% correct on regular words versus 53% for exception words, and disabled readers score 78% on regular and 49% on exception words. Most important is the finding that both groups show nearly the same size difference (28 and 29%) between the word types. Although most disabled and normal readers were tested with different words, it was possible to compare smaller groups of older disabled ($n = 23$) and younger normal ($n = 26$) readers who read the same list. The older disabled readers score 77% correct on the regular words vs 45% for exception words. The younger normal readers score 77% correct on the regular words and 40% on the exception words. The difference between the disabled and normal readers' regularity effect (33 vs 37%) is not significant. This result is consistent with Barron's (1980) report of a similar sized regularity effect in his error data for normal and disabled readers.

From the perspective of the dual encoding model, the substantial size and similarity of the regularity effect for both groups would suggest that they both use the phonological path to advantage in reading difficult regular words. But this interpretation seems to conflict with the substantial group difference observed in the phonological lexical decision task and the oral nonword reading task. One possible resolution of this conflict between theory and data may be based on a distinction between *use* of the phonological path and the subjects *skill* in using that path. Although the disabled readers are far below the normal readers in phonological skill, even the younger disabled readers are able to read 58% of the pseudohomophone nonwords from the phonological task correctly. It seems likely that at least some disabled readers would apply their limited phonological coding ability to aid in reading difficult words, and it is not clear that the application of less accurate or efficient phonological coding processes would necessarily lead to a significantly smaller regularity effect. For example, if a disabled reader were biased to use the phonological path rather than the orthographic path because of intense instruction in phonics, that subject might show a regularity effect that is larger than the regularity effect for normal readers with superior phonological skill. The distinction between use and skill in phonological coding will be supported in the following section when we look at within-group differences in the regularity effect for disabled readers.

Another possible cause of the similar regularity effects for disabled and normal readers is that the regular word advantage is due at least in part to their advantage in orthographic coding that is independent from phonological coding. In addition to being phonologically regular, regular words often have more common orthographic structures and these common structures could result in better processing and memory for their specific letter patterns in direct lexical access (Carr, Posner, Pollatsek, & Snyder, 1979; Massaro, Taylor, Venezky, Jastrzembski, & Lucas, 1980; Singer, 1980). The commonality of orthographic patterns was relatively balanced for the easy list of regular and exception words (e.g., *maid–said*), where there is no regularity effect for either group. In the difficult list where there is a similar regularity effect for both groups, the orthographic patterns for the exception words are less common than for the regular words.

A problem with the above orthographic familiarity hypothesis for the regularity effect is that the commonality of orthographic structures and their pronounceability are confounded in our difficult regular words. Massaro, Venezky, and Taylor (1979) separated orthographic structure associated with pronounceability (e.g., *drunet*) and structure based on high single-letter positional frequency in strings that were not pronounceable (e.g., *rdnuet*). Adults were influenced by both types of structure in letter-detection tasks. This led Massaro and Taylor (1980) to ask whether poor readers, because of a phonological coding deficit, might be significantly less sensitive than good readers to the orthographic structure associated with pronounceability. The results of their study were mixed on this question. Good- and poor-reading college students were nearly identical in their facilitation from the two types of orthographic structure. However, poor readers in the sixth grade showed less facilitation than good sixth-grade readers from orthographic structure associated with pronounceability. This later result was not significant in an overall analysis of variance that included two other structure conditions, so replication is needed. If the difference is confirmed, it would indicate a poor-reader deficit for sensitivity to the orthographic structure associated with pronounceability in a task that did not explicitly require phonological coding.

We do not wish to argue the null hypothesis for differences between normal and disabled readers in their response to orthographic regularity. The point is that both the disabled and normal groups show a substantial regularity effect for accuracy in reading words and it seems likely that any difference between the groups is quite small. In contrast, there is a substantial and significant difference between the groups when phonological coding is explicitly required, suggesting that most of the regularity effect is unrelated to the subjects' phonological skill. This view is further supported in the following study of individual differences in the regularity effect within the disabled group.

IV. INDIVIDUAL DIFFERENCES IN READING DISABILITY

This section and the following section on eye movements focus on analyses of individual differences within the disabled group. Similar analyses have been performed within the normal group, but in general, their reading style differences were not as strong and most of the correlations were not significant. Individual differences in reading style may be more salient among disabled readers because they develop unique strategies to deal with their reading problems.

Two seminal studies of individual differences in reading style influenced our selection of tests and initial hypotheses (Baron & Strawson, 1976; Boder,

1973). We begin with Baron and Strawson's distinction between "Phonecian" and "Chinese" styles by comparing the disabled readers' regularity effect with their phonological and orthographic coding skill. The second part of this section considers Boder's apparently related distinction between "dyseidetic" and "dysphonetic" disabled readers that was based on her analysis of their spelling errors. The correlations between the coding skills, regularity effects, and patterns of spelling errors support a dimension of individual differences in reading style that is based on the subjects' relative use of the phonological and orthographic paths in reading. This dimension is further supported by the analysis of eye movements in text presented in the fifth section. In the final section we discuss the normal distribution of individual differences in reading style and their etiology.

Two general approaches are used in our analyses of individual differences. First, correlations between variables are computed within the three age groups described in the previous group analyses of the regularity effect. A statistical motivation for this approach is that the different age groups vary substantially in their performance levels and variance on some of the tasks (see Table V). The computation of z scores across the whole sample could obscure important individual differences that may be observed within the separate age groups. Also, some individual differences in reading style observed among younger disabled readers are not present in the older subjects. To simplify the presentation of the age effects, only the results for the oldest and youngest thirds of the sample are presented here. In most analyses where reading style correlations for the youngest and oldest thirds were significantly different, the middle age group yielded correlations that were between those of the youngest and oldest groups.

The second general analytic approach is to observe individual differences in reading style that are independent from reading ability. Reading ability was controlled statistically by partialing out variance associated with the subjects' word recognition score on the PIAT. Thus, the correlations reported in this and the following section are based upon the subjects' performance on each variable relative to the linear effects of their word recognition scores. The simple correlations of each variable with PIAT word recognition prior to partialing are presented in the tables in parentheses.

A. Phonological Skill, Orthographic Skill, and the Regularity Effect

Baron and Strawson (1976) reported that normal readers who were selected for good phonological and poor orthographic skill (Phonecians) showed a regular word advantage in latencies, while others who were selected for good orthographic and poor phonological skill (Chinese) did not.

The Phonecian and Chinese subjects were extreme groups selected from a larger sample of college students, but Baron and Strawson thought of them as part of a continuous, single Phonecian–Chinese dimension of individual differences. Our analyses included data from all subjects rather than the extreme groups so that the variance in reading style could be estimated for the entire disabled population. In addition, we observed the independent relations of phonological and orthographic skill with the regularity effect and separately with regular and exception word reading.

The subjects' phonological and orthographic skill were computed from the number of correct responses in the phonological and orthographic tasks. The regularity effect, or relative-regular-word advantage in accuracy, was computed by subtracting the subjects' z scores for number of correct exception words from their z scores for number of correct regular words in the easy lists (see Table IV). Thus, a positive difference score would indicate a relatively strong regular word advantage in accuracy. Separate analyses were also performed with response latencies in the phonological, orthographic, and regular-exception word tasks. None of the theoretically interesting correlations described below for errors was significant in the latency data. The high error rates in these tasks limit the interpretation of the latencies, so only the accuracy data are reported here.

The correlation between the disabled subjects' regularity effect and phonological skill is $r = .10$ ($p > .05$) for the youngest subjects and $r = -.01$ ($p > .05$) for the oldest subjects (see Table VI). Thus, there is no significant relation between the regularity effect and phonological skill. A similar nonsignificant correlation between the regularity effect and phonological skill is present within the youngest group for 34 subjects whose phonological skill was estimated from the number of nonwords read aloud ($r = .05$, $p > .05$).

In contrast to the null results with phonological skill, orthographic skill is significantly correlated with the regularity effect ($r = -.31$, $p < .05$, for younger subjects; $r = -.36$, $p < .01$, for older subjects, see Table VI). The negative direction of these correlations indicates that subjects who perform well on the orthographic task relative to their word recognition on the PIAT are less likely to show a regular word advantage in accuracy. However, the interpretation of the regularity-effect-difference scores is limited by reliability problems arising from the combined error variance of the component scores. Conclusions drawn from the difference scores need further support and interpretation from the separate correlations between orthographic skill, regular word accuracy, and exception word accuracy. Examination of the component regular and exception word correlations in Table VI indicates that exception word accuracy contributes most of the variance in the regularity effect that is correlated with orthographic skill (r

TABLE VI

Individual Difference Correlations for Disabled Readers' Regularity Effect and Decoding Skills[a]

(PIAT rec.)	Reg. words (.76)	Exc. words (.72)	Reg.-exc. difference (.04)	Phon. skill (.58)	Ortho. skill (.55)
Reg. words (.43)		.64**	.36**	−.32*	.33*
Exc. words (.33)	.44**		−.48**	−.38**	.57**
Reg.-exc. difference (.10)	.50**	−.56**		.10	−.31*
Phon. skill (.23)	.15	.16	−.01		−.17
Ortho. skill (.20)	.03	.40**	−.36**	.07	

[a]Younger disabled readers above the diagonal ($n = 41$) and older disabled readers below ($n = 50$). All correlations are partialed on the subjects' PIAT word-recognition scores. Simple correlations with PIAT rec. are in parentheses across the top for young and down the side for old subjects. * $p < .05$; ** $p < .01$.

exc. = .57 vs r reg. = .33 for younger subjects; r exc. = .40 vs r reg. = .03 for older subjects). Regression analyses indicated that exception word accuracy predicts a significant amount of variance in orthographic skill after taking regular word variance into account, but regular word variance is not significant after taking exception word variance into account. Thus, better orthographic skill acts primarily to reduce the error rate for exception words, and thereby reduce any regular word advantage in accuracy.

How do the observed correlations between phonological skill, orthographic skill, and the regularity effect fit with the dual encoding model? The absence of a relation between phonological skill and the regularity effect in the present within-group analyses, and the absence of a significant group difference in the regularity effect in the previous section seem inconsistent with Baron and Strawson's (1976) view that subjects with better phonological skill should show a stronger regularity effect. However, as we suggested in the previous section, there may be individual differences in the *use* of the phonological path in reading that are independent from the subjects phonological *skill*. From this perspective, subjects who tend to make relatively greater use of the phonological path in reading, regardless of their phonological skill, might show a larger regularity effect. The following examination of the relation between performance in the orthographic task and the regularity effect will support this hypothesis.

The significant negative correlations between orthographic skill and the regularity effect are consistent with Baron and Strawson's (1976) view that Chinese style readers who have strong orthographic images should show a smaller regularity effect. From the perspective of the dual encoding model, if a subject has strong orthographic codes relative to their word recognition (remember that the linear effects of PIAT word recognition were partialed out), they should have relatively less difficulty processing exception words that presumably are better read through the direct orthographic path.

The subjects' accuracy in the orthographic task may also have implications for their use of the phonological path. Low accuracy in the orthographic task could result from the inappropriate use of the phonological path in this task as well as from any weakness in the subjects' orthographic codes. For example, subjects confronting the stimulus pair (*rane–rain*) could use a phonological code to achieve the same lexical response from either member of the pair, but this strategy would often lead to an incorrect response in the orthographic forced-choice task. Evidence from another study in progress with the orthographic task indicates that subjects often are able to give a correct oral response for the forced-choice pairs even though they choose the orthographically incorrect letter string (*rane*) as the word.

In summary, the present results suggest that reading style differences among disabled readers may be based on their differential use of the phonological and orthographic paths to the lexicon. A reciprocal relation is hypothesized wherein subjects with good orthographic codes tend to use the orthographic path in reading while those subjects with poor orthographic codes tend to use the phonological path, regardless of their phonological skill. While the observed correlations between orthographic accuracy and the regularity effect are consistent with this view, converging evidence is needed to support the implied relation between poor performance in the orthographic task and greater use of phonological path. The following analyses will show that younger subjects with relatively weak orthographic codes produce more phonologically accurate spelling errors. Then, in the next section, eye movement analyses will provide converging evidence for individual differences in the subjects' use of phonological and orthographic paths.

B. Phonological Skill, Orthographic Skill, and Spelling Errors

What does spelling have to do with reading? In general, spelling skill is correlated with reading skill. For the disabled and normal readers in the present study, the 4.4 grade-level discrepancy in word recognition on the PIAT is mirrored by a 3.8 year discrepancy in PIAT spelling (see Table I).

However, the correlation between reading and spelling is far less than perfect, and there are many good readers who are relatively poor spellers (cf. Frith, 1980). Among disabled readers there are relatively few good spellers, and researchers have attempted to use the specific types of spelling errors to classify different subtypes of disabled readers (cf. Boder, 1973; Camp & McCabe, 1977; Mitterer, 1982).

Boder (1973) relied primarily on spelling errors to distinguish two major groups of disabled readers that seem somewhat analogous to the Phonecian and Chinese subjects of Baron and Strawson (1976). One subgroup was classified as "dyseidetic." In Boder's clinical description, the dyseidetic subjects were able to phonologically decode regular words and nonwords by slowly sounding them out, but their sight reading vocabulary was small and they had great difficulty reading exception words. Their spelling errors tended to be phonologically similar to the test word although they were often quite different visually, and regular words were more often read and spelled correctly than exception words. In general, the dyseidetics "manifest weaknesses in visual perception and memory for letters and whole word configurations, or gestalts, with resulting disability in developing a sight vocabulary, although they have no disability in developing phonic skills" (Boder & Jarrico, 1982, p. 7).

A second subgroup was classified as "dysphonetic." These subjects could read both regular and exception words that they knew by sight, but they were deficient in sounding out unknown words and nonwords. In contrast to the dyseidetic subjects, the dysphonetic subjects showed little difference in their ability to read exception and regular words. The dysphonetics' spelling errors were distinctly nonphonological, although they might be visually similar to the target word, and the dysphonetics were able to spell regular and exception words equally well by sight. In general, the dysphonetics "have difficulty integrating written symbols with their sounds, with resulting disability in developing phonic word-analysis skills. They have no gross deficit, however, in visual gestalt function" (Boder & Jarrico, 1982, p. 7). Baron (1979) and Treiman et al. (1983) have noted the apparent similarity of Boder's dysphonetic and dyseidetic subtypes to their Chinese and Phonecian style readers.

Boder (1973) described a third "mixed" group comprising the most severely disabled readers who were deficient both in sight reading and phonological decoding. In a recent report, Rosenthal, Boder, and Callaway (1982) estimated that the incidence of the different subtypes in the dyslexic population was 60% dysphonetic, 20% dyseidetic, and 20% mixed. Although the three groups were described as extreme, qualitatively distinct subtypes that resulted from individual differences in basic gestalt and linguistic skills, the data were not presented in sufficient detail to evaluate Boder's clinical descriptions of the subtypes or their etiology.

In the present study we evaluated the types of spelling errors made by disabled readers to see if individual differences in the error patterns were related to differences in reading processes. Since a detailed description of Boder's (1973) test was not available when we began the research, we used the Camp and McCabe (1977) test of reading and spelling patterns which is based on the Boder approach, and is quite similar to the test recently published by Boder and Jarrico (1982). It consists of a list of 20 spelling words selected for the subjects' reading grade level. About 50% of the words on the list could be read correctly within 2 seconds for each word. The reading vocabulary level is determined with an alternate list of 20 words that was used in analyses of the regularity effect for difficult words presented in the previous section. The spelling test was given by first presenting the word in isolation, then it was used in a sentence, and finally it was read again in isolation. The subjects wrote out their spellings, and the experimenter asked for clarification of spellings that were not legible.

Both the Camp and McCabe (1977) and the Boder and Jarrico (1982) tests use dichotomous scoring procedures for classifying spelling errors and subjects into the dyseidetic and dysphonetic categories. These dichotomous divisions appeared somewhat arbitrary, so a scoring procedure was developed for analyzing several specific characteristics of each spelling error and for rating each error on a more continuous scale for their phonological and visual similarity to the target word. Phonological similarity was simply the degree to which the spelling sounded like the target. Visual similarity was based on the number of salient visual characteristics in common with the target such as number of letters and appropriately placed ascenders and descenders, but it also was a subjective rating. Each spelling error was assigned two numbers from 1 (low) to 10 (high) to separately indicate phonological and visual similarity to the target word. The ratings were averaged across spelling errors to obtain mean visual and phonological similarity scores for each subject. One rater evaluated the spelling errors for all subjects using this scoring system. A smaller group of subjects' errors was also scored by a second rater to obtain rater-reliability estimates. The rater reliabilities were .85 for the phonological rating and .82 for the visual rating across the reading disabled subjects. The mean number of errors that were made by the older and younger groups were 12.0 and 10.8, respectively, out of the 20 spelling words.

Correlations are presented in Table VII for the younger and older disabled readers' number of words spelled correctly, visual similarity ratings, phonological similarity ratings, phonological skill, and orthographic skill. The phonological and visual ratings of the spelling errors are strongly correlated, and their correlations with other variables are quite similar. This is consistent with the raters' subjective impression that a clear dissociation between visual and phonological similarity was rarely observed. It might be possible to observe a stronger dissociation by using words selected specifically for this purpose, but there were not enough suitable stimuli in the Camp and McCabe lists. It appeared that both the phonological and visual ratings indicate the general similarity of a misspelled word to the target word. Note that the similarity ratings are not simply equivalent to spelling skill defined by the number of words spelled correctly, at least for the younger subjects. Their correlations between the spelling ratings and number of words correctly spelled do not approach significance (see Table VII).

Significant age differences are present between several correlations when the oldest and youngest thirds of the disabled readers are compared. The results for the youngest subjects presented above the diagonal in Table VII will be described first. These correlations are based on 38 of the youngest subjects (mean age = 9.9 years) who have complete data for all of the relevant variables.

1. Phonological Skill and Spelling Ratings for Younger Subjects

Phonological skill is positively correlated with the similarity ratings of spelling errors, although only the correlation with phonological similarity is significant (see Table VII). In addition, for the 32 of these subjects whose phonological skill could be estimated from oral nonword reading errors, the correlations are $r = .32$, $p < .05$, with the phonological rating and $r = .47$, $p < .01$, with the visual rating. Thus, those subjects whose phonological skill is relatively good compared to their word recognition make

TABLE VII

Decoding Skill and Spelling Error Rating Correlations[a]

(PIAT rec.)	Number correct (.34)	Phon. rating (.54)	Vis. rating (.61)	Phon. skill (.61)	Ortho. skill (.55)
Number correct (.09)		.01	.11	.13	−.12
Phon. rating (.45)	.26*		.74**	.29*	−.48**
Vis. rating (.34)	.42**	.77**		.23	−.47**
Phon. skill (.23)	.01	.09	−.05		−.08
Ortho. skill (.20)	.19	.15	.14	.07	

[a]Younger disabled readers above the diagonal ($n = 38$) and older disabled readers below ($n = 50$). Simple correlations with PIAT rec. are in parentheses across the top for young and down the side for old subjects. *$p < .05$; **$p < .01$.

spelling errors that are more phonologically and visually similar to the target word. This result contrasts with the nonsignificant correlations between phonological skill and reading style defined by the regularity effect in the previous study and by eye movements described in the following section. Individual differences in spelling styles may be more closely related than reading style to phonological skill. Other researchers have suggested that spelling is more directly supported than reading by phonological processes (Barron, 1980; Bryant & Bradley, 1980; Frith, 1979; Treiman, 1984).

2. Orthographic Skill and Spelling Ratings for Younger Subjects

In striking contrast to the positive correlations with phonological skill, orthographic skill is negatively correlated with both similarity ratings (see Table VI). Thus, subjects who are better in the orthographic task relative to their word recognition have lower similarity ratings for their spelling errors. Conversely, subjects with relatively weak orthographic codes produce spelling errors that are more phonologically and visually more similar to the target word. Mitterer (1982) recently reported some results that are consistent with these correlations. He gave young disabled readers a yes–no lexical decision task that included pseudohomophones (e.g., *rane*) as foils. This is similar to the type of decision that our subjects had to make in the forced-choice orthographic task. Some of Mitterer's disabled readers were more likely than others to mistakenly identify the pseudohomophones as words. In a separate spelling task, these subjects' spelling errors tended to be more phonologically similar to the target word.

Our explanation for the negative correlation between orthographic skill and the spelling ratings is that subjects who have relatively weak orthographic codes tend to use phonological codes in spelling (and reading). Their greater use of phonological codes in spelling results in errors that are more phonologically and visually similar to the target. However, there are two possible problems with this explanation. First, it is not obvious why subjects with relatively strong orthographic codes could not use them to advantage in spelling, thus producing a positive correlation between orthographic skill and the spelling ratings. The reason may be that these younger subjects are quite limited in their reading experience, and although their orthographic codes are relatively stronger than those of their peers in a task that involves word *recognition,* they are still not strong enough to support the reasonable spelling of relatively unfamiliar words in a *production* task. However, these subjects may use their relatively strong orthographic codes to produce perfectly accurate spellings for more familiar words.

The second apparent problem with our explanation is that subjects who have relatively strong orthographic skill do not necessarily have weaker

phonological skill. In fact, the correlation between accuracy in the phonological and orthographic tasks is not significant (see Table VII). Why then
would the subjects high in orthographic skill show less tendency to use their
apparently equivalent phonological coding skills to produce more reasonable spellings of unfamiliar words? The answer to this question requires
further elaboration of the dual encoding model and consideration of the
different ways in which subjects might read nonwords.

3. Two (or More) Phonological Processes in Reading and Spelling

Performance in the phonological task may be based on two different
phonological paths to the lexicon, each of which allows the reading of nonwords, but dominant processing in one is associated with good orthographic
skill and low similarity ratings for spelling errors while dominant processing
in the other phonological path is associated with poor orthographic skill
and spelling errors that are more similar to the target.

Recent models of reading have emphasized parallel and interactive processing between the different memory systems depicted in Fig. 1 (cf. Mc-
Clelland & Rummelhart, 1981). These interactions could be represented in
Fig. 1 by making all of the arrows bidirectional between the different memory systems. In this type of model, there are at least two possible ways to
read nonwords. First, subjects could use the mediating phonological path
to the lexicon already described wherein grapheme–phoneme rules are used
to produce the sound of a nonword. Second, the sound of a nonword could
be determined by direct activation of words or parts of words in the lexicon
that are similar to the nonword. The activation of these lexical items could
then feed back to phonological memory and support the phonological decoding of nonwords. Glushko (1979) and Kay and Marcel (1981) have argued that this is how older normal readers typically derive phonological
codes for both words and nonwords.

Baron's model of reading (1977) included both prelexical and postlexical
activation of phonological codes, and he distinguished several different ways
in which the prelexical activation of phonological codes might occur. These
ranged from small-unit grapheme–phoneme correspondence rules, to larger
subword units, to words that could exist, disembodied from their meaning,
in phonological memory. Treiman *et al.* (1983) presented evidence that normal readers use both large and small unit rules to access sound codes when
reading sentences, but they left open the question whether the large units
activated phonological memory prelexically, postlexically, or both. However, the prelexical–postlexical question can not be decided here, and it may
not be important for the following account of our results.

Regardless of whether the phonological codes used in reading are generated prelexically, postlexically, or both, the critical issue may be the subjects' differential use of small and large units in decoding words and nonwords. Individual differences in orthographic skill may reflect the subjects' differential skill in the use of small and large units in reading and spelling. Those subjects who have relatively good orthographic codes may tend to access the lexicon directly with word units. They may also be able to use relatively large word or subword units either pre- or postlexically to access phonological memory for decoding nonwords. In contrast, subjects with relatively poor orthographic skill may depend less on the use of large units in either direct lexical access that is required for good performance in the orthographic task, or in the generation of phonological codes for the phonological task. Instead, they may rely more on the use of small-unit grapheme–phoneme rules to achieve an equivalent level of nonword reading and word recognition.

Although either small or large units could be used to derive the correct pronunciation for a nonword in our tests of phonological coding, the large and small unit phonological processes may not be equally useful for spelling unfamiliar words in younger children. When strong orthographic codes are not available for spelling a word, it may be easier to use a limited set of grapheme–phoneme conversion rules in reverse as phoneme–grapheme conversion rules in spelling. In fact, the use of these rules in both directions is often explicitly taught in programs that emphasize phonics training (Perfetti, 1984a). However, because these rules are not adequate for many words and it is not always clear from the sound which of the possible phoneme-grapheme correspondences are appropriate, precisely correct spellings often require specific orthographic knowledge. Thus, it is interesting to note that the similarity ratings for spelling errors are not correlated with the number of words spelled correctly. The overapplication of common phoneme-grapheme small-unit rules would sometimes lead to spelling errors, sometimes correct spellings, and usually spelling errors that are reasonably similar to the target word.

Subjects who are relatively unfamiliar with phonics rules and who read nonwords more by analogy or through larger units may have greater difficulty reversing these phonological processes to produce reasonable spellings for unfamiliar words. These subjects may be able to spell a number of familiar words accurately through their superior orthographic codes, but they would be at a severe disadvantage in spelling words that were unfamiliar. Thus, they show lower similarity ratings for their spelling errors. However, it is possible that older disabled readers may be able to utilize their greater orthographic knowledge more directly to spell unfamiliar words through the reverse application of the large-unit codes they use in reading.

This hypothesis will be tested by comparing correlations between orthographic skill and spelling for the younger and older groups.

4. Age Differences in Relations between Coding Skills and Spelling Ratings

Correlations for the 50 oldest disabled readers (mean age = 15.4 years)
are presented below the diagonal in Table VII. In contrast to the younger
disabled readers, there are no significant correlations between the spelling
ratings and phonological or orthographic skill. Fisher's z tests indicated
that the older readers' correlations of spelling ratings with orthographic
skill are significantly different from those of the young readers. This difference should be interpreted with caution because the Cronbach-ALPHA
reliability (Cronbach, 1951) for the orthographic task was lower for the
older than for the younger subjects (.46 vs .83), probably because there are
ceiling effects on this task for the older subjects. Nevertheless, it is interesting that both similarity ratings correlate positively with orthographic skill
in the older group as opposed to the negative correlations in the younger
group. If the positive correlations in the older group could be confirmed
with a more reliable measure of their orthographic skill, it would suggest
that the basis for spelling performance shifts toward orthographic codes in
older disabled readers. This wold be consistent with Ellis's (1982) hypothesis that orthographic strategies in spelling are dominant in normal adult
readers. The absence of a significant correlation between phonological skill
and spelling ratings in the older group is also consistent with this hypothesis. Cronbach-ALPHA reliabilities were identical (.69) for phonological
skill in the younger and older groups.

Another indication of a developmental shift in spelling processes is the
significant correlations between the number of words spelled correctly and
the similarity ratings for the older subjects (see Table VII). Recall that these
correlations are not significant for the younger subjects. Fisher's z tests
indicated that the correlations were significantly different between the
younger and older groups for the visual similarity rating but not for the
phonological rating. The significant correlation between spelling accuracy
and visual similarity of spelling errors suggests that the processes involved
in spelling known and unknown words are more similar in the older group.

In addition to the above evidence for developmental changes in spelling
processes, some studies have suggested that there are parallel developmental
changes in the relation between phonological coding and lexical access in
reading. The relation is quite strong for very young readers. Firth (1972)
reported that the ability to read nonwords in a group of 91 6 year olds
accounted for 75% of the variance in their reading ability. In our youngest
group, the correlation between phonological skill and word recognition on

the PIAT was $r = .61$. This is quite high considering that the reliability of our phonological measure was .69. In contrast, the correlation for the older group ($r = .23$), was not significant, and it was significantly different by Fisher's z test from the correlation for the younger group. Other research has indicated that normal children decrease their dependence on phonological coding as they increase in age (Doctor & Coltheart, 1980; Reitsma, 1983c; Snowling & Frith, 1981), although there is not complete agreement with this conclusion (see Jorm & Share, 1983, for a review of conflicting studies).

5. Summary

The data presented in this section suggest that the younger disabled readers vary in reading and spelling styles based on their differential use of phonological and orthographic codes. Some subjects seem to use small-unit phonological codes in reading and spelling while other subjects rely more on large-unit orthographic codes. This view has been supported by the correlations between orthographic skill and the regularity effect and between orthographic skill and the spelling ratings. However, the preceding measures of individual differences in reading and spelling styles may not be ecologically valid as indicies for style differences when reading text for comprehension. In the following section we present a study of disabled readers eye movements when reading stories. The subjects' eye movement patterns reveal reading style differences in text that correlate meaningfully with their performance in the orthographic task and their spelling ratings.

V. EYE MOVEMENT READING STYLE

Eye movement analyses were included in the study for two reasons. First, it seemed that individual differences in word coding processes might be expressed in patterns of visual attention while reading text. Letter identification while reading is limited to a rather narrow span of about six to eight characters to the right and two to four characters to the left of the fixation in normal readers (Rayner, 1984; Underwood & McConkie, 1983), and disabled readers, as a group, are not significantly different from normal readers in their span of letter processing (Underwood, 1982). Therefore, the direction of gaze is a good indication of the words and parts of words that are being attended during a fixation (Just & Carpenter, 1980; Kliegl, Olson, & Davidson, 1982). We hypothesized that subjects who use small-unit rules for phonological coding in lexical access would show a more sequential left-to-right pattern of eye movements within and between words than subjects who accessed the lexicon through the direct path.

The second reason for studying eye movements was that some researchers have reported that basic oculomotor deficiencies may cause reading problems. These reports range from the extreme claim that abnormal eye movements are the "key to dyslexia" (Pavlidis, 1981), to Pirozzolo and Rayner's (1978) view that abnormal eye movements may be a factor for a "visual-spatial" subtype of disabled readers.

The disabled readers' eye movements were monitored while they read short stories of about 200 words at their reading grade level from the Spache Diagnostic Reading Scales (1963). One story was read aloud and another was read silently. Eight factual comprehension questions were asked at the end of each story. Subgroups of younger disabled and normal readers were also tested in a nonreading tracking task to see if there were any basic differences in general oculomotor skill.

Further details of our methods in the eye movement tasks and group comparisons between disabled and normal readers are presented in Kliegl (1982) and in Olson, Kliegl, and Davidson (1983a,b). In general, comparisons between the present disabled and normal groups show that the disabled readers make more fixations, slightly longer fixations, and proportionately more regressions. These results are consistent with many previous eye movement studies of group differences between good and poor readers (see Pirozzolo & Rayner, 1978; Tinker, 1958, for reviews). The novel contribution of the present research is its analysis of within-group differences in reading style based on matching patterns of fixations to the underlying text.

A. The "Plodder–Explorer" Dimension of Eye Movement Reading Style

Two eye movement parameters proved to be particularly useful for observing individual differences in reading style. They are the percentage of the subjects' eye movements that regressed to previous words in the text, and the percentage of forward eye movements that skipped words. The between-word regressive and progressive word-skipping eye movements were added together to represent a reading style dimension. At one end there are the "plodder" subjects who display relatively few regressions between words or word-skipping forward movements. They tend to move steadily forward, with more frequent forward saccades within the words and to the immediately following word. At the other end of the reading style dimension are the "explorer" subjects. They display relatively more regressions to previous words and forward word-skipping movements, and relatively fewer intraword and word-to-word progressive movements. These two types of readers might have equivalent word-recognition scores and they might finish reading the text in the same amount of time, but their patterns of visual attention were significantly different. The plodder and explorer subjects were also different on other important variables that we have been considering throughout the article. It should be emphasized that the plodder–explorer dimension was normally distributed and there was no evidence of distinct subtypes in eye movement reading style.

Before discussing the correlations of other variables with the plodder–explorer dimension, it may be helpful to observe the actual percentages of different types of eye movements that are obtained for subjects at different ends of the dimension. This was accomplished by dividing subjects on the plodder–explorer dimension at the median (which was .1 SD from the mean), and computing separate mean percentages of the different eye movements for subjects at the low (plodder) and high (explorer) ends. There were 37 subjects in the younger group and 41 subjects in the older group who had useable eye movement data.

Table VIII presents the mean percentages of six different types of eye movements that were matched to the underlying text, In addition, mean forward and regressive saccade lengths that were calculated independently from the underlying text are presented in number of character spaces. The last two variables are the mean fixation duration and the number of words read per second. The correlations of each of the percentages with the plodder–explorer dimension are presented in parentheses. The means in Table VIII are based on eye movements in the oral reading task. A similar pattern of eye movement percentages on the plodder–explorer dimension is present in the silent reading task.

Some justification is needed for adding the between-word regression and word-skipping percentages. (Actually the subjects' word-recognition-adjusted z scores for these percentages were added.) A pragmatic justification is that the correlations with the variables in Table IX are generally stronger when the two eye movement percentages are added than when either is considered alone. Also, the pattern of correlations is generally similar for the two types of eye movements across these variables. Finally, the between-word regressions and word-skipping movements are positively correlated with each other for old-subjects-oral (.28), old-subjects-silent (.32), young-subjects-oral (.35), and young-subjects-silent (.37) conditions. Multiple regression models tested whether word skipping and regression percentages entered separately do a better job of accounting for variance in the other variables than the plodder–explorer dimension. They do not.

Relations between the percentages of the six word-based eye movements are reciprocal. Since the percentages of between-word regressions and word skipping are higher for explorer subjects, their percentages must be lower on some of the other types of eye movements. In Table VIII it can be seen

TABLE VIII

Means for Eye Movement Percentages and Related Variables in Plodders and Explorers and Correlations with the Plodder–Explorer Dimension[a]

	Young			Old		
	Plodder ($n = 18$)	(r)	Explorer ($n = 19$)	Plodder ($n = 21$)	(r)	Explorer ($n = 20$)
Word to word (w.)	40.9%	(−.57)	35.0%	40.1%	(−.83)	31.0%
Word skipping	7.2%	(.82)	10.7%	12.3%	(.80)	19.2%
Regress between w.	14.6%	(.82)	19.4%	13.1%	(.80)	17.5%
Progress within w.	22.1%	(−.49)	18.7%	19.2%	(−.56)	14.8%
Regress within w.	10.3%	(.30)	11.2%	9.7%	(.27)	11.1%
Line switch (total)	4.8% (100%)	(.11)	5.1% (100%)	5.5% (100%)	(.31)	6.6% (100%)
Fixation duration (msec)	411	(−.30)	372	332	(−.45)	293
Words read per second	1.04	(−.10)	1.15	1.52	(−.25)	1.73
Progressive saccade	4.44	(.70)	5.16	5.35	(.65)	6.57
Regressive saccade	4.67	(.16)	4.95	4.95	(−.09)	4.76

[a]Percentages are mean values for subjects above and below the median on the plodder–explorer dimension. Progressive and regressive saccades are in number of characters spanned. Values in parentheses are correlations of the variable with the plodder–explorer dimension. All correlations larger than $r = .26$ are significant ($p < .05$).

that they are significantly lower than the plodders in word-to-word and within-word progressive movements. The explorers also tend to have shorter fixation durations and longer forward-saccade lengths, but they are not significantly different in reading rate. This indicates that they make slightly more eye movements than the plodders, but they finish reading the text in about the same time. How are these different eye movement reading styles related to the other variables we have been studying?

The first part of this section is concerned with the relations between eye movements and the disabled readers' coding skills and spelling ratings. The second part is concerned with eye movement relations to verbal intelligence, semantic errors, and comprehension of the text. Correlations with each of the relevant variables are presented for the younger and older groups in Table IX, separated for oral and silent stories.

B. Eye Movements, Coding Skills, and Spelling Ratings

The correlations for the young disabled readers in the oral stories are discussed first, followed by their performance in the silent condition. Then the results for the older subjects are presented.

1. Young Subjects in the Oral Reading Condition

Recall that in the spelling analyses, the similarity ratings of spelling errors and orthographic skill are negatively correlated for the younger group (see Table VII). In Table IX, it can be seen that these measures are also oppositely related to the younger subjects' eye movements. Those readers whose spelling similarity ratings are higher and those who are relatively poor in the orthographic task tend to be on the plodder end of the eye movement dimension. Hierarchical regression analyses indicated that the orthographic task and the spelling ratings mostly overlap in the variance they account for in the plodder–explorer dimension. This suggests that performance in both tasks is based on the same underlying individual differences in coding processes.

It was argued in the spelling section that poor performance in the orthographic task and the associated higher spelling similarity ratings indicate a

TABLE IX

Correlations for Coding Skills, Spelling Ratings, Comprehension, Semantic Errors, and Verbal Intelligence with the Plodder–Explorer Dimension for Younger and Older Subjects in Oral (O) and Silent (S) Stories.[a]

	Ortho. skill	Phonol. skill	Visual spelling rating	Phonological spelling rating	Comprehension	Semantic errors	Kaufman verb. IQ
Young (O) plodder–explorer	.54**	−.25	−.38*	−.46**	.10	.31*	.56**
(S)	.39**	−.02	−.21	−.33*	.15	.15	.40**
Old (O) plodder–explorer	.11	−.08	.11	−.10	.23	.21	.58**
(S)	.13	−.16	.28*	−.03	.30*	.34*	.50**

[a] $n = 37$ in young group and 41 in old group. $*p < .05$; $**p < .01$.

greater tendency to use small-unit phonological coding in lexical access and spelling. In relation to eye movements, greater use of small-unit phonological coding in lexical access would yield a plodder style of reading because the subject sequentially attends to the grapheme–phoneme correspondence patterns in words rather than the larger orthographic images for whole words. Thus, plodders show significantly higher percentages of within-word and word-to-word progressive eye movements (see Table VIII).

Separate analyses of the eye movement percentages indicate that both between-word regression and word-skipping components of the plodder–explorer dimension account for significant variance in orthographic skill and the spelling ratings. However, for the within-word and word-to-word movements, only the within-word progressions are significantly related to orthographic skill ($r = -.46$), and phonological spelling ratings ($r = .29$). The respective correlations in the silent condition are $r = -.34$, and $r = .41$, and again there are no significant correlations with the word-to-word progressive movements. Although word-to-word progressive movements are the modal pattern and they show significant variance in relation to the plodder–explorer dimension, their variance is not related to individual differences in coding and spelling. Also, there are no significant correlations with the percentages of intraword negative movements and line switches, or with mean length of negative saccades.

Mean length of positive saccades is strongly correlated with word skipping ($r = .68$ oral, $r = .65$ silent), for obvious reasons. It is also positively related to between-word regressions ($r = .46$ oral, $r = .36$ silent), and it is negatively related to intraword-positive movements ($r = -.52$ oral, $-.80$ silent). Thus, it is not surprising that mean-forward-saccade length relates to orthographic skill and the spelling ratings in much the same way as the plodder–explorer dimension. For the young subjects, the correlations with mean-forward-saccade length are orthographic skill, $r = .45$ oral, $r = .43$ silent; visual rating, $r = -.26$ oral, $r = -.22$ silent; phonological rating, $r = -.36$ oral, $r = -.43$ silent. It is apparent that this single eye movement parameter, which is based on a relatively simple calculation of mean-forward-saccade length independent from the underlying text, captures much of the variance in reading style for these variables. However, we will continue to discuss the data for the plodder–explorer dimension and the specific eye movement percentages because they give a better indication of the dynamics of individual differences in reading style.

The eye movement correlations with verbal intelligence will be discussed later. For now, it is important to note that orthographic skill and the spelling ratings predict variance in the plodder–explorer dimension independently from verbal intelligence. Hierarchical analyses indicated that orthographic skill and verbal intelligence account for about 20% independent variance in the plodder–explorer dimension after taking the other variable into account. Their multiple correlation with the plodder–explorer dimension is .70. Adding the subjects' phonological or visual spelling ratings to the model raises the multiple r nonsignificantly to .71. This is an impressive amount of variance considering the reliability of the measures. A conservative estimate of the reliability of the explorer–plodder dimension was obtained by correlating the subjects' position on this dimension in the oral and silent stories ($r = .77$). Since the tasks of oral and silent reading are different, reliability within the same condition should be higher. This is quite remarkable for such a brief reading task. The stories were only about 200 words in length and the mean reading time was only about 3 minutes. However, this yielded about 300 to 600 eye movements per subject for the calculation of the different eye movement percentages.

In spite of the apparent power of the eye movement measures to detect individual differences in reading style, phonological skill is not significantly correlated with the plodder–explorer dimension when measured by the forced-choice task ($r = -.25$ oral, $r = -.02$ silent), or by the oral nonword reading task ($r = -.18$ oral, $r = -.10$ silent). However, there were small but significant correlations for phonological skill in the forced-choice task with the percentage of within-word-progressive movements in both oral ($r = .27$) and silent ($r = .30$) conditions, and there were also small but significant correlations with mean-forward-saccade length ($r = -.29$ oral, $r = -.33$ silent).

The relation between phonological skill, defined by the ability to read nonwords, and reading style, presently indicated by the plodder–explorer dimension, seems to be quite small compared to the eye movement relations with the use of small-unit phonological coding and the strength of orthographic codes. Some research has suggested that phonological skill might be more related to reading style in subjects younger than ours (cf. Mitterer, 1982). The reason for this may be that very young readers have very limited orthographic knowledge and their reading of nonwords may depend more on the use of small-unit grapheme–phoneme conversion rules.

2. Young Subjects in the Silent Reading Condition

The correlations with the plodder–explorer dimension in Table IX are consistently but not significantly lower in the silent condition than in the oral condition for younger readers' orthographic skill and the spelling ratings. Perhaps the added stress of reading aloud accentuates individual differences in style associated with differences in coding processes. It is also possible that children's coding processes in silent reading are generally less phonological. Treiman *et al.* (1983) suggested that this may be true for normal adult readers. However, the different patterns of eye movements in oral and silent reading do not indicate a major change in coding processes. From the oral to the silent condition, regressions between words declined from 17.1 to 15.6%, word skipping movements increased from 9 to 10.1%, and intraword positive movements declined from 20.3 to 19.5%. None of these differences is significant. Thus, there is no indication from the subjects' eye movements that there is a difference in small-unit phonological coding between the oral and silent reading conditions.

3. Eye Movements, Spelling Ratings, and Coding Skills in the Older Group

As in the previous developmental comparisons for the spelling ratings, there are no significant relations for orthographic skill, visual spelling rating, or phonological spelling rating to the older subjects' eye movements. Differences in the size of the correlations between the age groups are significant by Fisher's z test for orthographic skill and phonological and visual spelling ratings in the oral condition. Only for orthographic skill could the reduced correlation for the older subjects be attributed to a substantial reduction in variance and reliability for the measure.

To review the developmental argument made before, the older subjects may be less likely to use small-unit phonological coding in lexical access because with their greater reading experience, they can depend more on large-unit orthographic codes. This would reduce the variance in small-unit phonological coding in the older subjects that could be related to individual differences in eye movements. The older subjects' lower percentages for within-word progressive eye movements and higher percentages for word skipping are consistent with this view (see Table VIII).

The absence of significant correlations between eye movements, spelling ratings, and coding skills in the older group might have led us to doubt the relevance of their eye movements to individual differences in reading style. However, the older subjects' strong correlation between the plodder–explorer dimension and verbal intelligence described below shows that eye movements are a valid measure of differences in reading style across a broad age range.

C. Verbal Intelligence and the Plodder–Explorer Dimension

We did not predict the correlations between the plodder–explorer dimension and verbal intelligence that appeared in both age groups (see Table IX). They were first observed at a slightly lower level for the WISC-R verbal subscale. The correlations in Table IX are based on a measure developed by Kaufman (1975) from his factor analysis of the WISC-R tests. Kaufman found that four of the WISC-R tests, Information, Vocabulary, Similarities, and Comprehension loaded on a verbal factor. Our measure of verbal intelligence is an unweighted average of these four tests, each of which was significantly correlated with the plodder–explorer dimension at a slightly lower level than the mean for the four tests. The other WISC-R tests loaded on two factors that Kaufman called Perceptual Organization and Freedom from Distractability. Neither of these is significantly related to the subjects' eye movements.

1. Younger Subjects

Analyses of the specific eye movement percentages in the younger subjects revealed similar correlations with verbal intelligence for word skipping and between-word regressions ($r = .51$, $r = .41$, respectively, for oral reading; $r = .39$, $r = .27$, respectively, for silent reading). The correlations between intraword-positive movements and verbal intelligence are $r = -.42$ (oral) and $r = -.56$ (silent). Again, as for the coding and spelling variables, there are no significant correlations with the word-to-word progressive movements, intraword-regressive movements, or the mean length of regressive movements, but the mean length of forward saccades correlated at $r = .53$ (oral) and $r = .56$ (silent) with verbal intelligence. The patterns of eye movement correlations with verbal intelligence in the younger group are similar to those with orthographic skill. A theoretical account for why the correlations are observed with orthographic skill and the spelling ratings has been presented, but the reasons for the similar correlations of eye movements with verbal intelligence may be different because verbal intelligence and orthographic skill each account for about 20% independent variance in the plodder–explorer dimension. We will return to this question after presenting the results for the older subjects.

2. Older Subjects

The pattern of component eye movement correlations with verbal intelligence is somewhat different for the older subjects. Word skipping and between-word regressions are similarly correlated with verbal intelligence ($r = .43$, $r = .52$, respectively, for oral reading; $r = .47$, $r = .39$, respectively, for silent reading). The correlations between the intraword-positive movements and verbal intelligence are $r = -.56$ in the oral condition and $r = -.21$ in the silent condition. Mean lengths of forward saccades are correlated at $r = .43$ (oral) and $r = .49$ (silent) with verbal intelligence. The main age difference is the older subjects' significant correlations between verbal intelligence and word-to-word progressive movements ($r = -.42$ oral, $r = -.53$ silent). The reason for this difference between the age groups is that the older subjects' saccades are generally longer, and they skip more words (see Table VIII). Thus, there is a much stronger trade off in the older group between the other eye movement percentages and word-to-word movements on the plodder–explorer dimension (see Table VIII).

3. Basis for the Verbal Intelligence Correlations

One possible reason the more verbally intelligent disabled readers tend to rely on a more exploratory approach is because they have the general knowledge and oral vocabulary that allows them to depend less on the use of phonological coding in reading words, and more on the use of context. The idea of less phonological coding for the more verbally intelligent subjects is only marginally supported by the direction of correlations for verbal intelligence with the younger subjects' orthographic skill ($r = .21, p > .05$), phonological skill ($r = -.23, p > .05$), and phonological spelling ratings ($r = -.35, p < .05$). However, processes indicated in the coding and spelling tasks were not measured in a situation where context could play a role. For example, the way a subject reads the word *rain* in the orthographic task could be different from his approach in the context of a story, depending on his verbal intelligence. There is some evidence to support this hypothesis from the reading errors the subjects made in the oral stories. The more intelligent explorer subjects tended to make errors that were more semantically appropriate in the text (see Table IX). However, the correlations were not very large and were significant in only two of the four conditions, perhaps because the subjects did not make enough errors in the short stories, which were adjusted for difficulty according to their word recognition scores.

The above explanation of the link between verbal intelligence and eye movements is based on the same relations of word decoding processes with eye movements that were described before. From this point of view, orthographic skill and verbal intelligence account for significant independent variance in the plodder–explorer dimension in the younger group because the two variables pick up on different sources of individual differences in word coding processes. But there may be other influences of verbal intelligence on eye movements.

In view of the greater use of context by the more intelligent explorers that was inferred above from their more semantically appropriate errors, we expected to find a correlation between eye movements and the subjects' performance on the comprehension test that was given after each story. It can be seen in Table IX that comprehension is significantly correlated with the plodder–explorer dimension only for the older subjects in the silent condition. Actually, these ambiguous results are not too surprising since the stories were short, the questions were few (eight), and they pertained to simple facts in the stories. Most subjects did quite well on the tests so ceiling effects may have obscured true individual differences in comprehension.

The strong relation between eye movements and verbal intelligence is intriguing and it invites further research with longer texts, more extensive analyses of the subjects' errors, more converging evidence on the subjects' differential use of small-unit phonological coding in text, and memory tests for the gist and surface structure of the text. One hypothesis to be tested in future research is that the more verbally intelligent subjects tend to make more exploratory eye movements because they are more concerned with monitoring their comprehension of the text and maintaining their memory for previous words. There is substantial evidence that disabled readers suffer from limitations in phonological memory (see the third section), that may be needed to integrate the words in a sentence for semantic interpretation (cf. Kleiman, 1975). The more intelligent disabled readers greater frequency of between-word regressions in text may be related to a memory restoration function.

D. Eye Movements in a Nonreading Task and the "Visual–Spatial" Subtype

Eye movements were also monitored in a tracking task to see if there is any difference in basic oculomotor function between or within groups that might account for the results in reading. Some eye movement researchers and reading therapists have argued that the abnormal eye movements observed in disabled readers during reading are a cause rather than an effect of their reading difficulties (cf. Punnett & Steinhauer, 1984). Generally there has been little evidence to support this causal interpretation (Pirozzolo & Rayner, 1978; Tinker, 1958), although Pavlidis (1981) has recently reported that abnormal eye movements in his tracking task were the "key to dyslexia." Pavlidis reported that his 12 disabled readers made many more eye movements and proportionally more regressions than normal readers in a simple tracking task, and the distributions for the two groups did not overlap.

Some of the present subjects were tested in a tracking task similar to the one used by Pavlidis (1981). Details of the methods and results of this test may be found in Olson et al. (1983b). Briefly, 34 disabled and 36 normal readers (mean age = 11 years) were asked to follow a point on the screen as it shifted sequentially to five positions from left-to-right and right-to-left. There are no significant differences between disabled and normal readers' tracking eye movements. Similar null results have been reported in two other studies (Brown, Haegerstrom-Portnoy, Adams, Yingling, Galin, Herron, & Marcus, 1983; Stanley, Smith, & Howell, 1983). Also, there are no significant correlations within the disabled group between tracking eye movements and Kaufman's verbal, perception, and distractability factors from the WISC-R, or any of the coding and spelling tasks.

Pirozzolo and Rayner (1978) have reported from a few case studies that there is a "visual–spatial" subtype of disabled reader whose eye movements are distinctly abnormal, but these individuals must be quite rare in the reading disabled population. Rayner (1983) has also recently reported that the "visual–spatial" subtype is very rare. His estimate is that the "visual–spatial" subtype includes less than 10% of disabled readers. To see if there was a small group of "visual–spatial" dyslexics in the present sample that might have been concealed in correlations for the whole group, 10% of the disabled readers were selected who had complete eye movement data and who had the high-verbal, low-performance pattern on the WISC-R that has been described as characteristic of the "visual–spatial" subtype (Pirozzolo, 1983). After controlling for the subjects' verbal intelligence, there were no significant differences in eye movements between the 12 high-verbal–low-performance subjects and the rest of the sample. Thus, there was no indication of a significant "visual–spatial" subtype with eye-movement problems.

As Rayner (1983) has suggested, the "visual–spatial" subtype is quite rare. The present results indicate that it probably accounts for far less than 10% of disabled readers in school-referred samples. Such cases might be more frequently observed in clinic populations, although Snowling (personal communication) has estimated that no more than one in 50 of her reading disabled patients have reading difficulties that might be related to visual–perceptual deficits. Thus, the frequent regressions and larger number of eye movements commonly observed for the vast majority of disabled readers seems to be due to their difficulty in reading, and the individual differences in eye movement reading style observed among our disabled readers reflect different ways of coping with their reading problem that are associated with their different word decoding strategies and verbal intelligence.

VI. DISTRIBUTION AND ETIOLOGY
OF READING DISABILITIES

There are two remaining questions to be addressed in this final section. The first is the distribution of reading disabilities in the population, and the second related question is the cause of reading disabilities.

A. Distribution Issues

Many previous efforts at subtyping disabled readers have drawn cases from clinics in large metropolitan areas. There is no way of knowing how representative these clinic samples may be of the general problem of reading disability in the schools (Snowling, 1983). Often, subtypes have been identified on the basis of one or a few individuals, with no indication of their frequency in the population. The present sample provided a unique opportunity to assess the frequency of different reading disabilities. About half of the children who were reading disabled in several Boulder area schools participated in the project. Although the sample was not exhaustive, there was no indication that it was biased. Those disabled readers and their parents who declined to participate in the project often cited the inconvenience caused by the three extensive test sessions.

Two issues are addressed from this sample regarding the distribution of reading disabilities. The first issue is the distinctiveness of levels of reading ability in the disabled sample compared to the rest of the population. The second issue is whether different reading disabilities consist of distinct subtypes or continuous distributions.

1. Distribution of Reading Ability in the Population

Some researchers who work with school samples view reading disability as the extreme low end of the normal distribution of reading ability in the population, excluding those poor readers who have obvious neurological problems (cf. Perfetti, 1984a). More commonly, reading disability or dyslexia is viewed as a distinct syndrome that is separate from the normal distribution of reading ability. The only evidence for the statistical separation of dyslexia from the normal distribution of reading ability is the analysis by Yule, Rutter, Berger, and Thompson (1974) of five large and exhaustive samples of English school children. They reported that while a normal distribution would predict that 2.28% of the children would read less than two standard deviations below the mean for their population, the average for the groups was about 4%. However, a closer inspection of their results suggests that this overrepresentation is probably an artifact of skew in three of the five samples where the mode was clearly above 0 standard deviation. This seemed to have been caused by ceiling effects in the reading tests for these three samples. The authors acknowledged that the reading tests for these groups may have been more sensitive to skill differences in the lower range, and variance in performance was limited in the high range. It seems likely that this accounts for the larger than expected proportion of readers that was more than two standard deviations below the mean in these three samples. In the two samples that did not have obviously skewed distributions and apparent ceiling effects, the number of readers two standard deviations below the mean was not significantly greater than expected from a normal distribution. A recent study by Rodgers (1983) used tests of reading ability that were selected to avoid ceiling and floor effects. No significant deviations were observed from a normal distribution for reading ability in Rodgers's sample of 8836 10 year olds above 70 IQ. This result questions the qualitative distinction made by many researchers between "dyslexic" and less severely disabled "poor" readers.

We do not have data on reading ability for all of the children in the Boulder schools, so it can't be demonstrated that the distributions of reading ability in our population is normal. However, we can address a slightly different but related question. The present sample contained a sufficient range of reading ability in the disabled group so that separate analyses could be done with the subjects that would meet the traditional criteria for reading disability or "dyslexia," and subjects that some researchers would describe as "poor" readers who are not sufficiently retarded to be identified as "dyslexic" (see Section II for selection criteria). If the "dyslexics" are an etiologically and distributionally distinct group, they might show some qualitative differences from the "poor" readers in their reading processes. We attempted to test this hypothesis by dividing the disabled readers into groups of "dyslexics" who were below 70% of their expected grade level and "poor" readers who were above the 70% criterion, but still well below their normal controls. This was an arbitrary division, since there was no indication of any bimodality for reading ability in the present disabled sample.

There are quantitative but not qualitative differences between the "dyslexic" and "poor" groups. For example, the "dyslexic" group averaged about 2 years lower in PIAT word recognition than the "poor" group, and they made about 5% more errors on both the phonological and orthographic coding tasks. Thus, the relative-phonological coding deficit is similar for both groups and both groups show a greater relative-phonological deficit than the normal readers. Also, separate analyses of within-group differences in reading style were performed for the "dyslexic" and "poor" readers. The same patterns of individual differences are present in both groups.

The above results are consistent with the view that many readers identified as "dyslexic" may be part of the normal distribution of reading ability. Later we will discuss the implications of this view for the etiology of reading disability. It should be emphasized that while the continuum view seems to be appropriate for the disabled readers tested in the present study, it does not exclude the possibility that there are some unique "dyslexics" that may contribute to a deviation from the normal curve that is difficult to detect statistically. The uniqueness of these subjects from other disabled readers would have to be demonstrated by behavioral, neurological, and genetic analyses.

2. Distinct Subtypes versus Dimensions of Individual Differences

A classic study by Kinsbourne and Warrington (1963) deliberately selected extreme cases of delayed readers to highlight differences. Others who have followed Kinsbourne and Warrington have cited their work as support for distinct subtypes, but Kinsbourne (1982) has recently cautioned that the underlying behavioral distributions may be continuous. He recommended multivariate approaches to the study of individual differences.

Boder's (1973) dichotomous classification of dyseidetic and dysphonetic readers suggests a very clear separation, resulting from distinctly different causes, and requiring distinctly different remediation techniques (Boder and Jarrico, 1982). However, the present study revealed essentially normal distributions of component reading skill and style differences in the present sample. Even where there are deviations from strict normality indicated by significant kurtosis or skew, there is no evidence for multimodality in the distributions. One example is from the analysis of spelling errors. While Boder described distinct dyseidetic and dysphonetic subtypes from her analysis of spelling errors, the present subjects' spelling errors vary on continuous dimensions of visual and phonological similarity. As in a recent study by Finucci et al. (1983), the disabled readers' errors are generally less phonologically similar to the target word than those of the normal readers. Within the disabled group, the ratings range continuously from moderate to low similarity with the target word. A division of this continuum into dyseidetic and dysphonetic subtypes would be arbitrary.

Recent approaches to subtyping disabled readers have used cluster and Q factor analyses of their performance on various tests (Doehring et al., 1981; Lyon & Watson, 1981; Naidoo, 1972; Petrauskas & Rourke, 1979; Satz & Morris, 1981; Vavrus, Brown, & Carr, 1983). These clustering approaches have yielded varying numbers of subtypes. At present there has been no attempt to integrate the subtyping results across the different studies. Within the study by Doehring et al., no relation was found between subtypes defined by reading tasks and those defined by language tests and neuropsychological tests on the same subjects. Some have suggested that further research is needed to validate and clarify the meaning of subtypes identified in cluster analyses (Fisk & Rourke, 1983; McKinney, 1984; Satz & Morris, 1981).

Cluster analyses were performed by Vogler, Baker, Decker, and DeFries

(1984) on the WISC-R subtests and other psychometric measures of cognitive and reading skills for the present subjects. After examining the results of several different clustering algorithims, it was concluded that although there were substantial individual differences in the test profiles, the clusters did not define distinct and homogeneous subtypes. Rather, the subjects' variation in performance patterns on these tests were better characterized by a multivariate continuum. It appeared that the clustering routines were defining clusters due to minor and possibly random departures from a continuous distribution. The presence of continuous distributions for individual differences in reading disability is seen below to have implications for their etiology.

B. Etiology of Reading Disabilities

Three types of evidence bear on the causes of different reading disabilities in the present sample. First is the continuous distributions described above. Second is the relation between differences in reading processes and basic cognitive skills. Third is the evidence from a few of our subjects that teaching method may have a major influence on their reading styles.

1. Etiological Implications of Subtypes and Continuous Distributions

Distinct subtypes suggest distinct causes for different reading disabilities such as different training programs, localized brain damage (cf. Coltheart, 1981; Saffran & Marin, 1977), or single gene inheritance patterns (Smith, Kimberling, Pennington, & Lubs, 1983). Continuous distributions suggest multiple causes and polygenic models of inheritance (DeFries & Decker, 1982). This is also true for the distribution of reading ability. If disabled readers are distinctly separate from the normal distribution of reading ability, single gene factors or some unique environmental insult would be likely. An alternate view is that due to polygenic inheritance patterns and/or continuously varying environmental influences, disabled readers are very low in the specific cognitive skills needed for normal reading, just as superior readers may be very high in these critical skills.

Of course it is possible that the distinct subtype view is correct for some disabled readers, but they could not be distinguished with the present behavioral measures. It is also possible that our selection criteria excluded subjects who might have fit one or more distinct subtypes. Evidence of brain damage resulted in the exclusion of a few children who were referred from the schools. Such disabled readers may be more frequent in clinic samples where distinct subtypes are often reported. Their exclusion from the present sample is in accord with commonly accepted definitions of reading disability or dyslexia.

2. Reading Style Differences and Basic Cognitive Resources

Boder and Jarrico (1982) cited several unpublished studies that found a link between the dyseidetic and dysphonetic classification of reading-disabled subjects and their different performance patterns on the WISC-R subscales. It was concluded that the observed individual differences in reading and spelling styles were caused by different patterns of cognitive deficit. Dyseidetics were reported to be lower in the WISC-R performance subscale than in the verbal subscale while dysphonetics were lower in the verbal subscale. However, a recent study in Holland by van den Bos (1984) classified reading disabled children as dysphonetic or dyseidetic and found no significant differences between these two groups of children in specially designed tasks that separated their visual and auditory processing abilities. A second study by Hooper and Hynd (1984) classified reading-disabled children with the Boder and Jarrico test and compared the dyseidetic and disphonetic subtypes' performance on the Kaufman Assessment Battery for Children (K-ABC). There were no significant differences between the subtypes in their K-ABC performance patterns that were consistent with Boder's (1973) cognitive deficit theory.

Boder's (1973) theory was evaluated in the present study by comparing the ratio of phonological skill to orthographic skill with the ratio of verbal IQ to performance IQ, after partialing out word recognition. The correlation for all disabled readers was $r = .01$. Next, the separate partial correlations of phonological skill, orthographic skill, phonological spelling ratings, and visual spelling ratings with performance IQ were calculated. Boder's theory predicts that subjects low in phonological skill and high in whole-word reading would tend to be stronger in the performance IQ subscale than subjects who are high in phonological skill and low in whole-word reading. However, none of the correlations with performance IQ was larger than $r = -.08$.

Apparently the differences between dyseidetic and dysphonetic reading and spelling patterns bear no relation to the visual–gestalt processing skills measured by the WISC-R performance subscale. This conclusion is consistent with Vellutino's (1979) view that basic visual–gestalt processing deficits do not make a significant contribution to reading disability. Of course there have been case studies reported in the literature where visual processing deficits were associated with reading problems, but these cases must be quite rare. To see if a few of the present subjects might fit Boder's (1973) dyseidetic visual-deficit theory, 12 disabled readers who had the greatest deficit in performance IQ were compared with the rest of the sample. As reported in the previous section for eye movements, they were not significantly different from the rest of the sample in their coding skills or reading styles.

Several of the studies that have used cluster techniques with various measures of verbal and perceptual skills have identified subtypes with perceptual or perceptual-motor impairment (cf. Lyon & Watson, 1981; Satz & Morris, 1981). For example, Lyon and Watson's largest of seven subtypes contained 32% of their disabled readers and was characterized by deficits in visual perception. We argued previously that cluster analyses could identify such a subtype that was not really distinct from the rest of the sample (Vogler *et al.*, 1984). In addition, our analyses indicate that perceptual performance is not significantly related to differences in reading style or the component reading skills.

Correlations were also calculated for the coding, reading, and spelling measures with Kaufman's (1975) verbal factor. The correlations with the plodder–explorer dimension have already been discussed. In addition, there was some indication of a trade-off between phonological skill and verbal intelligence in the present sample that was opposite the relation hypothesized by Boder (1973). In the age subgroups used for the individual-difference analyses, the correlation between Kaufman's (1975) verbal factor and phonological skill was significantly negative for the older subjects ($r = -.28$). The correlation was also negative but not significant for the younger group ($r = -.23$). For the 59 younger disabled readers whose phonological skill could be estimated from their oral nonword reading, this measure of phonological skill was negatively correlated with Kaufman's verbal factor ($r = -.28$). While these negative correlations are not very strong, they suggest that there is an interaction between basic phonological coding skills and higher level verbal skills in determining the subjects ability to recognize words. The more verbally intelligent children tend to have better oral vocabularies, and they may have more reading experience. This may supplement their weak phonological skills and bring them to a given level of word recognition that less intelligent readers would have to rely more on phonological skill to reach.

3. Environmental Influences on Individual Differences in Reading Style

Kinsbourne (1982) has suggested that some poor readers, regardless of their basic deficit, may appear similar to Boder's (1973) dyseidetics with their slow and painstaking phonological decoding of words, because they have been overinstructed in a phonics approach such as that emphasized by the Orton-Gillingham method. Unfortunately, reliable data on precisely how the present subjects were taught to read were not available, but some anecdotal examples suggest a strong role for training methods. In a current study of reading disability in families, two brothers were tested. One showed a strong explorer reading style in eye movements while the other was a plodder. When these patterns were shown to their parents, they volunteered the information that the two boys had been taught to read by very different methods. The plodder had been taught with a heavy emphasis on phonics, and the younger explorer, who was making more rapid progress in learning to read, was being encouraged to develop his sight-reading skills and to use context as an aid in word decoding. Both children attended the same school, but the approaches of their individual teachers were quite different.

A second example suggests that individual differences in reading style may sometimes be overtly strategic, and subjects may sometimes vary their phonological reading strategies depending upon their perception of the task demands. After plodding through the oral reading task, painstakingly sounding out unknown words with only moderate success, one disabled reader mentioned after the test series that he read for us as he did in school, but he read differently when reading his comic books for pleasure. Then he did not worry about making mistakes that did not sound like the target word and would often guess the word's identity from context. His special education teacher at school discouraged this approach and was trying to teach him phonics (without much success). When he was asked to read some additional paragraphs aloud in his normal pleasure mode, this subject shifted his eye movement reading style from the plodder to the explorer end of the dimension. Observations of other subjects have indicated that sometimes reading styles may shift from explorer to plodder within a paragraph, particularly when mistakes in word decoding lead to obvious inconsistencies in the text.

There may be other more subtle influences on reading style. Francis (1982) suggested from her studies of beginning readers that general personality differences and learning styles may be influential. For example, the cautious learner who attends to every detail may be more likely to use a phonics approach. It may be necessary to consider several diverse sources of variability to understand the etiology of each child's disability and to account for the distribution of different reading styles among disabled readers.

VII. SUMMARY AND NEW DIRECTIONS IN RESEARCH

Individual differences in reading disability were explored through the analysis of component reading processes and related cognitive skills. Reading theory provided a framework for the selection of tests and for understanding the relations between variables. Although the observed individual differences do not seem to form distinct subtypes, they do indicate substantial variability in reading processes and related cognitive skills within the disabled population.

The subjects' use and skill in the phonological and orthographic paths to the lexicon were studied in detail. Comparisons between the disabled and normal groups reveal a deficit for disabled readers in phonological coding that is substantially greater than their deficit in orthographic coding. The deficit in phonological coding seems to be the most distinctive characteristic of the disabled group. Along with some related problems in basic linguistic skills, it may be the cause of most severe deficits in reading ability that are not related to low intelligence or poor education.

Individual differences in orthographic skill converge with differences in the subjects' regularity effect, spelling error patterns, and eye movements to support a reading-style dimension within the disabled group that is independent from reading ability. Orthographic skill and the use of small-unit phonological codes are reciprocally related on this dimension. Disabled readers with relatively poor orthographic skill show greater use of the small-unit phonological path to the lexicon. In addition, there is a link between verbal intelligence and reading style. In contrast to disabled readers with relatively high verbal intelligence, those with low verbal intelligence show greater use of the small-unit phonological path by their plodding eye movements in text.

Developmental changes in reading and spelling styles lead to different patterns of individual differences for younger and older disabled readers. Differences in orthographic skill and spelling indicate substantial variance in the use of the small-unit phonological path for younger subjects, but these differences are not significantly related to reading style in the older disabled readers. We hypothesized that with greater reading experience, there is a decline in the use of the small-unit phonological path, and greater dependence on the orthographic path.

Figure 3 summarizes our view of the reading-style dimension along with the orthogonal dimension of reading ability. A normal curve is drawn to represent the continuity of the reading style dimension and its essentially normal distribution in the present sample. Different performance patterns are presented for each end of the dimension, along with the inferred use of the phonological and orthographic paths to the lexicon.

The dimensions in Fig. 3 may account for much of the variance in reading disability, but several theoretical and practical questions remain to be answered. First, there may be important individual differences among disabled readers in reading and auditory comprehension processes. Measures in the present study focused primarily on word decoding. This choice was

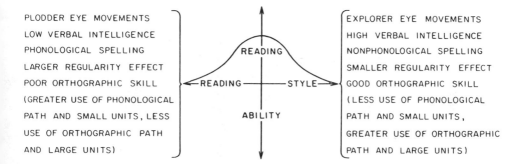

Fig. 3. Dimensions of reading style and reading ability.

made because testing time with the subjects was limited and there was substantial evidence from previous research that word decoding is the major factor contributing to the low levels of reading ability in the disabled population (for a review, see Stanovich, 1982). Nevertheless, there is variability in reading comprehension within the disabled sample that is independent from their word recognition, and comprehension of text is ultimately the best practical definition of reading ability. A complete model of individual differences in reading disability must take variance in comprehension into account (cf. Vavrus *et al.,* 1983; Maria & MacGinitie, 1982). The PIAT comprehension and the eye movement tests probably were not adequate for this purpose. We could determine that the "word-caller" syndrome that has been characterized as having normal word decoding with extremely poor comprehension is quite rare in our school sample. Only one subject seemed to show this pattern. Among the other disabled readers, there are small but significant correlations with comprehension for eye movements and verbal intelligence. These relations are currently being explored with more thorough measures of reading comprehension in longer texts.

A second remaining question concerns the etiology of reading disability and individual differences in reading style. Evidence continues to accumulate for the importance of basic language skills in learning to decode words (Venezky, Shiloah, & Calfee, 1972; Liberman *et al.,* 1974; Bradley & Bryant, 1983), but the origins of variance in these skills remain to be determined. One view is that reading disability is influenced by genetic factors (cf. DeFries & Decker, 1982). Individual differences in reading style may also have a genetic component. The genetic hypothesis is currently being tested in a study of reading disability in families and twins. In addition, environmental influences need to be more thoroughly evaluated. Evidence from a few cases in the present study indicated the influence of teaching methods on reading style in the disabled group, but most research on the consequences of teaching methods has only evaluated group differences in reading ability for normal classes (Perfetti, 1984b).

The consequences of early individual differences in reading style among disabled readers for their subsequent reading achievement are unknown. Some of the older subjects who were identified in a previous study as reading disabled showed improvement in reading ability compared to the rest of the sample while others declined (DeFries & Baker, 1982). Unfortunately, there were no measures of reading style for these subjects when they were first tested. In a current family study, we are retesting some disabled readers who were young subjects in the present study. The stability of their reading styles and relations to changes in reading ability across age are being evaluated.

Basic research on individual differences should ultimately suggest ways for the optimal remediation of different reading disabilities. It seems likely that teaching all disabled readers with the same method would not result in the maximum benefit for each individual. Although many researchers have acknowledged this possibility, there is little hard evidence on the best way to deal with different cases. The most common prescription is to put a heavy emphasis on phonics training, perhaps because this addresses the greatest deficiency in most disabled readers, and there is some indication that this may be the best approach for most children in the schools (Perfetti, 1984a). However, some of the present disabled readers who were the weakest phonological decoders had received extensive training in phonics, apparently with little benefit. We do not know how well they would have read without this training, but there is some evidence from a pilot study by Lyon (1983) that disabled readers with the weakest language skills did not benefit from phonics instruction, while those who were somewhat stronger in language skills showed substantial improvement in word recognition after phonics training.

Two recent studies have trained prereaders and beginning readers in the phonemic analysis skills that may be important for learning to phonologically decode words (Bradley & Bryant, 1983; Treiman & Baron, 1983). Both studies suggest a causal link between prereaders' training in the phonemic analysis of speech sounds and their later reading ability in the early grades. Children at risk for reading disability because of poorly developed language skills might benefit from phonemic analysis training prior to or in conjunction with reading instruction. Long ago, Huey (1908) noted the dependence of reading on language skills and advocated waiting until the child was sufficiently strong in language to learn to read without undue difficulty. Since Huey's advice is generally ignored and most schools begin the same reading instruction for all children around 5 or 6 years of age, early training in phonemic analysis for those children at risk may help reduce the negative impact of this policy.

ACKNOWLEDGMENTS

This research was supported by USPHS program project Grant HDMH11681-01A1, Richard Olson, co-investigator. We thank John DeFries, project director, Sadie Decker, project coordinator, and David Shucard, coinvestigator, for the collegial interaction that made this project possible. DeFries and Decker supervised the recruitment of subjects and psychometric testing. We also thank Linda McCabe for her supervision of the Camp and McCabe spelling test, graduate assistants Susan Davies and Barbara Wise for their contributions to all phases of the research, and Jan Keenan for her comments on earlier drafts of the manuscript. The final version of the manuscript benefited from the comments of Jon Baron, Elena Boder, Tom Carr, Uta Frith, Vicki Hanson, Marcel Kinsbourne, John Mitterer, Chuck Perfetti, Keith Rayner, Maggie Snowling, Keith Stanovich, Becky Treiman, and the Editor, Gary Waller.

REFERENCES

Allport, A. Word recognition in reading. In P.A. Kolers, M. E. Wrolstad, & H. Bouma (Eds.), *Processing of visible language* (vol. 1). New York: Plenum, 1977.

Andrews, S. Phonological recoding: Is the regularity effect consistent? *Memory and Cognition,* 1982, **10**, 565–575.

Bakker, D. J. Hemispheric differences and reading strategies: Two dyslexias? *Bulletin of the Orton Society,* 1979, **14**, 84–100.

Baron, J. Mechanisms for pronouncing printed words: Use and acquisition. In D. LaBerge & S. J. Samuels (Eds.), *Basic processes in reading: Perception and comprehension.* Hillsdale, New Jersey: Erlbaum, 1977.

Baron, J. Orthographic and word specific mechanisms in children's reading of words. *Child Development,* 1979, **50**, 60–72.

Baron, J., & Strawson, C. Orthographic and word-specific mechanisms in reading words aloud. *Journal of Experimental Psychology: Human Perception and Performance,* 1976, **2**, 386–393.

Baron, J., Treiman, R., Wilf, J. F., & Kellman, P. Spelling and reading by rules. In U. Frith (Ed.), *Cognitive processes in spelling.* New York: Academic Press, 1980.

Barron, R. W. Visual and phonological strategies in reading and spelling. In U. Frith (Ed.), *Cognitive processes in spelling.* New York: Academic Press, 1980. Pp. 195–215.

Benton, A. L., & Pearl, D. (Eds.), *Dyslexia: An appraisal of current knowledge.* London and New York: Oxford Univ. Press, 1978.

Besner, D., Coltheart, M., & Davelaar, E. Basic processes in reading: Computation of abstract letter identities. *Canadian Journal of Psychology,* 1984, **38**, 126–134.

Boder, E. Developmental dyslexia: Prevailing diagnostic concepts and a new diagnostic approach. In H. Myklebust (Ed.), *Progress in learning disabilities* (Vol. 2). New York: Grune & Stratton, 1971.

Boder, E. Developmental dyslexia: A diagnostic approach based on three atypical reading-spelling patterns. *Developmental Medicine and Child Neurology,* 1973, **15**, 663–687.

Boder, E., & Jarrico, S. *The Boder test of reading-spelling patterns: A diagnostic screening test for subtypes of reading disability.* New York: Grune & Stratton, 1982.

Bradley, L., & Bryant, P. E. Difficulties in auditory organization as a possible cause of reading backwardness. *Nature (London),* 1978, **271**, 746–747.

Bradley, L., & Bryant, P. Visual memory and phonological skills in reading and spelling backwardness. *Psychological Research,* 1981, **43**, 193–199.

Bradley, L., & Bryant, P. Categorizing sounds and learning to read, a causal connection. *Nature (London)* 1983, 301, 419–421.

Briggs, P., & Underwood, G. Phonological coding in good and poor readers. *Journal of Experimental Child Psychology,* 1982, **24**, 93–112.

Bronner, A. F. *The psychology of special abilities and disabilities.* Boston: Little Brown, 1917.

Brown, B., Haegerstrom-Portnoy, G., Adams, A. J., Yingling, C. D., Galin, D., Herron, J., & Marcus, M. Predictive eyemovements do not discriminate between dyslexic and control children. *Neuropsychologia,* 1983, **21**, 121–128.

Bryant, P. E., & Bradley, L. Why children sometimes write words which they do not read. In U. Frith (Ed.), *Cognitive processes in reading and spelling.* New York: Academic Press, 1980.

Byrne, B., & Shea, P. Semantic and phonetic memory codes in beginning readers. *Memory and Cognition,* 1979, **7**, 333–338.

Camp, B. W., & McCabe, L. *Denver reading and spelling test.* Unpublished manuscript, University of Colorado Medical Center, 1977.

Carr, T. H. Building theories of reading ability: On the relation between individual differences in cognitive skills and reading comprehension. *Cognition,* 1981, **9**, 73–114.

Carr, T. H., Posner, M. I., Polatsek, A., & Snyder, C. R. R. Orthography and familiarity effects in word processing. *Journal of Experimental Psychology: General,* 1979, **108**, 389–414.

Cohen, R. L., & Netley, C. Short-term memory deficits in reading disabled children, in the absence of opportunity for rehearsal strategies. *Intelligence,* 1981, **5**, 69–76.

Coltheart, M. Lexical access in simple reading tasks. In G. Underwood (Ed.), *Strategies in information processing.* New York: Academic Press, 1978.

Coltheart, M. Reading, phonological encoding and deep dyslexia. In M. Coltheart, K. Patterson, & J. C. Marshal (Eds.), *Deep dyslexia.* London: Routledge & Kegan Paul, 1980.

Coltheart, M. Disorders of reading and their implications for models of normal reading. *Visible Language,* 1981, **15** (3), 245–286.

Critchley, M. *The dyslexic child.* London: Heinemann, 1970.

Cronbach, L. J. Coefficient alpha and the internal structure of tests. *Psychometrica,* 1951, **16**, 297–334.

Davidson, B. J., Olson, R. K., & Kliegl, R. *Individual differences in developmental reading disability.* Unpublished manuscript, University of Colorado, 1983.

DeFries, J. C., & Baker, L. A. Colorado family reading study: Longitudinal analyses. *Annals of Dyslexia,* 1982, **33**, 153–162.

DeFries, J. C., & Decker, S. N. Genetic aspects of reading disability: A family study. In R. N. Malatesha & P. G. Aaron (Eds.), *Reading disorders: Varieties and Treatments.* New York: Academic Press, 1982.

Denkla, M. B., & Rudel, R. G. Rapid "automatized" naming (R.A.N.): Dyslexia differentiation from other learning disabilities. *Neuropsychologia,* 1976, **14**, 471–479.

Denkla, M. B. Minimal brain dysfunction and dyslexia: Beyond diagnosis by exclusion. In M. E. Blaw, I. Rapin, & M. Kinsbourne (Eds.), *Topics in child neurology.* New York: Spectrum, 1977.

Doctor, E. A., & Coltheart, M. Children's use of phonological encoding when reading for meaning. *Memory & Cognition,* 1980, **8**, 195-209.

Doehring, D. G., Trites, R. L., Patel, P. G., & Fiedorowicz, C. A. M. *Reading disabilities.* New York: Academic Press, 1981.

Ehri, L. C. The role of orthographic images in learning printed words. In J. F. Kavanagh & R. L. Venezky (Eds.), *Orthography, reading, and dyslexia.* Baltimore: Univ. Park Press, 1980.

Ehri, L. C., & Wilce, L. S. The mnemonic value of orthography among beginning readers. *Journal of Educational Psychology,* 1979, **71**, 26-40.

Ellis, A. W. Spelling and writing [and reading and speaking]. In A. W. Ellis (Ed.), *Normality and pathology in cognitive function.* New York: Academic Press, 1982.

Finucci, J. M., Isaacs, S. D., Whitehouse, C. C., & Childs, B. Classification of spelling errors and their relationships to reading ability, sex, grade placement, and intelligence. *Brain and Language,* 1983, **20**, 340-355.

Firth, I. *Components of reading disability.* Unpublished doctoral dissertation, University of New South Wales, 1972.

Fisk, J. L., & Rourke, B. P. Neuropsychological subtyping of learning disabled children: History, methods, implications. *Journal of Learning Disabilities,* 1983, **16**, 529-531.

Fletcher, J. M., Satz, P., & Vellutino, F. R. Unitary deficit hypothesis of reading disabilities: Has Vellutino led us astray? *Journal of Learning Disabilities,* 1979, **12**, 155-159.

Francis, H. *Learning to read.* London: Allen, 1982.

Frederiksen, J. R. Component skills in reading: Measurement of individual differences through chronometric analysis. In R. E. Snow, P. A. Federico, & W. E. Montague (Eds.), *Aptitude, learning, and instruction.* Hillsdale, New Jersey: Erlbaum, 1980.

Frith, U. Reading by eye and writing by ear. In P. A. Kolers, M. E. Wrolstad, & H. Bouma (Eds.), *Processing of visible language.* New York: Plenum, 1979.

Frith, U. Unexpected spelling problems. In U. Frith (Ed.), *Cognitive processes in spelling.* New York: Academic Press, 1980.

Frith, U. Experimental approaches to developmental dyslexia: An introduction. *Psychological Research,* 1981, **43**, 97-109.

Gleitman, L. R., & Rozin, P. The structure and acquisition of reading I: Relations between orthographies and the structure of language. In A. S. Reber & D. L. Scarborough (Eds.), *Toward a psychology of reading.* Hillsdale, New Jersey: Erlbaum, 1977.

Glushko, R. J. The organization and activation of orthographic knowledge in reading aloud. *Journal of Experimental Psychology: Human Perception and Performance,* 1979, **5**, 674-691.

Golinkoff, R. M., & Rosinski, R. R. Decoding, semantic processing, and reading comprehension skill. *Child Development,* 1976, **47**, 252-258.

Gordon, H. W. The learning disabled are cognitively right. *Topics in Learning and Learning Disabilities,* 1983, **3**, 29-39.

Guttentag, R. E., & Haith, M. M., Automatic processing as a function of age and reading ability. *Child Development,* 1978, **49**, 707-716.

Hall, J. W., Wilson, K. P., Humphreys, M. S., Tinzmann, M. B., & Bowyer, P. M. Phonemic similarity effects in good versus poor readers. *Memory & Cognition,* 1983, **11**, 520-527.

Harris, A. J., & Jacobson, M. D. *Basic elementary reading vocabularies.* New York: MacMillan, 1972.

Henderson, L. *Orthography and word recognition in reading.* New York: Academic Press, 1982.

Hooper, S. R., & Hynd, G. W. *Differential diagnosis of subtypes of developmental dyslexia with the Kaufman assessment battery for children (K-ABC)*. Manuscript under review, 1984.

Huey, E. B. *The psychology and pedagogy of reading*. New York: Macmillan, 1908.

Humphreys, G. W., Evett, L. J., & Taylor, D. E. Automatic phonological priming in visual word recognition. *Memory & Cognition,* 1982, **10**, 576–590.

Ingram, T. T. S., Mason, A. W., & Blackburn, I. A retrospective study of 82 children with reading disability. *Developmental Medicine and Child Neurology,* 1970, **12**, 271–281.

Jansky, J., & de Hirsch, K. *Preventing reading failure*. New York: Harper, 1972.

Johnson, D. J. Remedial approaches to dyslexia. In A. L. Benton & D. Pearl (Eds.), *Dyslexia: An appraisal of current knowledge*. London and New York: Oxford Univ. Press, 1978.

Johnson, D. J. Persistent auditory disorders in young dyslexic adults. *Bulletin of the Orton Society,* 1980, **30**. 268–276.

Johnson, D. J., & Myklebust, H. *Learning disabilities: Educational principles and practices*. New York: Grune & Stratton, 1967.

Johnston, R. Phonological coding in dyslexic readers. *British Journal of Psychology,* 1982, **73**, 455–460.

Jorm, A. F. Specific reading retardation and working memory: A review. *British Journal of Psychology,* 1983, **74**, 311–342.

Jorm, A. F., & Share, D. L. Phonological recoding and reading instruction. *Applied Psycholinguistics,* 1983, **4**, 103–147.

Just, M. A., & Carpenter, P. A. A theory of reading: From eye fixations to comprehension. *Psychological Review,* 1980, **87**, 329–354.

Katz, R. B. *Phonological deficiencies in children with reading disability: Evidence from an object-naming task*. Unpublished Ph.D. dissertation, University of Connecticut, 1982.

Katz, R. B., Shankweiler, D., & Liberman, I. Y. Memory for item order and phonetic recoding in the beginning reader. *Journal of Experimental Child Psychology,* 1981, **32**, 474–484.

Kaufman, A. S. Factor-analysis of the WISC-R at eleven age levels between 6 ½ and 16 ½ years. *Journal of Consulting and Clinical Psychology,* 1975, **43**, 135–147.

Kay, J., & Marcel, A. One process, not two, in reading words aloud: Lexical analogies do the work of non-lexical rules. *Quarterly Journal of Experimental Psychology,* 1981, **33A**, 397–413.

Kinsbourne, M. The role of selective attention in reading disability. In R. N. Malatesha & P. G. Aaron (Eds.), *Reading disorders: Varieties and treatments*. New York: Academic Press, 1982. Pp. 199–214.

Kinsbourne, M., & Warrington, E. K. Developmental factors in reading and writing backwardness. *British Journal of Psychology,* 1963, **54**, 145–156.

Kleiman, G. M. Speech recoding in reading. *Journal of Verbal Learning and Verbal Behavior.* 1975, **14**, 323–339.

Kliegl, R. *On relations between cognition and reading style: Individual differences and developmental trends*. Unpublished Ph.D. dissertation, University of Colorado, Boulder, 1982.

Kliegl, R., Olson, R. K., & Davidson, B. J. Regression analysis as a tool for studying reading processes: Comment on Just and Carpenter's eye fixation theory. *Memory & Cognition,* 1982, **10**, 287–295.

Kochnower, J., Richardson, E., & DiBenedetto, B. A comparison of the phonic decoding ability of normal and learning disabled children. *Journal of Learning Disabilities,* 1983, **16**, 348–351.

Kucera, H., & Francis, W. N. *Computational analysis of present day American English*. Providence, Rhode Island: Brown Univ. Press, 1967.

LaBerge, D., & Samuels, S. J. Toward a theory of automatic information processing in reading. *Cognitive Psychology,* 1974, **6**, 293-323.

Liberman, I. Y., Shankweiler, D., Fisher, F. W., & Carter, B. Reading and the awareness of linguistic segments. *Journal of Experimental Child Psychology,* 1974, **18**, 201-212.

Loftus, G. R. On the interpretation of interactions. *Memory & Cognition,* 1978, **6**, 312-319.

Lyon, G. R. Subgroups of learning disabled readers: Clinical and empirical identification. In H. Myklebust (Ed.), *Progress in learning disabilities* (Vol. V.). New York: Grune & Stratton, 1983.

Lyon, R., & Watson, B. Empirically derived subgroups of learning disabled readers: Diagnostic characteristics. *Journal of Learning Disabilities,* 1981, **14**, 256-261.

McClelland, J. L., & Rumelhart, D. E. An interactive activation model of context effects in letter perception: Part I. An account of basic findings. *Psychological Review,* 1981, **88**, 375-407.

McConkie, G. W., & Rayner, K. The span of the effective stimulus during a fixation in reading. *Perception & Psychophysics,* 1975, **17**, 578-586.

McCusker, L. X., Hillinger, M. L., & Bias, R. G. Phonological recoding and reading. *Psychological Bulletin,* 1981, **89**, 217-245.

McKinney, J. D. The search for subtypes of specific learning disability. *Journal of Learning Disabilities,* 1984, **17**, 43-50.

Malatesha, R. N., & Aaron, P. G. (Eds.), *Reading disorders.* New York: Academic Press, 1982.

Mann, V. A., Liberman, I. Y., & Shankweiler, D. Children's memory for sentences and word strings in relation to reading ability. *Memory & Cognition,* 1980, **8**, 329-335.

Maria, K., & Macginitie, W. H. Reading comprehension disabilities: Knowledge structures and non-accommodating text processing strategies. *Annals of Dyslexia,* 1982, **32**, 33-60.

Mark, L. S., Shankweiler, D., Liberman, I. Y., & Fowler, C. A. Phonetic recoding and reading difficulty in beginning readers. *Memory & Cognition,* 1977, **5**, 623-629.

Massaro, D. W., & Taylor, G. A. Reading ability and utilization of orthographic structure in reading. *Journal of Educational Psychology,* 1980, **72**, 730-742.

Massaro, D. W., Taylor, G. A., Venezky, R. L., Jastrzembski, J. E., & Lucas, P. A. Letter and word perception: Orthographic structure and visual processing in reading. Amsterdam: North-Holland, 1980.

Massaro, D. W., Venezky, R. L., & Taylor, G. A. Orthographic regularity, positional frequency, and visual processing of letter strings. *Journal of Experimental Psychology: General,* 1979, **108**, 107-124.

Mattis, S., French, J.H., & Rapin, I. Dyslexia in children and young adults: Three independent neuropsychological syndromes. *Developmental Medicine and Child Neurology,* 1975, **17**, 150-163.

Mitterer, J. O. There are at least two kinds of poor readers: Whole-word poor readers and recoding poor readers. *Canadian Journal of Psychology,* 1982, **36**, 445-461.

Moore, M. J., Kagan, J., Sahl, M., & Grant, S. Cognitive profiles in reading disability. *Genetic Psychology Monographs,* 1982, **105**, 41-93.

Naidoo, S. *Specific dyslexia.* London: Pitman, 1972.

Olson, R. K., Kliegl, R., & Davidson, B. J. Eye movements in reading disability. In K. Rayner (Ed.), *Eye Movements in reading: Perceptual and language processes.* New York: Academic Press, 1983.(a)

Olson, R. K., Kliegl, R., & Davidson, B. J. Dyslexic and normal readers' eye movements. *Journal of Experimental Psychology: Human Perception and Performance,* 1983, **9**, 816-825.(b)

Olson, R. K., Davidson, B. J., Kliegl, R., & Davies, S. E. Development of phonetic memory in disabled and normal readers. *Journal of Experimental Child Psychology,* 1984, **37,** 187–206.

Parkin, A. J. Phonological recoding in lexical decision: Effects of spelling-to-sound regularity depend on how regularity is defined. *Memory & Cognition,* 1982, **10,** 43–53.

Parkin, A. J., & Underwood, G. Orthographic vs. phonological irregularity in lexical decision. *Memory & Cognition,* 1983, **11,** 351–355.

Pavlidis, G. Th. Do eye movements hold the key to dyslexia? *Neuropsychologia,* 1981, **19,** 57–64.

Pavlidis, G. Th. The "Dyslexia syndrome" and its objective diagnosis by erratic eye movements. In K. Rayner (Ed.), *Eye movements in reading: Perceptual and language processes.* New York: Academic Press, 1983.

Perfetti, C. A. *Reading ability.* London and New York: Oxford Univ. Press, 1984.(a)

Perfetti, C. A. Individual differences in verbal processes. In R. Dillon & R. R. Schmeck (Eds.), *Individual differences in cognition.* New York: Academic Press, 1984.(b)

Perfetti, C. A., & Hogaboam, T. The relationship between single word decoding and reading comprehension skill. *Journal of Educational Psychology,* 1975, **67,** 461–469.

Petrauskas, R. J., & Rourke, B. P. Identification of subtypes of retarded readers: A neuropsychological, multivariate approach. *Journal of Clinical Neuropsychology,* 1979, **1,** 17–37.

Pirozzolo, F. J. *The neuropsychology of developmental reading disorders.* New York: Praeger, 1979.

Pirozzolo, F. J. Eye movements and reading disability. In K. Rayner (Ed.), *Eye movements in reading: Perceptual and language processes.* New York: Academic Press, 1983.

Pirozzolo, F. J., & Rayner, K. The neural control of eye movements in acquired and developmental reading disorders. In H. Avakian-Whitaker & H. A. Whitaker (Eds.), *Advances in neurolinguistics and psycholinguistics.* New York: Academic Press, 1978.

Posnansky, C. J., & Rayner, K. Visual-feature and response components in a picture-word interference task with beginning and skilled readers. *Journal of Experimental Child Psychology,* 1977, **24,** 440–460.

Punnett, A. F., & Steinhauer, G. D. Relationship between reinforcement and eye movements during ocular motor training with learning disabled children. *Journal of Learning Disabilities,* 1984, **17,** 16–19.

Rayner, K. Eye movements, perceptual span, and reading disability. *Annals of Dyslexia,* 1983, **32,** 163–174.

Rayner, K. Visual selection in reading, picture perception, and visual search: A tutorial review. In Bouma, & Bouwhuis (Eds.), *Attention and performance.* Hillsdale, New Jersey: Erlbaum, 1984.

Reitsma, P. Printed word learning in beginning readers. *Journal of Experimental Child Psychology,* 1983, **36,** 321–339.(a)

Reitsma, P. Word-specific knowledge in beginning reading. *Journal of Research in Reading,* 1983, **6,** 41–56.(b)

Reitsma, P. Sound priming in beginning reading. *Child Development,* 1983, in press.(c)

Rodgers, B. The identification and prevalence of specific reading retardation. *British Journal of Educational Psychology,* 1983, **53,** 369–373.

Rosenthal, J. H., Boder, E., & Callaway, E. Typology of developmental dyslexia: Evidence for its construct validity. In R. N. Malatesha & P. G. Aaron (Eds.), *Reading disorders: Varieties and treatments.* New York: Academic Press, 1982.

Rudel, R. G. Residual effects of childhood reading disabilities. *Bulletin of the Orton Society,* 1981, **31,** 89–102.

Saffran, E. M., & Marin, S. M. Reading without phonology: Evidence from aphasia. *Quarterly Journal of Experimental Psychology,* 1977, **29,** 515–525.

Satz, P., & Morris, R. Learning disability subtypes: A review. In F. J. Pirozzolo & M. C. Wittrock (Eds.), *Neuropsychological and cognitive processes in reading.* New York: Academic Press, 1981.

Seymour, P. H. K., & Porpodas, C. D. Lexical and non-lexical processing of spelling in dyslexia. In U. Frith (Ed.), *Cognitive processes in spelling.* New York: Academic Press, 1980.

Shankweiler, D., Liberman, I. Y., Mark, L. S., Fowler, C. A., & Fisher, F. W. The speech code and learning to read. *Journal of Experimental Psychology: Human Learning and Memory,* 1980, **5,** 531–545.

Siegel, L. S., & Linder, B. A. Short-term memory processes in children with reading disabilities. *Developmental Psychology,* 1984, **20,** 200–207.

Singer, M. H. The primacy of visual information in the analysis on letter strings. *Perception & Psychophysics,* 1980, **27,** 153–162.

Singer, M. H., & Crouse, J. The relationship of context-use skills to reading: A case for an alternative experimental logic. *Child Development,* 1981, **52,** 1326–1329.

Smith, S. D., Kimberling, W. J., Pennington, B. F., & Lubs, H. A. Specific reading disability: Identification of an inherited form through linkage analysis. *Science,* 1983, **219,** 1345–1347.

Snowling, M. J. Phonemic deficits in developmental dyslexia. *Psychological Research,* 1981, **43,** 219–234.

Snowling, M. J. The comparison of acquired and developmental disorders of reading: A discussion. *Cognition,* 1983, **14,**105–118.

Snowling, M. J., & Frith, U. The role of sound, shape, and orthographic cues in early reading. *British Journal of Psychology,* 1981, **72,** 83–87.

Spache, G. D. *Diagnostic reading scales.* New York: McGraw Hill, 1963.

Stanley, G., Smith, G. A., & Howell, E. A. Eye movements and sequential tracking in dyslexic and control children. *British Journal of Psychology,* 1983, **74,** 181–191.

Stanovich, K. E. Individual differences in the cognitive processes of reading. I: Word decoding. *Journal of Learning Disabilities,* 1982, **15,** 485–493.

Tinker, M. A. Recent studies of eye movements in reading. *Psychological Bulletin,* 1958, **55,** 215–231.

Treiman, R. Individual differences among children in spelling and reading styles. *Journal of Experimental Child Psychology,* 1984, in press.

Treiman, R., & Baron, J. Phonemic-analysis training helps children benefit from spelling-sound rules. *Memory & Cognition,* 1983, **11,** 382–389.

Treiman, R., Freyd, J. J., & Baron, J. Phonological recoding and use of spelling-sound rules in reading sentences. *Journal of Verbal Learning and Verbal Behavior, 1983,* **22,** 682–700.

Underwood, R. N. *The span of letter recognition of good and poor readers* (Technical Rep. No. 251), University of Illinois at Urbana-Champaign, July, 1982.

Underwood, N. R., & McConkie, G. W. *Perceptual span for letter distinctions during reading* (Technical Rep. No. 272), University of Illinois at Urbana-Champaign, April, 1983.

van den Bos, K. P. Letter span, scanning, and code matching in dyslexic subgroups. *Annals of Dyslexia,* 1984, in press.

Vavrus, L. G., Brown, T. L., & Carr, T. H. *Component skill profiles of reading ability: Variations, tradeoffs, and compensations.* Paper presented at the meeting of the Psychonomic Society, San Diego, Calif., Nov. 1983.

Vellutino, F. *Dyslexia: Theory and research.* Cambridge, Massachusetts: M.I.T. Press, 1979.

Venezky, R. L. *The structure of English orthography.* Paris: Mouton, 1970.

Venezky, R. L., & Massaro, D. W. The role of orthographic regularity in word recognition. In L. Resnick & P. Weaver (Eds.), *Theory and practice of early reading.* Hillsdale, New Jersey: Erlbaum, 1979.

Vogler, G. P., Baker, L. A., Decker, S. N., DeFries, J. C., & Huizinga, D. H. *Cluster analytic classification of reading disability subtypes: Evidence for a multivariate continuum.* Manuscript under review. Institute for Behavioral Genetics, University of Colorado, Boulder, 1984.

Wolf, M. The word-retrieval process and reading in children and aphasics. In K. Nelson (Ed.), *Children's language* (Vol. 3). New York: Gardner, 1981.

Yule, W., Rutter, M., Berger, M., & Thompson, J. Over- and under-achievement in reading: Distribution in the general population. *British Journal of Educational Psychology,* 1974, **44,** 1–12.

LONGITUDINAL STUDIES OF READING AND READING DIFFICULTIES IN SWEDEN

INGVAR LUNDBERG

Department of Psychology
University of Umeå
Umeå, Sweden

I. INTRODUCTION

Current reading research is almost totally dominated by American and British contributions. The generality of the insights from this impressive work might, however, be hampered by the fixation to a single language, a specific orthography, specific school traditions, and specific cultural patterns. The relativity of the findings is sometimes highlighted in contrasting analyses of radically different scripts (e.g., Hung & Tzeng, 1981). Sometimes it is proposed that reading difficulties are a minor problem in countries with orthographies characterized by a closer grapheme–phoneme correspondence than the English orthography, as for example in Finland where the script has a uniform letter–sound relationship. Nevertheless, a substantial proportion of children in Finland are reported to have difficulties in learning to read and write (Kyöstiö, 1980). Swedish orthography seems to take an intermediate position on the regularity scale perhaps closer to the Finnish end point than the complicated English one. Yet reading and spelling difficulties are of major educational concern in Sweden.

With the exception of Malmquist's studies (Malmquist, 1958, 1981) nothing has really been reported on reading research in Sweden to an international audience, mainly due to lack of interest in reading among Swedish researchers in education. This is rather surprising with regard to the increasing concern among politicians, school managers, parents, and the general public. It has been estimated that some 20% of students leave the Swedish 9-year compulsory school with reading proficiency below the average level of grade 6, a level of skill which is regarded as clearly insufficient to meet minimum requirements of literacy in modern, postindustrial society.

Learning problems have, of course, been recognized by the educational research community. However, the earlier focus on individually related deficits has been replaced by a more sociologically oriented approach where learning problems are regarded as reflections of socioeconomic crises in society. This level of analysis has not provided teachers with useful guidelines for daily work with reading disabilities. Nevertheless, the shift of perspective has had an impact on educational practice. Utmost efforts have been made to integrate remedial teaching with regular school work, with the result that remedial classes of various kinds and clinics for special education are rapidly being phased out. In this educational atmosphere the attitudes toward testing and assessment also have become strongly negative.

Under the increasing pressure from concerned policy makers and school managers it seems as if the pendulum now has swung and some scope is being left for a closer analysis of the reading process and the individually related obstacles for acquiring literacy. As in other parts of the world the reading process has recently become an attractive challenge for cognitive psychologists and linguists in Sweden. The change of climate has also affected medical researchers which was reflected in a recent Wenner-Gren symposium in Stockholm on dyslexia (Zotterman, 1982).

Before we report our empirical work a few more specific remarks on the instructional practice of beginning reading in Sweden seem appropriate.

A. The Swedish School System

Compulsory education starts when the child is 7 years old and includes 9 years of schooling. Almost 100% of the schools are public, and the teaching is regulated by a master plan common to all schools in the country. Teachers are trained in state colleges with uniform admission policies and standards of quality. The remarkable homogeneity of the school system is further promoted by the lack of social stratification in most Swedish municipalities. With the exception of a few metropolitan districts residential areas are mixed with people from all kinds of social strata. Tax and income policies have brought about considerable economic equality. Thus, on the whole the variation among schools is small in comparison with most countries as far as teaching standard and socioeconomic background of the pupils are concerned.

The class size in the first grades has a maximum of 25 pupils. However, the actual mean size for the whole country is presently not more than 18 pupils. In the first grade, moreover, the class is often divided into two groups for some 10 hours of the children's weekly schedule of 20 hours, which gives the teacher good opportunities for individualized teaching.

Special education is handled in a most flexible way where governmental subsidies to local municipalities can be used in ways that best meet local needs at individual school units. Thus, special teachers may be used for individual tutoring of children with reading difficulties, for remedial teaching in clinics, or, if more desirable, as counselors to regular teachers in the regular classroom work. There is also a general trend of trying to break the traditional isolation of individual teachers and establish teams of teachers.

According to a firmly established tradition in Sweden, children should not be subjected to any formal reading instruction before the school start, neither in preschool institutions nor at home. At present about 110,000 children or more than one-sixth of all children in the age 1–7 years old are attending day care centers. In the last preschool year almost 90% of all children are enrolled in kindergarten for at least 3 hours per day. By tradition the emphasis in Swedish child care service is on social, emotional, and esthetic development rather than on intellectual preparation for school work. Thus, a majority of Swedish children enter school by the age of 7 without any reading ability.

B. Methods of Reading Instruction

Methods of reading instruction are fairly uniform in the first grades. All existing basal readers systems in Sweden are designed to keep some balance between analytic and synthetic methods from the very beginning. Listening, speaking, reading, and writing are integrated from the start, which is in contrast to the normal practice in for example the United States where writing is usually introduced later in the program. In Sweden writing is supposed to support the teaching of reading. Phonemic segmentation and sound blending is emphasized early by the majority of teachers. Lately some version of the language experience approach has caught the attention of many Swedish teachers in the elementary grades. Mostly it is used as a supplement to traditional methods and the phonics elements are retained as an important part of the new approach.

C. Orthography

The phonics emphasis in Swedish reading teaching is probably a reflection of the rather regular orthography. Although the grapheme–phoneme correspondences are quite consistent, at least in comparison with English, there are some significant exceptions causing problems, especially in spelling and to some extent also in reading. Some sound segments can be represented in the orthography in a great number of ways. Take for example the /ʃ/ sound which can be spelled in the following ways: *stj, sj, skj, sk, sch, ch, sh, g, si,* or *ti.* The /j/ sound is spelled as *j, g, gj, hj, lj,* or *dj.* Vowels such as /o/ are quite randomly spelled *o* or *å,* and /ɛ/ is spelled *ä* or *e.* The morphophonemic character of the orthography can be illustrated by *hög* (high) and *högt* (highly) were *gt* is pronounced *kt.* Especially hard hurdles are the principles for doubling consonants, which also is one of the main sources of misspellings. The rules are very complicated and include many exceptions. The normal case is that consonants are doubled after short vowels such as *hat* /haːt/ and *hatt* /hat/. In unstressed syllables, however, short vowels do not need double consonants (ok*t*ober) or (måna*d*). A number of other exceptions are governed by morphological rules. As many German languages Swedish is also characterized by heavy clusters of consonants in initial as well as in final position, e.g., *strand, skälmskt,* or in middle position in compound words such as *falsktskrikande.* Phonotactic reductions and assimilations are also common, e.g., Lundberg is pronounced Lu*m*berg in rapid normal speaking.

The specific hurdles of Swedish orthography are for most pupils relatively easily overcome, at least in reading. Spelling problems, however, are often observed even in the upper grades. To estimate the incidence of specific reading disabilities in Sweden is not easy. The cut-off limit is largely arbitrary and a matter of pedagogic convention. Special educational support is given to about one-fifth of the pupils, but only a minority of them should probably be regarded as dyslexic in a more restricted sense. Thus, there is no real basis for comparing the incidence of dyslexia in Sweden with other countries with different orthographic structures.

This is the general background to the project which will be reported in the present article. Except for its more provincially related ambition to contribute to a badly needed improvement of special education in Sweden it may contain some features of more general interest: The reading problems are studied in a "purer" context than in many other places. The school system is comprehensive with a late school start (7 years). It is very homogeneous as far as socioeconomic factors and teachers' training are concerned As was already mentioned, the Swedish orthography is rather regular. The design of the project is longitudinal where a large group is followed through several years in school. It is multidimensional, and a number of analytic tools have been used which normally are not seen in current dyslexia research. It has some potentialities for cross-national comparisons. Already from the start the project was coordinated with similar efforts in Norway and Denmark. (In fact the original intiative to a longitudinal dyslexia project was taken by Prof. Gjessing in Bergen, Norway.)

In the present report the following issues are of primary concern:

1. How can the variance in reading and spelling among pupils in the first school years be explained in terms of factors such as cognitive and linguistic development, socioemotional adjustment, age, sex, class size, residential area.

2. What are the main differences between students who quickly develop reading and spelling skills and those who develop at a slow rate?

3. What are the characteristic cognitive and socioemotional profiles of underachievers in reading and spelling as compared to normal children?

4. Is it possible to identify specific subtypes of reading-disabled children?

5. How is the long-term development of reading-disabled children?

Apart from its more scientific aims, the project also had practical aims, the intention being to help to bring about concrete improvements to clinical investigations into remedial education, and in this connection we have developed quite a number of new diagnostic methods. We have also been anxious to make concrete suggestions, not always firmly based on empirical evidence, regarding the planning of educational assistance for children with reading disabilities.

II. GENERAL DESIGN

A. Subjects

The investigation was carried out in the community of Umeå, an administrative and educational center of the northern region of Sweden with about 80,000 residents. The community includes an urban part without any specific social stratification, surrounding rural districts with farming and forestry and a few minor industrialized places with paper mills. Some 700 children or two-thirds of the total population of school beginners in 1977 took part in the study, most of them being born in 1970. The selected group can be regarded as reasonably representative of the total population of school beginners in Umeå. A random sample of nonselected classes was later checked on reading and spelling performances and the obtained results did not significantly deviate from the selected classes. A majority of the children had attended preschool or kindergarten before entering school, but so far there is no direct link between these programs and the regular school program. Only a few of the children had gained any reading ability before school with the help of parents or older siblings or in any other informal ways.

The project can be divided into two parts: one is concerned with a description of the whole population (screening studies) and the other has its focus on a subgroup of reading-disabled children.

The screening studies provided the basis for selection of underachievers for further intensive diagnostics and remedial work. We also hoped that a *comprehensive and longitudinal description* along several important dimensions of a large and representative group of children during the first school years would yield some new insights into the complicated network of interacting factors of critical importance for the development of basic reading and spelling skills in school. The screening studies also provided *reference data* necessary for evaluating the development of our specific target group with learning disabilities. Inherent in the screening program is also an interesting potential for cross-national comparison within Scandinavia.

B. Screening Studies

After about 7 months in grade 1 the first screening study took place with a comprehensive survey of cognitive functions (Raven), reading, spelling, school attitudes, self-concept, sociometric status, and teacher assessments of linguistic development, motor skills, social and emotional adjustment, reading, writing, and underachievement.

C. Instruments

The teacher ratings were essentially based on "The Pupil Rating Scale" developed by Myklebust (1971) for the purpose of identifying learning-disabled children. The Swedish version included four areas: Language comprehension, Language production, Motor development, and Behavior in school (including socioemotional adjustment). Each area consisted of several more specific rating dimensions with 5-point scales. The teachers were carefully instructed how to handle the scales. A period of 5 weeks was available for careful observations to obtain a reliable basis for the ratings. Despite the lack of interrater reliability data the scales seem to have been handled consistently by the teachers. Evidence for this judgment is the remarkable agreement of patterns in the repeated screening study 2 years later. Similar scales have also been used in the Norwegian and Danish parts of the project with essentially the same results as in Sweden.

A few weeks later the teachers also rated the pupils' achievements in reading, writing, and mathematics. Moreover, they tried to give numerical estimates of the degree of over- or underachievement of each pupil, i.e., they related the actual performance to what could be expected from their evaluation of the pupil's intelligence level.

More formal assessments were also included in the screening program. As a nonverbal measure of intelligence a version of Raven's progressive colored matrices was used with 33 items (Raven, 1965). A reading test measured speed and accuracy of silent decoding of unrelated words. It consisted of 400 words each related to one of four drawings. Reading achievement was measured as the number of correctly matched drawings in successive 5-minute intervals up to 15 minutes. The retest reliability after 6 months was .84. The first spelling test consisted of 30 words all of which were contained in the basal readers. To avoid ceiling effects the spelling test had to be changed considerably in the later screening occasions.

Socioemotional adjustment was also assessed by some more formal instruments. Sociometric status was obtained by the conventional method of asking each child to mention the three children in the class whom he/she preferred to have as playmates in an imagined play situation. At a later occasion the question concerned working companions. Self-esteem or self-concept was assessed by an instrument the design of which to some extent was inspired by an American scale (Meyerowitz, 1962). The child was requested to express his/her agreement with the opinions or actions of two phantasy figures, the Flag and the Balloon child, who operated in various situations in school. School attitudes were assessed with a rating scale where the child pointed to one of several faces expressing various degrees of sadness or happiness when confronted with activities in school.

Parts of this assessment program (reading test, spelling test, and Raven) were repeated at the beginning of grade 2 (about 6 months later) to stabilize the basis on which underachieving pupils were selected for closer study and to provide a measuring point for the general follow-up study. The last broad survey of the entire population took place halfway through grade 3, using partly modified and partly new instruments adapted to the current developmental level. This survey covered cognitive functions (Raven), word decoding, reading, comprehension, spelling, school attitudes, level of aspiration, self-concept, sociometry, and teacher assessments of the same kind as in grade 1. Finally, a majority of the population was given a spelling test in grade 5 and the underachievement group and its matched comparison group of normal readers were given two reading tests.

III. SOME RESULTS FROM THE SCREENING STUDIES

The great number of screening variables (about 30 in grades 1 and 3, respectively) and all possible interrelations between them contain an overwhelming amount of information. Here we will focus only on a few questions. The first concerns how to explain the interindividual variance in basic skills in reading and writing. The second concerns the development of these skills over the first school years. Later the screening data will also be used to evaluate the progress of the underachievers. For each individual a general index of basic skills (here called Basics 1) was defined as the unweighted sum of z-scores on the reading test results from grades 1 and 2, spelling tests from grades 1 and 2, and teacher assessments of reading and writing from grade 1. (Basics 1 = z reading test 1 + z reading test 2 + z spelling 1 + z spelling 2 + z rated reading + z rated writing.) Each z-value is computed as the difference between an individual's score on the specific variable and the mean score for the whole population on that variable. This difference is divided by the standard deviation of the population scores. Since the mean of z-scores of a given variable is 0, the mean of the general basics index is also 0.

A. AID Analysis

In the first exploratory step we applied the AID technique (Sonqvist, Baker, & Morgan, 1973) to get an overview of the most critical configuration of factors that can explain the variance of basic skills. The main purpose of this analysis was to identify and segregate a set of subgroups from the population which are the best we can find for maximizing our ability to predict the dependent variable (basics). Essentially the AID technique is a sophisticated tabularic method for bringing some order in data. The variance of the criterion measure is analyzed such that a nonsymmetric branching process is developed to partition the population into a series of subgroups with maximum homogeneity with respect to the dependent variable. The computer program looks for the predictor variable which after dichotomization yields the lowest within group sums of squares. Starting again from the obtained subgroups the program proceeds by looking for the next subgrouping with the lowest within group sums of squares. The progressive splitting continues until specified criteria concerning group size and sums of squares have been met. Assumptions of linearity, additivity, and metric level, normally important in multivariate methods, need not be fulfilled.

Except for the already mentioned screening variables some other predictors were also included in the analysis, such as sex, age (3-month intervals), class size, and residential type (rural, urban). Figure 1 presents the results of the first analysis based on screening 1 and 2.

When reading an AID diagram one can start to the far left where the whoie population under concern is located. We then proceed to the right and follow the different branchings toward smaller and smaller subgroups. One should notice that the subgroups on a given split level are different in at least two ways: first they have different means on the criterion measure—the variable we want to "explain," and second, they are different on some critical predictor variable, specified at the split point. Now, let us start with group 1, the population. It has 705 individuals and a mean value of 0 on basics (according to the definition of the composite index). The whole group is first divided into two subgroups—number 2, a low group with a basics mean of -1.7 and number 3, a high group with a mean of $+3.5$. The groups also differ on language comprehension (group 2 has values in the range 0–6, and group 3 in the range 7–13). The next split for each of these groups is also based on language comprehension. Thus, groups 4, 5, 8 and 9 are established. As we proceed further, however, new critical factors appear. Following the lowest branching we end up in group 14 with a basics mean of -10.9. This group consists of 15 boys with an extremely low level of language production (1) and low language comprehension (0–4). On the other extreme we find group 19 with a mean of $+6.3$, a group with high Raven scores, excellent socioemotional adjustment, and good language comprehension (8–13). Interactions among the variables are also seen in the diagram. Take for example group 18, which contains individuals with superior basic skills. However, their Raven scores are low. These children seem to have been able to offset their limited cognitive potentialities with

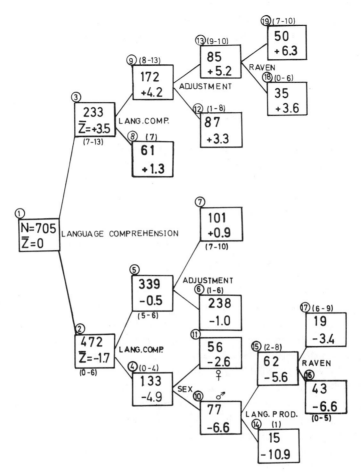

Fig. 1. AID analysis of basic skills measured in grade 1 and 2.

very good socioemotional adjustment and with a high level of language comprehension. In contrast to this group we find in group 17 children with high Raven scores who nonetheless have low levels of reading and writing achievement (−3.4). These pupils are boys with a low level of language comprehension. The detection of such interactions is one of the assets of AID.

The most conspicuous finding of the AID analysis is the strong priority of the *language factors,* especially the language comprehension variable. This variable comprises the sum total of teacher assessments of different aspects of the pupil's ability to apprehend and comprehend the spoken language in different situations. The assessments were made during a 3-week observation period, before any other tests were administered, so that they cannot have been influenced by the results of the latter.

Before drawing firm conclusions a word of warning concerning the use of AID seems justified. Researchers using AID have not paid enough attention to the question of cross-validation. There is a considerable risk to capitalize on chance when the tree structures are developed in a given set of data. Slight changes might cause drastic differences in outcome. Here, however, we are on firmer ground, because practically identical structures have been obtained from Norwegian data ($N=3400$) and also from the screening in grade 3 with partly different tests where the outcome was strikingly similar to the structure presented here. In all cases oral language comprehension seems to be the most critical factor in reading and spelling. The evidence also indicates that learning-disabled children show pervasive and enduring language problems across a wide variety of language dimensions. To this question we will return later.

It is also important to note that some variables of significant loadings in the pedagogical debate did not contribute to the explanation of the basics variance, e.g., self-concept, school attitudes, level of aspiration, sociometric status, age, class size, residential area. In order to penetrate the impact of these variables more subtle analyses are required which will do justice to the interaction of different factors. The effect of *sociometric status,* for example, is only apparent in comparisons between extreme groups, in that the most isolated pupils seem to have more than average difficulty in coping with basic skills at school.

In the case of *sex differences* regarding basic skills we find that girls have a slight but significant lead. Dividing the material into different levels of language comprehension, however, one finds a very pronounced difference at the lowest level of language comprehension, while in the group with a high level of language comprehension, girls and boys read and write with more or less equal proficiency.

B. Path Analysis

The AID method seemed to have been a useful exploratory tool in revealing the most critical factors behind basic skills. Although more than 50% of the variance has been "explained" the description has been rather primitive. Our next step had a more theoretical flavor. Despite the nonexperiment nature of the screening nothing prevents an attempt to logically order the variables in a simple causal model and to work out the quantitative implications of such a model. Our first very modest attempt is presented in Fig. 2. On this stage of causal modeling the longitudinal potential has not been utilized and the following analysis has primarily an illustrative

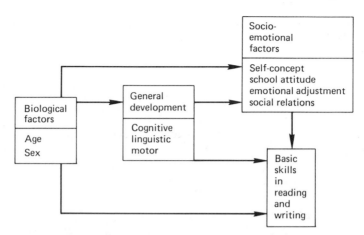

Fig. 2. Determinants of basic skills: hypothetical structural relations.

function while we are waiting for the final implementation of the LISREL program (Jöreskog & Sörbom, 1980) into our computer system.

The level of basic skills is assumed to be directly or indirectly determined by three groups of variables. First in the causal chain there are some given biological factors such as age and sex (of course sex differences are socially or culturally determined as well. However such factors exert their influence very early in life). The next step concerns some general developmental characterictics, such as cognitive, linguistic, and motor development. This group of factors is supposed to be relatively unaffected by school and is primarily determined by the interaction of biological factors and home or preschool environment. A third group of factors concerns socioemotional conditions. At this stage of theorizing strong simplifications are necessary. Here, for example, we disregard the reasonable possibility of mutual influences between the sets of factors.

Information about the relative importance of various determinants of reading and spelling ability has practical relevance only if it can add knowledge about the causal structure behind the actual learning process. The interpretation, in action-oriented terms, of the analysis is impossible without some basic theoretical assumptions about the levels on which different factors operate and about their degree of logical priority in relation to the criterion variable. "Explained" variation in the regression sense does not necessarily permit causal interpretations and may, at least partially, be an artifact. For intervention purposes, quantitative estimates are needed of what may be the effect of changes in factors conceived as determinants.

Path analysis is an analytical tool that permits a causal interpretation of a postulated model (e.g., Land, 1969). It does not purport to demonstrate causality; it merely works out the logical and quantitative implications of the model assumptions. It is a more acceptable procedure when estimating the relative importance of various factors than a conventional stepwise multiple regression analysis, since it takes into account also the operation of indirect and spurious effects. Provided certain formal requirements are fulfilled (recursivity, additivity, linearity, and metric data) the system can be determined by sets of regression equations. The obtained standardized beta coefficients are called path coefficients and measure the expected change in standard deviation units of the dependent variable (basics), that results from one standard unit change in a determinant. The results of our path analysis are summarized in Fig. 3.

Above each arrow the path coefficient is given. The strongest direct effect on basic skills is obtained from the linguistic variables, especially language comprehension. This was the case in the AID analysis as well, but now we

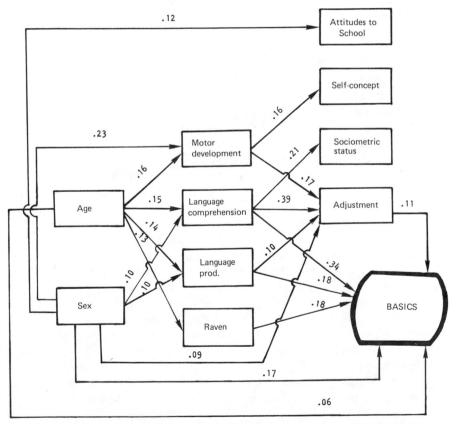

Fig. 3. Results of the path analysis. Path coefficients are given above the causal arrows.

have a more precise expression of its impact. We can also see that socio-emotional factors have a rather modest influence on basic skills. Only adjustment as rated by the teachers seems to have a direct effect. Also cognitive level as measured by Raven and sex are significant determinants. Norwegian data have been analyzed in the same way and essentially the same picture emerges, with language comprehension having the strongest impact.

The present illustration of the application of path analysis was based only on data from the first screening studies. Path analysis should be regarded as a special case of structural equation models with some serious limitations clarified by Rogosa (1979). A considerable increase in complication, relevance, and explanatory power will be obtained when the longitudinal potential of the project is exploited in the causal modeling work. Right now we are implementing the LISREL program (Jöreskog & Sörbom, 1980) into our computing system which will provide superior sophistication and rigor in evaluating the fit of our models.

C. The Development of Basic Skills

To interpret a curve of the development over the school years of a skill such as reading or spelling is a most complicated matter, the main problem being the measurement or scaling of the dependent variable (see, e.g., Wohlwill, 1973). In models of the reading process where the development of qualitatively different stages is emphasized, quantitative comparisons between points separated in time may even become absurd.

In the case of reading we had the possibility to use the same measuring stick at three different occasions, a test of silent word reading with a response format of multiple choices of a series of pictures. The number of correctly decoded words were recorded over successive 5-minute periods. This test was used in grade 1, grade 2, and grade 3, which does not mean that an interpretable developmental process can be traced. However, the same test was used in two Danish communities and partly in Norway, which means that some comparative information is available.

In Fig. 4 we can see how reading proficiency improves over the school years. (In the Danish investigation only the 10-minute level was recorded.) Swedish pupils are quite superior to the Danish pupils in grade 1. The figure does not include Norwegian data, but at the 15-minute limit the Swedish average in grade 1 is 152 and the Norwegian 138, a difference which is clearly significant. Swedish reading instruction in grade 1 therefore seems to progress more rapidly than in the other municipalities. Smaller classes and favorable grouping arrangements may also have contributed toward the difference. In grade 3, however, the Swedish lead appears to be reduced.

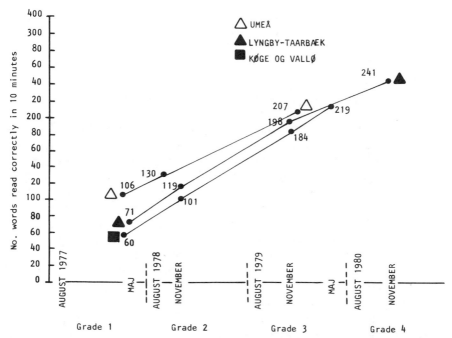

Fig. 4. The development of word reading over the first school years in three Scandinavian communities.

No corresponding differences have been established in the Raven scores, which suggests that we are faced here with pedagogically induced variations. Perhaps the somewhat closer grapheme–phoneme correspondence of the Swedish orthography also plays a role.

D. The Change from Basics 1 to Basics 3

To express the change or development of a skill from one occasion to a second as a difference or gain score implies several problems. (For a critical discussion of the use of gain scores see, e.g., Cronbach and Furby, 1970.) There are problems with reliabilities of the two measures and problems with regression effects due to nonperfect correlation between the two measures. High values on the first measurement tend to be lower (regress toward the mean) at the second occasion and low initial values are naturally expected to be higher on the second occasion. Thus, to the extent that the correlation deviates from 1, simple gain scores will overestimate the development of the low achievers and underestimate the progress of pupils with high initial values.

One way of avoiding this problem is to express the change in relation to the regression line. Thus, each individual is assigned a residual value (deviation from the regression line) that expresses his/her relative change with due regard to the regression effect. This index of relative change will be used when the progress of the dyslexic children is evaluated (see below). Here we will look at the extreme groups of children with the most positive development of basic skills in reading and writing and the group with the most negative (relatively speaking) development. The correlation between the general index of basic skill, in grade 1 and 2 (basics 1) and the corresponding index in grade 3 (basics 3) is computed. With reference to the regression line two 5% confidence limits are defined (Hays, 1973, p. 648), the upper one delimiting the pupils with marked positive development and the lower one demarcating those with extreme negative development. The bands are slightly bent, upward and downward, respectively, due to the varying densities of the column distributions. Thus, a positive group of 34 cases and a negative group of 32 cases were selected out of a total of 637 cases. It should now be recognized that the initial level of basic skills was about the same in the two groups. However, there was a substantial difference in the basics 3 level.

No specific factor or configuration of factors seemed to clearly characterize the two groups. The socioeconomic family background was slightly better in the positive group; no special school or class was overrepresented in any of the groups. A discriminant analysis (Klecka, 1980) was performed to find out which of the screening variables in grades 1 and 2 discriminate the positive and negative extreme groups best. Again language comprehension and language production are the critical variables. This is somewhat surprising since the explanatory function is not the same. Actually, the groups do not differ on initial basics level. They differ in developmental *rate* which appears to be predictable on the basis of language factors.

Another critical factor is *sex*. The positive group includes 21 girls and only 13 boys, while the balance is reversed in the negative group with 21 boys and only 11 girls. This pattern is significant ($\chi^2 = 4.96, p < .05$). As in most other countries the schools in Sweden seem to offer a more congenial and supportive place for girls than for boys.

A corresponding extreme group analysis was performed with the *self-concept* variable. From several sources, questionnaires and teacher assessments, all items referring to academic self-concept were collected and constituted the basis for defining a general index, one in grade 1 and one in grade 3. Now the total number of cases was 544. As before the residual values were taken as change indicators. The confidence band now included 51 cases of which 28 appeared in the extreme positive region and 23 in the negative. The positive group contained 21 boys and only 7 girls which is in remarkable contrast to the actual situation in basics. The negative group contained 12 girls and 11 boys. Thus, the relationship between basic skills and self-concept seems to be complicated. Perhaps this pattern of sex differences reflects some fundamental difference in the way boys and girls are treated in school, the different patterns of feedback that they get on their schoolwork. Teachers tend to give girls feedback on the basis of the intellectual quality of their work. Boys, in contrast, are more likely to be evaluated on the basis of conduct or trivial things like neatness, sloppy handwriting, or lack of motivation. This leads boys to become more independent of teacher's opinion, while girls, when they encounter failure, may become more distressed and disrupted.

IV. UNDERACHIEVEMENT

The ultimate concern of the present project was to gain a better understanding of reading disabilities. It is now time to more directly focus on this problem. Certainly it is tempting to get involved in complicated arguments concerning the proper definition of dyslexia (e.g., Valtin, 1978–79; Benton & Pearl, 1978). In Umeå the socioeconomic variance among children is comparatively small and most children are offered fairly competent and adequate teaching during the first school years. Thus, some hotly debated exclusion criteria are not applicable to our population. We took our departure from the common experience among teachers that now and then they meet students with surprisingly hard problems in learning to read and write despite adequate development in other fields of learning. Thus, underachievement constituted our basis for selecting a group of reading-disabled children for further diagnosis and treatment.

A. Regression Model

Underachievement was here defined as a stable and significant discrepancy between expected achievement level in reading and/or spelling and the level actually observed in the first screening studies. The expectation was based on the general cognitive level as measured by Raven's progressive matrices, a nonverbal test justified in this context.

To avoid the pitfalls of regression effects discussed above the residuals in relation to the regression line were used. However, we are faced with at least two problems of principle with the regression approach. First, there is a question of arbitrary statistical judgment in defining the region of critical values of the residuals. By pure convention we choose a 10% confidence band. Second, how should the risk be handled that an individual obtains a critical residual value merely by unfortunate coincidence. Instead of a doubtful formal correction for lack of reliability we decided to repeat the critical measurements after an interval of about 6 months. Only the pupils who fell in the critical zone on both occasions and thus displayed stable underachievement were included in the final group for further study. This careful strategy minimized the risk of committing false alarms at the expense of missing true cases.

We also required an additional criterion of stability or consistency—a shift from underachievement in reading to underachievement in spelling, or vice versa, was not accepted. Consistency was required in at least one of the variables. Our statistically defined procedure now implies that underachievement can occur at all levels of cognitive ability.

With our procedure, 49 pupils out of a total of 705 came to be defined as stable underachievers. Following consultations with the teachers, three pupils who displayed certain grave disturbances were excluded. Of the remaining 46 pupils (6.5% approximately), 38 were boys and 8 girls. This conspicuous imbalance between the sexes tallies well with similar international studies in which both biological and social psychological explanations are usually put forward to account for the striking differences between the sexes. We will refrain from speculations of our own for the time being.

B. Selection of Control Children

For reasons of comparisons a matched control group of normal children was selected with an attempt to keep some basic factors constant. The immediate pedagogical environment, including teacher and schoolmates, is certainly of critical importance for the development of basic skills in reading and writing during the first school years. Since the underachievers were unevenly distributed over the 44 school classes involved in the project (4 or 5 cases in some classes and none in several classes) it seemed reasonable to select the control children from exactly the same classes as the underachievers. A second critical factor is of course cognitive ability. Here matching might imply severe methodological problems, especially if the test is verbally loaded (Valtin, 1978–79). Raven's nonverbal character, however, partly avoids the pitfalls and a matching on this variable seems justified. As we have seen, sex is an important factor. Thus for each child in the underachieving group a corresponding "twin" for the control group was selected from the same class, of the same sex, and with approximately the same sum score from the two Raven testings, but, of course, with a reading and spelling proficiency corresponding to their intellectual level, i.e., very close to the regression line.

C. Underachieving and Control Children Compared

One of the first questions we asked was whether the two groups differed in terms of socioeconomic background factors, for it is a widespread and perhaps well-founded view that pupils with problems at school often come from problem homes. In the introductory remarks we also noted the tendency to discuss learning disabilities within a social–political context. But our interviews of parents of the underachieving children in their homes revealed a fairly normal picture with very few signs of social or economic problems. In most cases it seemed difficult to put the pupil's learning problems down to shortcomings of the domestic environment. This impression was confirmed by a closer analysis. Hard data were available concerning educational level of both parents, occupational status, and family income. The socioeconomic level was compared as follows. For a given combination of educational level, occupation, and income in an underachievement case we looked for a corresponding case in the control group. This search procedure was made independently by two persons with almost complete agreement. Thus, 33 cases could be successfully matched out of a total of 46 pairs. In the remaining 13 pairs we found a negligible superiority of educational status on the part of the control group parents. The size of the residuals (index of underachievement) was not related to the socioeconomic level. The reasonable conclusion was that underachievement was connected more with individually related than with social problems. It is indeed a handicap to the individual and not a mere artifact of an inappropriate social demand placed upon him.

D. Comparison on Screening Variables

The dyslexic group and the control group were compared in a number of respects and as is seen in Figs. 5 and 6 considerable differences were found for nearly all variables except Raven, of course, which was one of the matching variables. In screening I and II word reading (OS 400) and spelling discriminate most between the groups as a consequence of the selection criteria. In Screening III some additional variables with considerable discriminative power are found, namely mathematics, sentence reading, and level of aspiration. On the whole, however, the differences between the groups are less pronounced in Screening III. A tempting but certainly premature interpretation of this fact would be to regard it as evidence of a successful intervention program which started after Screening II or 1 year or more before Screening III. To avoid the pitfalls of regression phenomena, however, more sophisticated data analyses and more information from the more intense individual inquiries are needed. We will later return to this question.

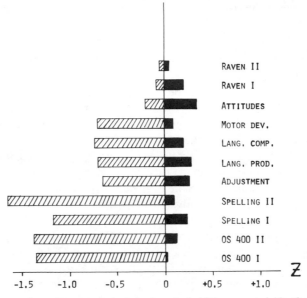

Fig. 5. Comparisons between dyslexic and control children on variables from Screenings I and II. Hatched boxes, dyslexic; solid boxes, control.

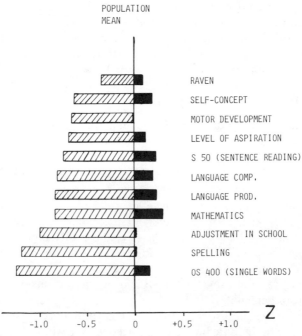

Fig. 6. Comparison between dyslexic and control children on variables from Screening III. Hatched boxes, dyslexic; solid boxes, control.

TABLE I

Isolated and Popular Children in the Control Group and in the Dyslexia Group

	Proportion 0 choices (isolated)		Proportion 5 choices (popular)	
	Play	Schoolwork	Play	Schoolwork
Control	.09	.04	.29	.34
Dyslexics	.20	.30	.17	.04

E. Sociometric Status

As an additional, more specific illustration of the screening comparisons we may look at the sociometric variables. Are there more socially isolated children in the dyslexic group than in the control group? Or conversely, what about highly popular children? Are there differences between different sociometric dimensions, i.e., do grade 1 children make valid distinctions in their sociometric choices? Table I gives the answers to these questions.

The dyslexic group contains a considerable proportion of completely isolated children (20–30%) while only a small proportion of the control children are isolated (4–9%). The proportion of very popular children is also much higher in the control group. As far as the play dimension is concerned the differences between the groups are smaller, which indicates that the children already in grade 1 make valid distinctions. Thus, we have now seen how a social variable is related to learning disabilities, although socio-emotional factors seemed to be of minor importance in the AID and path analyses of the whole population reported above.

V. DIAGNOSTIC PROGRAM IN GRADE 2

The screening studies were not particularly intended to reveal new insights concerning reading/spelling and its difficulties. More detailed diagnoses of the underachieving pupils hold some promise, however, provided the selection of procedures is guided by some theoretical conceptions of the reading process and the sources of obstacles for acquiring literacy. Our diagnostic program is outlined in Fig. 7. The control group was given a limited set of the diagnostic tests.

A critical part of the program is the analysis of *direct symptoms in reading and writing.* Here a number of individual subtests are given, including oral reading of a set of carefully selected words, silent reading, reading comprehension, listening comprehension, spelling from dictation, the effect of practice, etc. (see Table II). Apart from testing decoding, automatization, and comprehension the test items provoke various kinds of errors in-

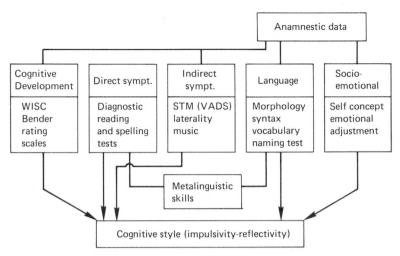

Fig. 7. Diagnostic program.

terpretable in terms of phonological problems or problems with orthographic structures, which at least in principle could yield a reasonable basis for subgrouping the dyslexic children.

Reading is primarily regarded as a language based skill which is reflected in the fourth box where we try to go closer to some basic *language skills.* In the first box some of the WISC subtests will give additional information for the language diagnosis.

An important bridge between language functions and reading is represented by "metalinguistic skills," i.e., the child's awareness of linguistic structures, especially the sound system, and his ability to manipulate or judge the abstracted formal aspects of language. In several studies we have demonstrated the importance of linguistic awareness to early reading and writing (Lundberg, 1978, 1982; Lundberg, Wall & Olofsson, 1980).

In recent years cognitive psychology has contributed much to our deeper understanding of dyslexia. The information processing approach has been especially fruitful. Several studies indicate limited processing capacity in *short-term memory* in dyslexic children (see, e.g., Torgeson, 1978–79). It is not quite clear, however, whether this bottleneck is a language-specific problem or of a more general kind. Without being able to solve this issue we still hoped to contribute to some understanding of memory functions in dyslexia by systematically varying sensory modality and response mode in digit span tasks. Unfortunately, neuropsychological assessments are mainly lacking in our program, which should be regretted in a project with the ambition of being comprehensive. In the last box the relevance of *so-*

TABLE II

Reading and Spelling Tests Used in the Diagnostic Program

Spelling
1. Dictation of letters.
2. Dictation of words
   a. Regular CVC or CVCV
      With nonplosive consonants
      Example: *fara*
   b. Regular CVC or CVCV
      With plosives
      Example: *bytet*
   c. Regular with consonant clusters
      Example: *strut*
   d. Irregular, word-specific spelling
      Example: *hjälp*/jelp/
3. Dictation of sentences.
4. Copying connected text
      Behavioral observations
      Memory
5. Effect of practice
      Practice on misspelled words from (2)
      Immediate effect and effect after 1 week

Oral reading
1. Letter reading
      Small and capital
2. Oral reading of words
      Equivalent to Spelling 2a–d
3. Oral reading of connected text
      Miscue analysis
      Comprehension questions
4. Oral reading of reversible words
      Examples: *ta, lat, mos, den*

Silent reading
1. Silent reading of connected text
      Comprehension test
      Reading speed
2. Proof reading
      Detection of misspelling in connected text

Listening comprehension
   A story is presented orally
      Free recall
      Prompted recall

cioemotional factors is recognized, especially different aspects of the child's self-concept. In the present report we will not discuss this aspect of dyslexia further.

Most of the test situations included in the program provided opportunities for assessing the child's conceptual or *cognitive style* as well, when he approached the various tasks and problems. We have especially focused on conceptual tempo or the dimension impulsivity–reflectivity as evaluated by test leaders, teacher assessments, and more directly with the help of MFFT (Kagan, 1966; Messer, 1976).

A detailed developmental, social, academic, and medical history was obtained from *interviews with parents* and teachers. In the present context we will not utilize the anamnestic data. However, the following finding seems to be of some relevance. In 17 of the 46 cases serious problems in language development were reported. Most of the remarks concerned children with low performance on the metalinguistic tasks. Problems of reading or spelling in the family (close relatives) were reported in more than half of the cases. Among the children with low scores on the metalinguistic tasks familial incidence was reported to a much higher extent. This finding, although it is based on a very crude method, underscores the need for subdividing learning-disabled children into more homogeneous subtypes in the search for familial–genetic determinants (Finucci, 1978).

Factor Analysis of Diagnostic Tests

Of the diagnostic tests used on the underachievers 20 were subjected to a factor analysis. Six factors with eigenvalues above 1 were extracted after varimax rotation, most variables having communalities between .70 and .80 (Table III). Some of the factors can be interpreted very easily, while others seem more obscure. On Factor 1 the tests with loadings above .50 included the different tasks on digit span with auditory presentation—oral recall having the strongest loading (.80). WISC vocabulary had a loading of .54. We interpreted the first factor as a memory factor. The second factor was very clear. Only the four metalinguistic tests had high loadings (.60–.80). Here we had clear support for the conception of linguistic awareness as an aspect of language development that could be treated separately from other language functions. On Factor 3 the total WISC score had a high loading together with the test on morphology. Perhaps this factor reflects general cognitive development. Factors 4 and 5 were less clear, but various verbal skills seemed to be involved. Finally, on Factor 6 only the coding subtest of WISC had a strong loading (.91).

The predictive value of the diagnostic tools was also clarified in a stepwise multiple regression analysis with the performance in grade 3 as criterion.

TABLE III
Rotated Factor Matrix (Varimax)

Test	I	II	III	IV	V	VI
				Factor		
Phoneme segmentation	.07	.83	.19	.03	.09	.18
Phoneme synthesis	.06	.82	.08	.19	.10	28
Position analysis	19	.59	.35	.32	−.03	.24
Phoneme subtraction	19	.64	.29	.20	.23	.05
Morphology	.16	.18	.73	.10	.07	−.35
Sentence completion	.19	.44	.12	−.04	.58	01
Syntax	−.02	.20	.10	.81	.20	−.10
WISC verbal: information	.55	.07	.22	.42	.29	−.15
WISC verbal: comprehension	.33	−.17	.18	.32	.68	27
WISC verbal: arithmetic	.23	.13	.59	.06	.42	.19
WISC verbal similarities	.09	.22	.39	.27	.68	02
WISC verbal: vocabulary	.54	−.01	.12	.53	.32	−.39
WISC performance: coding	−.01	.06	−.04	−.01	.12	.91
WISC total	.00	.25	.73	.48	.09	.15
Bender	−.35	−.33	−.17	−.65	.11	−.28
Latencies	−.04	−.30	−.50	.22	−.42	.09
Digit span: auditory stimulus—oral response	.80	−.03	.28	−.14	.07	−.12
Digit span: visual stimulus—oral response	.69	.33	−.17	.20	.10	.22
Digit span: auditory stimulus—written response	.48	.12	.67	.16	02	.01
Digit span: visual stimulus written response	.78	.26	.26	11	.23	.07

First, we investigated which of the tests apart from the reading and spelling tests were most related to reading in grade 3. In order of importance the following four variables yielded a multiple correlation of .72 (about half of the reading variance is explained): phoneme and syllable subtraction (a metalinguistic task) (simple $r = .48$), visual–auditory digit span, WISC total, Bender. The correlation should be evaluated in the light of the fact that some restriction of range is induced by the general low reading level of the group under investigation.

As far as writing in grade 3 is concerned the multiple correlation with a small set of diagnostic tests in grade 2 is still more impressive (.84). Also here the subtraction test and VADS take the lead followed by some of the verbal tests.

The critical importance of metalinguistic skills has now been confirmed again. In the subtraction test the subject is asked to tell the experimenter what is left of a word when a part (a phoneme or syllable) is deleted (e.g., *lo* from melody). We have used this task in earlier studies and obtained a remarkable discriminatory power (Lundberg, 1982). Apart from the ability to analyze words into components it also seems to require some general processing capacity, including attention, short-term memory, and system- atic search strategy. Perhaps the test reveals a critical bottleneck in some learning-disabled children.

My co-worker, Margit Tornéus, is now studying the metalinguistic de- velopment in great detail relating it to patterns of reading and spelling er- rors. She is also trying to solve the "chicken and egg" problem, i.e., demonstrating if there is any causal priority in the metalinguistic variable. In an experimental setting the effect of systematic training of metalinguistic skills is studied. By applying the LISREL program she has the possibility of testing the fit of a specific causal model concerning the relationship be- tween linguistic awareness, cognitive development, language development, reading, and spelling.

VI. SUBGROUPING OF READING DISABILITIES

There is now increasing recognition that reading retardates comprise a heterogeneous rather than a homogeneous population. Clinical as well as statistical evidence has been accumulated during the past decades (Ingram, 1960; Kinsbourne & Warrington, 1963; Johnson & Myklebust, 1967; Boder, 1973; Mattis, French, & Rapin, 1975; Denckla, 1977; Myklebust, 1978; Pi- rozzolo, 1979; Doehring, Trites, Patel, & Fiedorowicz, 1981). In Scandi- navia Gjessing (1980) has independently suggested a subtyping model strongly similar to Boder's classification and also based on functional anal- ysis of direct symptoms in oral reading and spelling.

The main subtypes of dyslexia according to Gjessing are auditive, visual, audio-visual, emotional, and pedagogical dyslexia. In *auditive dyslexia* the main symptoms are metaphonological problems with confusions of similar phonemes, difficulties with segmentation and sound blending, and partic- ular problems in decoding long words and words with clusters of conso- nants. The main problems in *visual dyslexia* concern direct perception and remembering of whole words. Reading is carried out with great effort and the words are sounded out rigidly as if they were seen for the first time. In *audio-visual dyslexia* both sets of symptoms are seen in the same individual. The remaining types are not as clearly revealed by direct symptoms in read- ing and spelling. More indirect evidence is needed to differentiate these sub- types.

Much inspired by Gjessing's model we have in the present project given particular emphasis to a qualitative analysis of how the child reads and spells. This approach offered us the essential guidelines for designing the remedial teaching, which followed the diagnostic phase. However, for research purposes statistical classification with its precise and objective character seemed preferable to subjective or clinical methods. Some investigators still doubt the evidence supporting the subgrouping hypothesis (e.g., Rutter, 1978). "Although patterns of subgroups may be delineated in the future, they are not evident at present" (Guthrie, 1978, p. 430). Satz and Morris (1981) have recently provided a critical and very clarifying review of subtype studies and convincingly demonstrated the limitations of clinical classification methods. Although the clinically defined subtypes show striking resemblances among different investigators (e.g., auditory or dysphonemic dyslexia and visual or dyseidetic dyslexia) and have a strong intuitive appeal, they must be viewed with caution until the rules for subtype classification are more clearly operationalized and validated against external criteria. Gjessing's approach, mentioned above, seems to be the most elaborated and explicit nonstatistical subgrouping procedure suggested so far. However, it still awaits validation against external criteria. Within the Norwegian part of the project there are promising potentialities to validation tests, also by the application of statistical methods such as ANOVA and MANOVA.

More recently, several attempts have been made to apply multivariate statistics in the search for subtypes (Doehring & Hoshko, 1977; Doehring *et al.,* 1981; Petrauskas & Rourke, 1979; Satz & Morris, 1981). However, the results from the statistical analyses should also be interpreted with caution, since the subtyping can vary as a function of the number and the kinds of tests used and the number and types of subjects tested.

Q-Factor Analysis

Our first attempt to find the hidden structure of the complex multivariate data set involved the application of Q-factor analysis (Overall & Klett, 1972; Nunnally, 1967; Doehring *et al.,* 1981) of those diagnostic variables that did not include direct measures of reading and spelling. The Q-technique is essentially an inverted factor analysis that groups children together who show similar patterns of performance. The measures of similarity are derived from the correlations between profiles. The correlation between the profiles of each possible pair of children is computed. In the conventional application of factor analysis a matrix of correlations between tests is analyzed. Now, the entries in the matrix are individuals rather than tests. It is well recognized that this technique is somewhat controversial. There are, for example, no objective rules for how to deal with cases where a given subject has significant loadings on several factors. Fleiss and Zubin

(1969) question the use of correlation as a measure of similarity between subjects. However, the study of Doehring *et al.* (1981) was very encouraging. They demonstrated a surprising effectivity and stability of the Q-technique, which yielded structures of impressing invariance over samples and clustering methods.

In our subgroup analyses we first started with the set of diagnostic variables which did not include direct measures of reading and writing under the assumption that the obtained subtypes would reflect homogeneity in some fundamental cognitive and linguistic characteristics of critical importance to reading and spelling. In the next step the Q-analysis was based on the different reading and writing tests, the prediction being that the individuals would group together in about the same way as in the first analysis. Finally we tried to apply a cluster analysis to test the invariance of the subtypes with a different technique.

In the first Q-analyses four factors were extracted together with the mirror-image of each factor, that is a total of eight factors. The mirror-factors were defined by loadings less than $-.50$. Of the 46 individuals 27 could be unambiguously referred to one of the factors, i.e., they had high loadings ($>.50$) on one factor and low on the rest ($<.30$). The remaining 19 cases had high loadings in more than one factor and were thus excluded from the subgroups. To give a simplified overview of the obtained structure the six factors extracted from the earlier mentioned R-analysis were used to characterize the subgroups.

Figure 8 shows the average factor score on each of the six factors for the different subgroups. (The mirror-groups must be inferred.) As mentioned earlier, factor 1 was interpreted as a short-term memory factor, factor 2 was metalinguistic, factor 3 general intelligence, factors 4 and 5 verbal factors, and factor 6 represented the coding subtest of WISC and might be interpreted as an attentional factor.

Subgroup 1 has no dramatic profile. Only a slight weakness in memory and general intelligence can be observed. Subgroup 2 is more characteristic with poor levels of memory and attention. Most of the members of this group also showed clear signs of impulsivity on the MFFT and the teacher ratings. Subgroup 3 also has extremely low memory functions, while their coding performance is adequate. The poor verbal level is in contrast to the comparatively well-developed metalinguistic ability. The remarkable dip in factor 5 with subgroup 4 is not easy to interpret, since the status of this factor is rather unclear (high loadings of some of the verbal subtests of WISC and sentence completion test). Common to all mirror groups is the low level of metalinguistic competence.

From this relatively clear structure it was reasonable to expect that a given

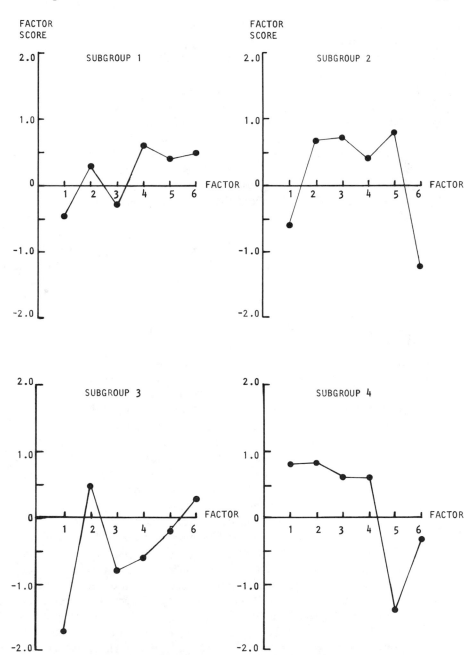

Fig. 8. Subgroup profiles over factors extracted from the diagnostic battery (except reading and writing tests).

profile in these basic functions would be reflected in the way various reading and writing tasks are approached.

In the next step 15 reading and spelling tests formed the basis for a Q-analysis. The battery included a number of spelling tests with systematic variation of phonological and orthographical complexity, a number of oral reading tests also varied along these dimensions, silent reading also including comprehension tests, reading of reversible words, detection of misspellings, etc. In this analysis 31 subjects could be classified into 6 subgroups (with the application of the same stop criterion as in the first Q-analysis). However, the expected patterning of profiles was not obtained. Only a few profiles seemed to fit into an interpretable pattern. Still worse was the fact that the subgroups from the first analysis did not remain in the second analysis. Only two individuals from factor 1 and two from factor 4 in the original analysis hung together in the reading/spelling profiles. The remaining children were scattered across all new factors or were impossible to classify in any specific reading/spelling factor. There are probably several reasons for this negative finding. First, Q-analysis might be an ill-suited tool for detecting reliable subgroups in the present case. Second, the intercorrelations among the reading/spelling tests are too high. Third, the subgrouping hypothesis might not be valid. One point of criticism against subgrouping studies raised by Satz and Morris (1980) was that no comparison group of normal readers is used. Then the obtained subtypes could be idiosyncratic to the specific target group of disabled readers. "One could not be sure that scalar or configural patterns in the normal readers would nor alter the subtype derivations" (Satz & Morris, 1981).

In the third step of our subgroup analysis we included the control group. Then only a subset of the diagnostic tests could be used. Instead of the Q-technique we applied a cluster analysis (Ward, 1963) where all subjects are classified. However, this technique was primarily sensitive to the absolute level on each test and thus the main partitioning divided most of the subjects into normals and underachievers. The groupings within the latter category were reasonably clear and partly replicated the pattern of our first Q-analysis with some profiles showing low metalinguistic competence, impulsivity, or poor attention. Of the 27 subjects classified earlier 17 were now grouped together in a similar way as before. Although this is not too impressive it may encourage a continuing search for stable and homogeneous subtypes. "It is only hoped that such studies reflect an awareness of the complexity of the problems being addressed and do not represent premature exercises using techniques that obscure rather than elucidate one's understanding of these children" (Satz & Morris, 1981). However, the problem is only partly a question of statistical sophistication. No real advance should be expected until our knowledge of the reading process has developed much further. Not until then are we in the position of selecting critical tasks and observations on which the subgrouping work should be based.

VII. THE REMEDIAL PROGRAM AND ITS EFFECT

A. Some Principles of Remedial Work

The obvious next step after diagnosing is to develop remedial guidelines. The methods which have been found to be most successful with dyslexic children are those which are "structured, sequential, cumulative and thorough" (Rawson, 1975). Our main departure was the functional analysis of the reading and writing of each individual child (Gjessing, 1980). An important feature of such analysis is to avoid mechanical classification of misspellings or reading errors in categories such as omissions, substitutions, reversals, etc. Instead a given error is interpreted in its functional context. If, for example, a child spells *sbider* instead of *spider* it is probably not a sign of poor phonological discrimination. The letter *b* in this context is certainly equivalent to the letter *p* as far as sound quality is concerned. The problem is rather one of poor feeling for orthographic regularities—*b* never occurs after *s* in initial position. A child showing many instances of similar problems is encouraged in systematic exercises to discover the orthographic regularities of the written language. Typical games could be "hangman" or visual search tasks where the target is a spelling pattern only occurring in a specific position within words. An effective search strategy then implies a selective focusing.

Other children may reveal serious problems with phonemic analysis and synthesis manifested in characteristic substitutions and simplifications of long words, sometimes also in a wild guessing strategy. Poor metalinguistic skills are often accompanying symptoms. Here the child is supposed to need many opportunities to discover the formal properties of language, especially the sound system. Rhyming, verses, puns, riddles, secret languages, mirror observations of one's articulation, looking for errors and slips of the tongue are all examples of games and exercises which have been found useful.

Certain teaching practices have been actively discouraged, for example, eye movement training, visual shape discrimination, nonverbal sound discrimination, attempts to change cerebral dominance, or other measures based on speculative neurology.

Our guidelines had not the character of a strict program, only that certain types of procedure predominated the actual practice, in most cases a phonics approach. The skill element of reading and writing was also strongly emphasized.

The responsible teacher was offered a rather thorough and detailed syllabus with several alternative options described. It did not contain a lot of "musts" or "shoulds" and left much to the teacher's own discretion. Reading and spelling were emphasized side by side as different aspects of the coding process.

The remedial support to each child was given within the ordinary school program without any extra time resources, which is the way special education is normally offered, either within the regular classroom or in special clinics. The special teachers were trained at the university over two semesters in evening courses, where theoretical rationale, diagnostic techniques, and intervention strategies were treated. Most teachers also took an active part in the design of material and exercises.

B. Evaluation of the Remedial Program

The evaluation of the effect of the remedial measures is an extremely difficult affair, even with a carefully designed experiment. From the available data, however, some indications of the effect are possible to discern. Of the 40 subjects available for follow up to grade 5, 23 were offered professional help by the special teachers in close contact with the university. The remaining 17 subjects were located in schools where the special teachers only had indirect contacts to the university. In the latter cases the guidelines were given by telephone and no regular checks on the progress were provided. These subgroups did not differ systematically on any known variable of relevance, except for the level of professional help. The groups also started from about the same level of basics 1. Thus, a kind of quasi-experimental condition had occurred which could be utilized for the evaluation.

As a first measure of change we used the residual values from the regression of basics 3 on basics 1 for the whole population. A positive residual then indicates unexpected fast progress over the treatment period (about 1 year) and a negative residual indicates slower progress than expected. In the first subgroup ($N=23$) with professional help 70% showed a positive development with an average residual value of $+.60$. In the informal group ($N=17$) 60% showed positive development with an average residual of $z = +.39$. The slow children in the first group (the remaining 30%) had an average of $-.53$, while the corresponding value in the informal group was $-.80$. The mean change was $+.25$ in the whole professional group and $-.10$ in the whole informal group. Thus, a larger proportion of children in the professional group developed positively than in the informal group and these children also showed a stronger positive change.

As a second comparison of the development we looked at the reading and spelling performance in grade 5. However, now regression data from the population were not available. Instead we compared the dyslexic children with the control group and noted which children reached a proficiency level one standard deviation unit below the mean of the control group, i.e., a level within the normal range of performance. Now, in the professional group more than half of the children (13) had reached that level in reading, while that was the case for only one-third (6) of the children in the informal group. In spelling the groups were quite similar with about 35% reaching an acceptable level in both groups.

The indications of the positive effects of our treatment program should, of course, be regarded with caution. Although the amount of training and general conditions were about the same in the two groups Hawthorne-effects might be the main source of difference between the groups.

As an additional attempt to evaluate the remedial program we selected a comparison group of retarded readers (no underachievement, i.e., their reading and spelling scores in grades 1 and 2 were outside the critical region for underachievement and were thus mostly in good accord with their Raven scores) who did not enjoy the benefit of our remedial guidelines. However, the matching on initial basics level was not very successful. The under-achieving group had a mean of -1.45 and a standard deviation of .61, while the group of retarded readers had a mean of -1.20 and a standard deviation of .46.

The average residual value of the latter group was very close to zero ($-.03$) which is the expected value of the population. The underachievers, including the professional and the informal subgroups, had an average value of $+.10$. Also this comparison must be treated with caution, since we know nothing of the base rate of improvement in a completely untreated group of underachievers. However, we have no indications in our data or from our practical experience that contradict a cautious optimism concerning the possibility of providing dyslexic children with positive help with a remedial approach based on the reading and spelling process itself. In any case, proponents of basic functions training (visual, auditory, motor) have not presented a convincing alternative.

VIII. THE LONG-TERM DEVELOPMENT
OF DYSLEXIC CHILDREN

Longitudinal studies of reading disabilities are scarce. An impressive follow-up investigation of the reading development of a large population of boys reported by Satz, Taylor, Friel, and Fletcher (1978) is a notable exception. They showed that disabled readers do not overcome their problems by grade 5. The slow development and the persistency of the handicap were also confirmed by Peter and Spreen (1979). Lundberg *et al.* (1980) showed that metalinguistic measures on nonreaders in kindergarten were highly predictive of later success or failure in reading. Our present data also support the rather pessimistic conclusions implied in the study by Satz *et al.* (1978). The developmental curves of reading and spelling over the five school years are almost parallel for the dyslexic and the control group with the latter lagging far behind. Within the dyslexic group the correlation between reading in grade 1 and grade 5 is as high as .60 despite the considerably restricted range.

As we already have seen, however, some indications of improvement have been recorded, especially among pupils subjected to professional help. But we should recognize that the amount of time spent on remedial teaching was quite modest and did not exceed what is normally offered in regular school work. According to experienced teachers the net amount of time devoted to practicing reading and spelling skills in Swedish schools seems to have diminished significantly over the past decades due to the introduction of many competing demands on the school program and to an increasing tendency to avoid homework. Now, Guthrie, Martuza, and Seifert (1979) among others have demonstrated the decisive importance of the time factor for developing basic skills in reading and writing. In comparison with the time spent on the task, variations in teaching methods seem to play a very subordinate role.

Indications of the lack of practice are provided by the oral reading tests in grade 5, where a majority of the dyslexic children showed poorly automatized word recognition. The reading test consisted of two parts; one required context-free reading of isolated words and the other required reading of connected discourse. Errors, hesitations, and rereadings were recorded as well as the reading speed. After the second task, comprehension and memory of the story was checked.

In the first task the word recognition could only be based on decoding of internal cues, i.e., information provided by the given word itself, either indirectly by phonological mediation or directly by word specific orthographic structures (e.g., Treiman & Baron, 1981). The second task provided rich external or contextual cues as well. Now, according to Stanovich (1980) an important difference between poor and good readers seems to be the following: Poor readers have great difficulties in decoding words on the basis of internal cues, one important reason being lack of automatization. When reading a connected discourse, however, they seem to be capable of compensating their poor graphic information processing by utilizing contextual information with a reading biased toward top-down control. But this utilization of context seems to demand mental resources or attentional capacity at the expense of comprehension. Good readers, on the contrary, have fully automatized and high-speed word recognition with minimum demand on controlled attentional processes which then are available for the complex inferences involved in genuine understanding. Our data seem to be in good accordance with this interactive model of reading.

The dyslexic group had an average error rate of 20% on the word reading test, while the mean for the control group was not more than 7%. The dyslexic children also showed far more hesitations and rereadings and their reading speed was only half as fast. However, the difference between dyslexics and controls was not of that dramatic kind in the context reading. For both groups the error rate decreased considerably (dyslexics: from 20 to 3%; controls: from 7 to 1%) but to a much greater extent for the dyslexic group, although the ratio of noncontextual/contextual word recognition errors is virtually identical for both groups. A large number of dyslexic children now seemed to read quite fluently and could not be discriminated from normal children probably to the satisfaction of most teachers. However, their comprehension was often poor. It is also doubtful whether their superficial graphic information processing and their heavy dependence on contextual cues is an acceptable strategy in the long run when unexpected and less familiar words are encountered. The poor word decoding is also reflected in spelling. Only 6 of the 40 dyslexic children reached the mean level of the control group on the grade 5 spelling test, most of them being far behind.

It seems as if the results from our grade 5 testing underscore an urgent need to invest more time in the remedial work with dyslexic children. Vast amounts of overlearning are recognized as a necessity in developing skills in most areas, e.g., music or sport. This should also be more widely recognized in reading and writing. Reading is probably best learned by reading. A basic educational concern is then to motivate the student to read. Reading research does not seem to be very helpful in guiding the teacher to select the right text at the right moment for a disabled reader. Probably, this belongs more to the artistic domain of education, where intuition, feeling, and professional devotion still are masters. However, some research-based ideas on how to develop automaticity have recently been proposed. Beck (1981) discusses the advantage of carefully planned repeated encounters of the same words in varying contexts. Samuels (1979) has demonstrated the usefulness of repeated readings of the same passage, where the successive discoveries of cues that compensate for the absence of prosody seem to be an essential element.

IX. SUMMARY AND CONCLUDING COMMENTS

The results presented in the present article are far from exhaustive. Scope limitation has forced us to be highly selective and to treat some parts of the project quite superficially, some significant findings not even being mentioned. Moreover, we are still eagerly waiting for our Scandinavian colleagues to provide the comparative basis from the affiliated projects. On the whole, nothing of what has been reported here seems to be exclusively related to conditions specific to the Swedish orthography or to Swedish school traditions. On the contrary, most of our results are largely in agreement with current Anglo-American reading research, although the employment of a broad assessment battery and the attempt to approach reading disabilities within a developmental context are comparatively unusual. We will now summarize our main findings and conclude our report with a few general comments on dyslexia research.

A. Summary of Results

First, we have found considerable variation among children in reading and writing already in the first school year, despite a most homogeneous school environment and home background. The variation was explained in terms of a broad spectrum of factors. By applying various multivariate techniques we arrived at the conclusion that language development had the most crucial role in accounting for individual differences in basic skills, the contribution of other variables such as motor development, social and emotional adjustment, school attitudes, self-concept, class size, etc. being small or insignificant.

The level of basic skills in grade 1 was highly predictive of later development. The extreme groups of children who either showed unexpected rapid development or slow development were compared along a number of dimensions. Also here language was the most critical determinant. Neither pedagogical environment (class) nor home background could explain the rate difference. However, a sex difference was observed favoring girls. In a corresponding contrast group comparison of the development of academic self-concept the pattern was reversed. A majority of the children with negative development were girls. This paradox was interpreted in terms of the different ways in which girls and boys are treated by teachers.

On the basis of the comprehensive population survey a minor group of dyslexic children (6.5%) was identified. However, it was made clear that estimates of the prevalence of dyslexia depend upon how it is defined. In the present case a statistical regression criterion of underachievement was applied. The dyslexic group differed from a matched comparison group of normal readers in a broad set of variables. Our attempts to delineate possible subgroups of disabled readers statistically were not very successful, which does not necessarily mean that the subgrouping hypothesis should be abandoned. A better understanding of the reading process, diagnostic tests based thereupon, and better developed multivariate techniques seem to be prerequisites for a more fruitful approach to subtype classification. The successful identification of more homogeneous syndromes will be expected to result in significant improvement in our ability to predict outcome and to institute appropriate remedial measures.

Based on a more or less clinical approach and some assumptions concerning the reading process we designed a remedial plan for each child. Some evidence of the positive effects of these measures was reported. However, the follow-up study indicates that most dyslexic children continue to lag far behind the normals even by grade 5.

On the basis of the evidence presented here and in many other studies it seems highly probable that relative deficiency in oral language skills is a central factor in the genesis of dyslexia. However, the particular facets of language development which are crucial in this respect must be specified. One important link between verbal problems and difficulties in learning to read seems to be related to linguistic awareness. A majority of retarded readers are impaired in their use of phonological codes for lexical access and have considerable difficulties in developing automatized word recognition. They often experience serious problems in segmenting spoken words into their constituent phonemes. Our attempts to train such skills already in kindergarten have been quite successful (Olofsson & Lundberg, 1983) although we do not know yet whether this training positively affects reading and spelling in school. At least we can predict with considerable success the preschool child at risk for future reading failure (Lundberg *et al.*, 1980).

Since we now have good reasons to believe that reading is essentially a metalinguistic task children should, early in school or even in kindergarten, be afforded rich opportunities to play with language, produce rhymes, to explain puns and riddles, to analyze utterances, and to make judgments about the appropriateness of language form and expressions in various contexts of communication. We have also emphasized the skill element in reading and writing and pointed out educational consequences of this insight.

B. Some Methodological Considerations

The typical experimental design in research on reading disabilities involves a comparison of the performance of retarded readers and a control group of normal readers on some task assumed to tap functions critical to learning to read, e.g., memory, cross-modal transfer, sequencing, etc. The observed deficits in the retarded readers are interpreted as basic causes of the difficulties. However, such conclusions are often unwarranted, since they are essentially based on correlational evidence, although the research may have a conspicuous experimental flavor.

The poor performance of dyslexics could alternatively be regarded as consequences of not having learned to read. A second alternative is that dyslexic children are characterized by some general immaturity of the central nervous system which may cause problems on many tasks of which some are quite irrelevant to reading.

There are at least two ways out of this much neglected correlational problem. The most obvious and direct, but also the most difficult way, is to set up a genuine experiment with adequate control measures taken, and active manipulation of independent variables, for example, experimentally designed training studies where the effect on reading is observed. Great care must here be exerted to separate specific and nonspecific influences (see, e.g., Olofsson & Lundberg, 1983). The second way is the one we have taken here. It is more indirect and involves longitudinal design. An important advantage of this approach lies in the possibility of untangling the complex effects of reciprocal influences. As already mentioned the LISREL methodology provides proper tools.

The longitudinal design implies ecological validity and may help to close the gap between reading theory and practice. The application of theoretical models of the reading process to educational settings has indeed been rather limited. Emphasis on the longitudinal development of teachable aspects of reading such as decoding, vocabulary or syntax comprehension and the disentanglement of the network or interrelated causal factors seems to be a fruitful research strategy. As an example of a promising reorientation of research on reading disabilities I would like to mention the work on metacognition by Wong (1982). In our follow-up study of the dyslexics we plan to include metacognitive variables.

Future progress in dyslexia research requires the integration of several approaches and we need more efforts to break down the barriers between cognitive psychology, developmental psychology, education, and neurology. We can expect a rapid growth of the knowledge of the neurological basis of dyslexia as new, noninvasive techniques become applied, such as measurement of cerebral blood flow or metabolism, electrophysiological techniques, and computerized tomography. However, no real significant and applicable advances of our knowledge of dyslexia will be made unless a proper understanding of the reading process is developed. Dyslexia is indeed a challenging riddle and we should not hope for simple solutions.

ACKNOWLEDGMENTS

This research was supported by grants from the Swedish National Board of Education, the municipality of Umeå, and the Secretariat for Nordic Cultural Cooperation. My co-workers

Margit Tornéus, Karin Taube, and Åke Olofsson are gratefully acknowledged. I also wish to thank the many children and teachers in Umeå who helped us.

REFERENCES

Beck, I. L. Reading problems and instructional practices. In G. E. MacKinnon & T. G. Waller (Eds.), *Reading research. Advances in theory and practice* (Vol 2). New York: Academic Press, 1981.

Benton, A. L., & Pearl, D. (Eds.), *Dyslexia. An appraisal of current knowledge.* London and New York: Oxford Univ. Press, 1978.

Boder, E. Developmental dyslexia: A diagnostic approach based on three atypical reading-spelling patterns. *Developmental Medicine and Child Neurology,* 1973, **15,** 663–687.

Cronbach, L. J., & Furby, L. How should we measure "change"—Or should we? *Psychological Bulletin,* 1970, **74,** 68–80.

Denckla, M. B. Minimal brain dysfunction and dyslexia: Beyond diagnosis by exclusion. In M. E. Blaw, J. Rapin, & M. Kinsbourne (Eds.), *Child neurology.* New York: Spectrum, 1977.

Doehring, D. G., & Hoshko, I. M. Classification of reading problems by the Q technique of factor analysis. *Cortex,* 1977, **13,** 281–294.

Doehring, D. G., Trites, R. L., Patel, P. G., & Fiedovowicz, C. A. M. *Reading disabilities. The interaction of reading, language, and neuropsychological deficits.* New York: Academic Press, 1981.

Finucci, J. M. Genetic considerations in dyslexia. In H. R. Myklebust (Ed.), *Progress in learning disabilities* (Vol 4). New York: Grune & Stratton, 1978.

Fleiss, J. L., & Zubin, J. On the methods and theory of clustering. *Multivariate Behavior Research,* 1969, **4,** 235–250.

Gjessing, H.-J. Reading disability: Diagnosis based on psycho-educational analysis of the learning function. *Forty-Fourth Yearbook. Claremont Reading Conference,* 1980.

Guthrie, J. T. Principles of instruction: A critique of Johnson's "Remedial approaches to dyslexia." In A. L. Benton & D. Pearl (Eds.), *Dyslexia. An appraisal of current knowledge.* London and New York: Oxford Univ. Press, 1978.

Guthrie, J. T., Martuza, V., & Seifert, M. Impacts of instructional time in reading. In L. B. Resnick & P. A. Weaver (Eds.), *Theory and practice of early reading.* Hillsdale, New Jersey: Erlbaum, 1979.

Hays, W. L. *Statistics for the social sciences* (2nd ed). New York: Holt, 1973.

Hung, D. L., & Tzeng, D. J. L. Orthographic variations and visual information processing. *Psychological Bulletin,* 1981, **90,** 377–414.

Ingram, T. T. S. Pediatric aspects of specific developmental dysphasia, dyslexia, and dysgraphia. *Cerebral Palsy Bulletin,* 1960, **2,** 254–277.

Johnson, D. J., & Myklebust, H. R. *Learning disabilities.* New York: Grune & Stratton, 1967.

Jöreskog, K. G., & Sörbom, D. *LISREL IV. Analysis of linear structural relationships by the method of maximum likelihood.* Chicago: National Education Resources, 1980.

Kagan, J. Reflection–impulsivity: The generality and dynamics of conceptual tempo. *Journal of Abnormal Psychology,* 1966, **71,** 17–24.

Kinsbourne, M., & Warrington, E. K. Developmental factors in reading and writing backwardness. *British Journal of Psychology,* 1963, **54,** 145–156.

Klecka, W. R. *Discriminant analysis.* Beverly Hills, California: Sage, 1980.

Kyöstiö, D. K. Is learning to read easy in a language in which the grapheme–phoneme correspondences are regular? In J. F. Kavanagh & R. L. Venezky (Eds.), *Orthography, reading, and dyslexia*. Baltimore: Univ. Park Press, 1980.

Land, K. C. Principles of path analysis. In E. F. Borgatta (Ed.), *Sociological methodology*. San Francisco: Jossey Bass, 1969.

Lundberg, I. Aspects of linguistic awareness related to reading. In A. Sinclair, R. J. Jarvella, & W. J. M. Levelt (Eds.), *The child's conception of language*. Berlin and New York: Springer-Verlag, 1978.

Lundberg, I. Linguistic awareness related to dyslexia. In Y. Zotterman (Ed.), *Dyslexia. Neuronal, cognitive, & linguistic aspects*. Oxford: Pergamon, 1982.

Lundberg, I., Wall, S., & Olofsson, A. Reading and spelling skills in the first school years predicted from phonemic awareness skills in kindergarten. *Scandinavian Journal of Psychology*, 1980, **21**, 159–173.

Malmquist, E. *Factors related to reading disabilities in the first grade of elementary school*. Stockholm: Almqvist & Wiksell, 1958.

Malmquist, E. Reading disabilities in Swedish children. In L. Tarnopol & M. Tarnopol (Eds.), *Comparative reading and learning difficulties*. Toronto: 1981.

Mattis, S., French, J. H., & Rapin, I. Dyslexia in children and young adults: Three independent neuropsychological syndromes. *Developmental Medicine and Child Neurology*, 1975, **17**, 150–163.

Messer, S. B. Reflection–impulsivity: A review. *Psychological Bulletin*, 1976, **83**, 1026–1052.

Meyerowitz, J. H. Self derogations in young retardates and special class placement. *Child Development*, 1962, **33**, 443–451.

Miles, T. R., & Ellis, N. C. A lexical encoding deficiency II: Clinical observations. In G. Th. Pavlidis & T. R. Miles (Eds.), *Dyslexia research and its applications to education*. New York: Wiley, 1981.

Myklebust, H. R. *The pupil rating scale. Screening for learning disabilities*. New York: Grune & Stratton, 1971.

Myklebust, H. R. Toward a science of dyslexiology. In H. R. Myklebust (Ed.), *Progress in learning disabilities* (Vol. 4). New York: Grune & Stratton, 1978.

Nunnally, J. C. *Psychometric theory*. New York: McGraw-Hill, 1967.

Olofsson, A., & Lundberg, I. Can phonemic awareness be trained in Kindergarten? *Scandinavian Journal of Psychology,* 1983, **24**, 35–44.

Overall, J. E., & Klett, C. J. *Applied multivariate analysis*. New York: McGraw-Hill, 1972.

Peter, B. M., & Spreen, O. Behavior rating and personal adjustment scales of neurologically and learning handicapped children during adolescence and early childhood: Results of a follow-up study. *Journal of Clinical Neuropsychology*, 1979, **1**, 75–92.

Petrauskas, R. J., & Rourke, B. P. Identification of subtypes of retarded readers: A neuropsychological, multivariate approach. *Journal of Clinical Neuropsychology*, 1979, **1**, 17–37.

Pirozzolo, F. J. *The neuropsychology of developmental reading disorder*. New York: Praeger, 1979.

Raven, J. *The coloured progressive matrices*. London: Lewis, 1965.

Rawson, M. B. Developmental dyslexia: educational treatment and results. In M. B. Rawson & D. D. Duane (Eds.), *Reading, perception, and language: Papers from the world congress on dyslexia*. Baltimore: York Press, 1975.

Rogosa, D. Causal models in longitudinal research: Rational, formulation, and interpretation. In J. R. Nesselroade & P. B. Baltes (Eds.), *Longitudinal research in the study of behavior and development*. New York: Academic Press, 1979.

Rutter, M. Prevalence and types of dyslexia. In A. L. Benton & D. Pearl (Eds.), *Dyslexia. An appraisal of current knowledge*. London and New York: Oxford Univ. Press, 1978.

Samuels, S. J. The method of repeated readings. *The Reading Teacher*, 1979, **32**, 403–408.

Satz, P., & Morris, R. Learning disability subtypes: A review. In F. J. Pirozzolo & M. C. Wittrock (Eds.), *Neuropsychological and cognitive processes in reading.* New York: Academic Press, 1980.

Satz, P., Taylor, H. G., Friel, J., & Fletcher, J. Some developmental and predictive precursors of reading disabilities: A six-year follow-up. In A. L. Benton & D. Pearl (Eds.), *Dyslexia: An appraisal of current knowledge.* London and New York: Oxford Univ. Press, 1978.

Sonqvist, J. A., Baker, E. L., & Morgan, J. N. *Searching for structure.* Ann Arbor, Michigan: Survey Research Center, Univ. Michigan, 1973.

Stanovich, K. E. Toward an interactive-compensatory model of individual differences in the development of reading fluency. *Reading Research Quarterly*, 1980, **16**, 32–71.

Torgeson, J. K. Performance of reading disabled children on serial memory tasks. *Reading Research Quarterly*, 1978–79, **14**, 57–87.

Treiman, R., & Baron, J. Segmental analysis ability: Development and relation to reading ability. In G. E. MacKinnon & T. G. Waller (Eds.), *Reading research: Advances in theory and practice.* (Vol. 3). New York: Academic Press, 1981.

Valtin, R. Dyslexia: Deficit in reading or deficit in research? *Reading Research Quarterly*, 1978–79, **15**, 201–221.

Vellutino, F. R. *Dyslexia. Theory and research.* Cambridge, Massachusetts: MIT Press, 1979.

Ward, J. H. Hierarchical grouping to optimize an objective function. *Journal of American Statistical Association*, 1963, **58**, 236–244.

Wohlwill, J. F. *The study of behavioral development.* New York: Academic Press, 1973.

Wong, B. Y. L. Strategic behaviors in selecting retrieval cues in gifted, normal achieving and learning disabled children. *Journal of Learning Disabilities*, 1982, **15**, 33–37.

Zotterman, Y. (Ed.), *Dyslexia. Neuronal, cognitive, and linguistic aspects.* Oxford: Pergamon, 1982.

LEARNING TO READ: A LONGITUDINAL STUDY OF WORD SKILL DEVELOPMENT IN TWO CURRICULA

ALAN LESGOLD,
LAUREN B. RESNICK, AND
KATHLEEN HAMMOND

Learning Research and Development Center
University of Pittsburgh
Pittsburgh, Pennsylvania

I. PROBLEMS IN READING

It is often assumed that reading is a very natural skill, one that is readily acquired by anyone who is willing to work hard at learning it. In fact, though, serious efforts to achieve universal literacy are quite novel (Resnick & Resnick, 1977). Many reports of high literacy in some earlier time are based upon low criteria, such as being able to read a fixed Bible passage or sign one's name. Others fail to consider less privileged members of a society in proclaiming the existence of universal literacy. In a sense, reading is a lot like driving a car. If one's expectations of success are low enough, it can appear that the skill is almost universal and that learning it requires nothing but practice. However, adequate driver performance in stressing situations such as driving on ice is not universal. Similarly, reading complex material with understanding is also not universal. Efforts are made to teach effective reading, and those efforts are partly successful. Presumably, if we knew more about how the skills of reading are learned, we could better teach them.

Continuing with our driving metaphor, we might think about how driving is taught. Surely, simple practice of the overall task of driving is a critical aspect of performance. We want drivers to have fully integrated capabilities to keep the car in the correct lane, watch for obstacles ahead, watch for dangers from sides and behind, maintain proper speed, operate windshield wipers, etc. Being able to do each of these things in isolation is not enough, though. Indeed, many of the people who are on the road today know about all of these subskills of driving but fail to coordinate them all into smooth overall performance. On the other hand, there are specific subskills of driving that many individuals simply lack, such as the winter driving skills mentioned above; these could be taught directly with considerable benefit.

One can imagine controversies over whether special subskills of driving should be taught in the context of overall driving practice or whether they should be taught separately. Presumably, most people would favor holistic instruction in driving, and there seems to be no reason why anyone would teach even a critical subskill *completely* outside the context of driving unless this was absolutely necessary. The analogy of this discussion of driving to reading should be apparent. Reading also involves many subskills. Some aspects of reading are exhibited by nearly all members of our society, but overall reading facility is nowhere near universal. Many favor a holistic approach to teaching reading, but, at the same time, there seem to be specific subskills on which performance is often nonoptimal.

The purpose of this article is to review some longitudinal data on the acquisition of reading skill. These data may bear on decisions that are made regarding one particular subskill, rapid word recognition. There is great controversy about whether to teach certain subskills of reading in isolation or as part of general reading practice. One reason for the controversy is that reading builds upon listening. In contrast with driving, where a novice must acquire a complex of mostly novel skills, reading involves the insertion of a new skill, visual word recognition, into a cluster of existing higher-level comprehension skills.[1] It seems quite reasonable that a nondriver would

---

[1] Of course, there are additional comprehension possibilities which first become feasible when information is being acquired visually rather than aurally.

need to learn *every* aspect of driving, but some believe that a nonreader needs only to learn to recognize words, after which he will, in some sense, be able to read.

In the sections that follow, we review first the alternate teaching approaches used in reading programs today and some elements of psychological theory that bear on these teaching approaches. Then, we discuss the longitudinal research approach we have employed. We believe it can provide useful information relative to several issues of theory and practice. This is followed by a presentation of the method and some outcomes of the study and their interpretation in terms of the issues raised earlier.

A. Teaching Positions

1. Code Approaches

Reading shares many skills with the listening capability that children develop at an earlier age. Everyone learns to listen (barring specific disabilities), but not everyone learns to read. This suggests that much of our effort to teach people to read should focus on the recognition of visually presented words. Words are composed of letters, and those letters occur only in a relatively small number of clusterings, which we might call syllables or spelling patterns. Those of an analytic bent might be moved to break up the task of learning to read according to the following rationale. We can consider reading as consisting of the skills that underlie listening plus word recognition skills. The listening skills are already appearing spontaneously by the time children begin to read, so effort should center on word recognition. The components of words are spelling patterns, so it makes sense to have children learn spelling patterns first and then learn words. Spelling patterns are composed of letters, so children ought to be able to recognize letters before they try to learn spelling patterns.

Such an approach eventually leads to instructional programs that start with subskill training and only later offer substantial experience with the coordinated act of actually reading text. In the context of the initial argument of this article, it might appear that such programs would not be very effective, since they apparently substitute specialized practice for experience with the integrated overall activity of reading. However, a number of meta-analyses of studies comparing reading program effectiveness have found that programs with a phonics component, that is, programs with specific instruction in symbol–sound correspondences, were somewhat more effective than programs which emphasized the integrated activity of reading exclusively (Chall, 1983; Resnick, 1979). Why might this be?

There are several possibilities. First, it may be that certain kinds of word recognition skills are not picked up in the normal course of "just plain reading," just as recovery from skids on icy roads is not picked up quickly in the course of "just plain driving." A second possibility is very similar: word recognition practice may be needed in greater amounts than is provided by just reading texts. That is, text reading may not provide very efficient practice for certain aspects of word recognition. Third, the achievement tests used in the studies that contributed to the meta-analyses were, for the most part, primary grades reading tests. These tests are aimed largely at word processing skills, so it is not surprising that they showed an advantage to teaching word processing skills directly.

Finally, it is possible that at the time most of the studies were done, we knew what to tell teachers about how to keep children engaged in reading-relevant word recognition practice, while perhaps we could give only vague guidelines to the teacher using more global teaching approaches. This last possibility deserves elaboration. An instructional system will be effective only if it keeps the learner engaged in an activity that can produce learning. The Chall study and other data have often been taken as indicating that *what* phonics or code-centered reading series teach is the best approximation to what children need to learn. It is also possible that such programs provide no closer an approximation to the optimal than global programs do, but that teachers generally do better at keeping children engaged with phonics materials.

2. Global Approaches

Of course, just as code-centered (phonics) approaches appeal to a theoretical viewpoint based upon a task analysis and decomposition of the reading act into component skills, holistic or global methods also appeal to some basic principles, which we have discussed above. Fischer, Burton, and Brown (1978) have perhaps made the strongest case. They point to the problem of learning to ski and note that skiing was formerly taught using a skill decomposition method. Each aspect of skiing was separately learned and practiced. Learning was slow. Then, skis started to be made in a graded series of lengths. Short skis allowed novices to engage in the integrated activity of skiing from the start, without significant risk. Learning became much more rapid. Similar experiences are reported by immersion-type language instruction approaches, such as the Israeli *ulpanim*. A few weeks of continually using a foreign language seem to be more productive than 2 years of classroom instruction that is distributed in small doses and involves subskill practice.

B. Research Issues

Past efforts to compare teaching approaches have too often involved efforts that resembled a horse race. One teacher would try to apply one teaching approach and a second would apply another. Whichever teacher got better results was declared the winner, and his/her aleatoric variation on a vague general principle was taken as evidence that the principle is valid. It is now clear that the choice of curricular approaches cannot be settled using horse-race comparisons. Whichever curriculum "wins" in a particular evaluation may have won for any number of reasons, including management effects, instructional effects, and completeness-of-coverage differences. A more productive approach would be to ask more limited and more controlled questions. In this article, we are concerned with the specific issue of the relationship of word recognition facility to overall comprehension success.[2] If we find, for example, that word recognition facility is an important precursor of achievement in comprehension-related aspects of reading, then there are a number of ways in which curricula might take account of this fact. If, on the other hand, we find that word recognition facility is simply a by-product of overall reading development, that it tracks comprehension achievement but does not precede it, then we will have dealt a strong blow to code-emphasis curricula—although there may still remain management advantages that must be studied separately.

Automaticity Theory

To motivate the specific results we report, we next discuss a particular theoretical viewpoint that is associated with the thinking of some designers of code-emphasis curricula. The longitudinal study we will report in this article was designed partly as a test of theoretical assertions by Perfetti and Lesgold (1977, 1979; Lesgold & Perfetti, 1978) regarding the role of word recognition efficiency in the overall process of comprehending a passage. If, during reading, part of the thinking capacity is given over to word recognition or word understanding, less capacity remains for joining concepts that need to become interrelated in the reader's mind. By automating word recognition and understanding through extensive practice, the mental capacity consumed by those simple processes can be decreased (cf. LaBerge & Samuels, 1974; Shiffrin & Schneider, 1977).

Stated this way, the automaticity argument seems obvious. However, there are two issues worth pointing out. First, there are only limited data to support the importance of word processing automaticity in reading. There are many studies showing that poor readers, at all ages, are slower than better readers at articulating individual words that they see in a visual display (Frederiksen, 1981; Jackson & McClelland, 1979; Perfetti & Lesgold, 1977). However, such correlational evidence must be regarded as relatively

[2]Of course, we also compared two different schools as well as two different curricula. Hence, we caution the reader to watch for qualitative differences in the data of the two groups that can speak to the validity of the conclusions we draw. Simple differences in overall achievement are no more meaningful when we show them than when others do.

weak. Poor readers may be poor because they do not practice very much; more practice might increase word recognition efficiency along with other aspects of reading skill. Second, there are few studies showing that everyday reading stresses the limits of one's processing capabilities, although in extreme cases, such as children who take perhaps 10 to 20 seconds to sound out a word, this seems likely. Put in a slightly different way, common sense and some weak correlational evidence suggest that getting more facile at word processing should be a necessary precursor of getting better at the higher level components of reading, but stronger evidence is needed.

II. THE NEED FOR LONGITUDINAL DATA

A longitudinal study can provide such evidence. By watching students develop their reading skills over time, we can ask the *causal* question: Is facility in word processing an important temporal precursor of improvements in overall reading skill? Of course, the temporal relationship is only one aspect of causal inference, but it is a step closer to where we would like to be. Existing data allow us to make causal inferences about word facility and overall reading achievement of the following very weak form: *the magnitude of A and B are strongly related.* A longitudinal study allows inferences of the form: *changes in A are followed closely in time by corresponding changes in B.* Of course, even in this more advanced form, it is possible that A and B are both precipitated by an outside cause (*C*), just as spring showers (*C*) produce both wet pavement (*A*) and, shortly thereafter, spring flowers (*B*). But, longitudinal research is a step in the right direction.

Problems in Longitudinal Studies

We set lofty goals for a longitudinal study of the development of reading skill when we started in 1976. We wanted to know how the process of learning unfolds, what some of the critical turning points in the process are, and what aspects of performance during the course of learning to read may be early signals that all is not going well and intervention is needed. We believed that two critical needs faced us in building a usable psychology of reading instruction: (1) to describe successive stages of competence and (2) to account for patterns of transition from one stage to another (cf. Glaser, 1976; Resnick, 1979). Although recent work on the psychology of reading had given us a much richer view of the details of skilled reading performance, we wanted to know more about the *processes of learning to read.*

A first requirement for understanding learning processes is a careful plotting of the actual trajectories of reading skill development in the primary grades. The information then available was based almost entirely on cross-sectional studies, in which children of different ages were compared on some set of reading-related tasks. As discussed above, cross-sectional research designs offer no way of studying individual courses of development, since each child is observed only a single time. In fact, changes in competence are never observed directly in cross-sectional research; instead, changes are inferred from observations made on children of different ages.

Another limitation of most past research on the development of reading skill was that there had been no effort to relate the course of skill development to differences in instruction. Quite typically, all subjects in a reading development experiment had been drawn from a single school or school system, and the instructional program the subjects used was not described in the research reports. We wanted, instead, to deliberately study two different curricula. While this still did not allow controlled observation of the effects of specific instructional components (which could be either differences in what is taught or the capabilities of different sets of students and teachers), it permitted us to discover aspects of learning which varied as a function of curriculum and other aspects which, at least for the range of curricula we examined, did not.

III. THE PRESENT STUDY

We set out to examine how word recognition automaticity develops, and how its development is related to the acquisition of comprehension skill. In particular, our longitudinal design allowed us to go beyond simple correlational analyses to consider the temporal relationships between word automaticity and text understanding skill. We included measures of word recognition speed and oral reading speed in our test battery, along with measures more closely related to comprehension, including the comprehension subtest from a standardized achievement test and tests of semantic judgment about word meanings and the meanings of sentences and paragraphs.

The overall study spanned a period of 5 years, with each cohort of children being followed for 4 years. The core data for each cohort were collected while the children were in first through third grade. Follow-up data were collected for another year in those cohorts where there were enough children remaining in the group to permit sensible interpretation of the data.

A. Children, Schools, and Curricula in the Study

Over this period, we have followed several cohorts of children in two different instructional programs. There was one large cohort in each program, plus smaller cohorts for pilot work and other special purposes. We began the study with over 300 children, to allow for inevitable attrition over the years of children whose families moved away. A total of approximately 80 children remained in the study through third grade.

The *Global-method* cohort children attended school in an urban suburb of 12,000 people, near a major city, with a large proportion of working-class families. Sixty percent were black and 40% were white. The cohort included about 50 children who stayed in the same school for all 3 years of primary reading, and who were still present for fourth-grade achievement testing. Achievement test results confirmed that this group was a representative sample of children for an urban setting. Their mean score on the reading portions of the Metropolitan Achievement Test, Primary Level, at the end of October of first grade corresponded to a grade equivalent of 1.1, a month behind the national average. By October of fourth grade their average scores on the Metropolitan Achievement Test (Total Reading) showed a grade equivalent of 4.3, slightly ahead of the national average.

The school based its primary reading curriculum on the Houghton Mifflin Basal reading program. Although the program was not formally individualized, there was substantial variation in the rate at which children progressed in the curriculum. There were several classrooms at each primary grade level, and there appears to have been some tracking by general ability level in assigning children to these classes. There were also several reading groups within each classroom to accommodate different rates of progress. Thus, most children were receiving instruction at a highly tailored rate.

The *Code-method* cohorts consisted of children in a similar social environment, with closely matching achievement, sex, and race demographics, who were taught using the New Reading System (NRS) developed at LRDC by Beck (Beck & Mitroff, 1972). This curriculum emphasizes word decoding skills along with comprehension skills. It was fully individualized. An important difference that we have noted between the curricula used in our two test sites is that there were explicit criteria in the NRS curriculum for movement from unit to unit. These were based almost completely on which words the children could read, not on their reading speed or any explicit assessment of comprehension. In contrast, children in the Global cohort moved as small groups, based upon teacher decisions about their overall reading performance. There were two Code cohorts. One contained 53 children, of whom about one-third remained after 3 years.[3] The second contained 56

[3]Both schools suffered unanticipated losses of students due to massive unemployment that developed in the area and to uncertainties about court-ordered desegregation plans. We have checked carefully for artifacts that these losses may have produced, and there appears to have been relatively uniform loss of students at all ability levels. Any potential artifacts are noted in the text.

children of whom 13 remained after 3 years. Since the two Code cohorts were in the same school, had the same teachers, and showed similar entering achievement profiles, they were combined for purposes of analysis and reporting. Table I summarizes the schedule for the study.

B. Measuring Development by Mastery

Most developmental studies chart growth as a function of age. In this study, however, the index of development is progress in the reading curriculum, not time. Our thinking was that by examining the performance of students with different levels of ability at points of apparently equal accomplishment, we would be more likely to detect individual differences that are not remediated by simply adjusting the rate of instruction. To this end we established a series of mastery landmarks in each reading curriculum, and each child was tested when he or she reached each landmark. For this purpose the curriculum was divided into segments or levels, each having one or two reading books with accompanying workbooks and related material. Each time a child reached a landmark point in the reading curriculum, he or she was given a battery of tests that assessed word recognition efficiency along with aspects of comprehension efficiency. This strategy allowed us to compare processing capabilities of children who had reached nominally equivalent levels in the curriculum at very different rates.

C. Types of Measures Used

To trace the development of word automation, we used a variety of measures that have proven useful in laboratory studies of the automation phenomenon. These included reaction times for oral reading of individual words and for judgments of word meanings. A further set of measures, used only at the more advanced test points, tested comprehension of sentences and

TABLE I
Schedule of Longitudinal Study

| Year | Cohert and Curriculum | | |
	Code Group B	Code Group C	Global Group D
1977–78	Grade 1	—	—
1978–79	Grade 2	Grade 1	Grade 1
1979–80	Grade 3	Grade 2	Grade 2
1980–81	Follow-up	Grade 3	Grade 3
1981–82	—	Follow-up	Follow-up

passages. To observe how children handled the multiple complexities of meaningful texts as their reading skill developed, samples of oral reading were collected and errors were coded for sensitivity to context and fidelity to the phonemic code. Finally, we included in our database subtest scores from the schools' regular achievement tests, which were administered to all children once a year.

1. Word Vocalization

The most straightforward efficiency measure was word vocalization speed. In this task a word is projected onto a small screen and the child must pronounce the word as quickly as possible. The first appearance of the slide on the screen triggers an electronic clock that runs until the child's voice triggers a voice-operated relay. Responses are recorded on tape. Accuracy scores and mean speed of correct responses were computed for each subject. This measure of word retrieval efficiency was included as an indicator of reading automaticity, on the assumption that as the child becomes able to recognize a word automatically, he or she also retrieves the phonological code more quickly.

2. Semantic Judgments

Children's speed and accuracy in making decisions about the meaning of words were examined in a category matching task. In this task the experimenter said the name of a category (e.g., *animal*), after which a word flashed on the screen. If the word was an instance of the category (e.g., *horse*), the child was to push the *yes* button. If it was not an instance of the category (e.g., *house*), the *no* button was to be pushed. This task was included as a measure of the automaticity of access to word meaning. Many researchers hold that words can be "recognized" in the sense of conveying a concept, even if they are not decoded completely (cf. Perfetti & Lesgold, 1979). That is, one can know what a word means in certain cases before one even knows what word has been seen. While this view is not universal, it seemed appropriate to have a measure of automaticity in processing the meaning of a word.

3. Control Tasks

As a control against the possibility that simple speed of performance might be correlated with reading achievement, simple response time and visual matching tasks were also used.

4. Oral Reading Rate and Error Analyses

The children also read short passages aloud at each test point. We recorded details of each error the child made, as well as the overall time it took to read each passage. The reading speed measures provide an overall index of passage reading efficiency, while the errors can tell us something about the nature of the reading process and especially the interaction of components of that process.

There were two types of passages written for each test level. Familiar passages contained sentences closely adapted from the children's readers and other curricular materials. Transfer passages were less tied to the sentence and phrase structures of the reading materials, and also contained many words (36% of the total) that were used only infrequently (less than 10 times in the reader just finished and less than 3 times in earlier readers). At each test point, the child read aloud one or more familiar passages and one or more transfer passages. Reading errors were analyzed qualitatively, following the procedure of Hood (1975–6) with slight refinements. Reading times were recorded and later converted to speed in words per minute.

5. Standardized Test Data

In the Global-method school, the Metropolitan Achievement Test was administered each year in October. In the Code method school, the Stanford Achievement Test was administered each year in April. We collected these annual standardized test data on all children. In addition, we were, with parents' permission, given any intelligence or readiness test scores the schools had for these children.

D. Results

1. Progress through the Curriculum

A major strategy for data analysis has been to divide each sample of children into three groups (high, medium, and low reading skill) on the basis of second and third grade reading comprehension scores. We can then "look backward" using the longitudinal data to show us the reading development patterns of successful and unsuccessful learners.

The high-skill group contained those children who scored at least one standard deviation above the sample mean on 1 year's test and above the mean on the other, or at least one-half standard deviation above the mean on both. The low-skill group included children who scored at least one standard deviation below the mean on one test and below the mean on the other, or at least one-half standard deviation below the mean on both. About 20–25% of the children were in each extreme group; the remaining children were placed in the medium-skill group.

There was considerable variability in the rate at which children progressed through the curricula. This can be seen in Table II, which shows the earliest and latest grade level at which Levels 3, 5, and 7 of the curricula were completed by the children in each ability subgroup. For the Code

TABLE II
Progress through the Curricula

| Group | Range of completion grade levels for | | | | | |
| | Level 3 | | Level 5 | | Level 7 | |
	Earliest	Latest	Earliest	Latest	Earliest	Latest
Global	1.4	2.2	1.9	2.9	2.8	4.0
Low[a]	1.5	2.2	1.9	2.9	2.9	4.0
Medium	1.4	2.2	1.9	2.9	2.8	4.0
High	1.4	1.8	1.9	2.4	2.8	3.0
Code	1.9	3.0	2.1	4.0	2.6	—
Low	2.3	3.0	3.5	4.0	4.0	—
Medium	1.9	3.0	2.4	4.0	2.9	4.0
High	1.9	2.2	2.1	2.9	2.6	3.6

[a]Because different criteria were used, cross cohort comparisons are inappropriate for magnitudes but reasonable for ranges.

group, the fastest high-ability children completed Level Seven 1.4 years ahead of the slowest low-ability children. Some low-ability children did not finish Level 7 even by the end of third grade. In the Global cohort, children advanced through levels with their reading groups, and reading placement was not perfectly correlated with our ability classification. This means that the patterns are less apparent in the table. Nevertheless, the spread between first and last completion of a given level ranged from .8 grade levels at Level 3 (1.4 for the earliest high-ability child to 2.2 for the latest low-ability child) to 1.2 grade levels at Level 7. The low groups progressed much more slowly than did the medium or high groups. However, about 15% of the children in either cohort who were classified as low skill on the basis of their test scores progressed through most of the curriculum at an average or above average rate. One low-skill child moved through the curriculum faster than the average high-skill child! Apparently, some children were able to satisfy their teacher that they were adequately learning the material in their regular lessons; otherwise, they would have been transferred to a slower paced group. Nonetheless, they did poorly on standardized tests later on.

2. Vocalization Latency

Results of the word vocalization task are shown in Figs. 1 and 2. Figure 1 shows mean response speeds for correct responses, while Fig. 2 shows mean accuracy levels. Consider the Global group (heavy lines) first. The low and medium Global groups started out taking half a second longer to say a word after it appeared on the screen than did the high group. Some

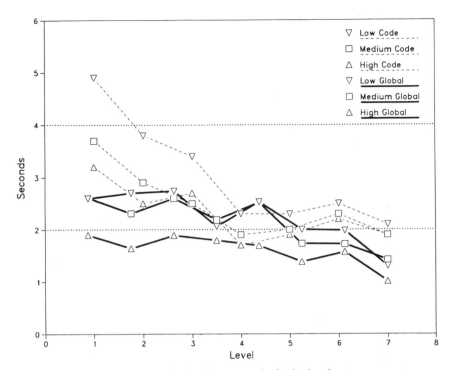

Fig. 1. Vocalization latency results for both cohorts.

difference in speed was maintained over all levels—although all skill groups speeded up by about .8 second by the final test point. There were also accuracy differences in the three groups throughout the study. The low-skill children averaged 40–60% correct, the medium-skill children about 70%, and the high-skill children 80–90%. In the Code cohort, the pattern was similar. An even greater initial speed difference was noted for the Code cohort. The Code children generally were slower at earlier test points than the Global children but showed a more pronounced speeding up as they progressed through the curriculum. In general, the Code students ended up somewhat slower than the Global students and were less accurate.

3. Semantic Judgment Latency

Latencies for the semantic (category) judgment task are presented in Fig. 3. In both cohorts, the low and medium groups took significantly longer than the high group at all test levels, but were not significantly different from each other. Note that all ability levels also showed an improvement in speed over time. Judgment speed dropped from a mean of 4.0 seconds

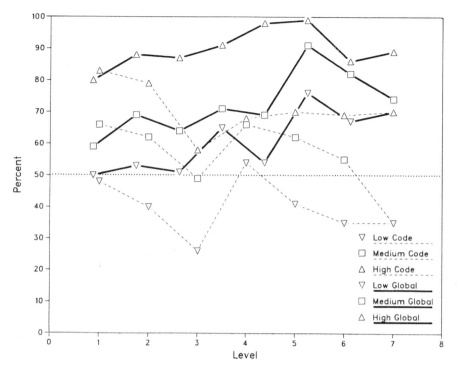

Fig. 2. Vocalization accuracy results for both cohorts.

to a mean of 2.1 seconds from Levels 1 to 7 for the Code cohort, and from 3.0 seconds to 2.0 seconds from Levels 1 to 8 for the Global cohort. The apparent increase in speed for the low-ability Code children at the last test point may be an artifact of sampling: only the fastest low-ability children finished in time to be tested before the end of third grade.

Accuracy of semantic judgments confirms the ability differences. The high ability subjects were more accurate than lower ability subjects. In the Global cohort, there was some rise over time in accuracy. Thus, on the average, these children were becoming both faster and more accurate. In the Code group, by contrast, there appears to have been a speed–accuracy tradeoff. As speed improved over time, accuracy dropped leaving these children at a lower accuracy level than their Global cohort peers at the end of 3 years.

4. Control Tasks

There were no ability-related effects and no significant changes over levels or between cohorts on either the visual matching or the simple reaction time tasks. This means that differences in speed of word vocalization and

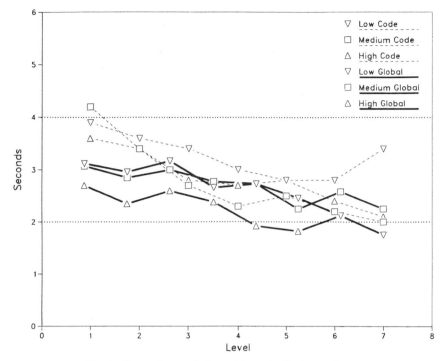

Fig. 3. Categorization judgment latencies for both cohorts.

semantic judgment cannot be attributed to a more general difference in reaction times among subjects.

5. Oral Reading Speed

Reading speed data are shown in Figs. 5 and 6. In both cohorts, there were substantial differences between the three ability levels in oral reading rates across the entire period of the study. At the first test point, early in first grade, the high-skill group was reading familiar passages at a rate of about 40 more words per minute than the low group. Although all subgroups gained in speed over levels, a substantial difference was maintained even at the end of third grade. A similar pattern of difference was obtained for the transfer passages, although all groups read them somewhat more slowly. These differences are particularly striking because the children in the lower groups took longer to reach each test point than children in the high-ability groups. They thus had more weeks or even months in which to practice at each reading level. Nevertheless they read more slowly at each level. The low groups remained at less than 30 words per minute on transfer passages through Levels 1 to 4 and increased slowly thereafter. This means that for

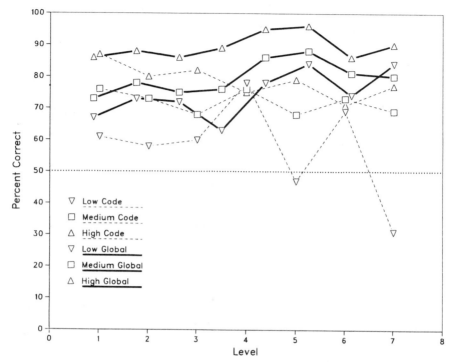

Fig. 4. Categorization judgment accuracy for both cohorts.

about the first 2 years of instruction these children were reading at a rate so slow that comprehension was all but precluded.

Both cohorts ended third grade with mean oral reading speeds between 110 and 120 words per minute on the familiar passages. However, there were substantial differences between cohorts in the early part of the primary curriculum. The Code group began at a mean of 26 words per minute and climbed steadily throughout the three grades. The Global group started at between 65 and 70 words per minute and stayed at that level until late second and early third grade, when they showed a sharp speed-up. It is possible that teachers in the Global classrooms we studied had higher speed/ efficiency criteria for progress through the curriculum than did the Code teachers. It is also possible that the overt decoding procedures (such as blending) that *Code* instruction mandates may slow down overall reading speed in the first months of learning to read.

On the transfer passages, shown in Fig. 6, the patterns were slightly different. The Global cohort showed initial performance that was similar to that of the Code group, but ended up slightly lower. Such a pattern might be expected because the initial NRS curriculum provides direct instruction in approaches that will permit decoding of the words in the transfer pas-

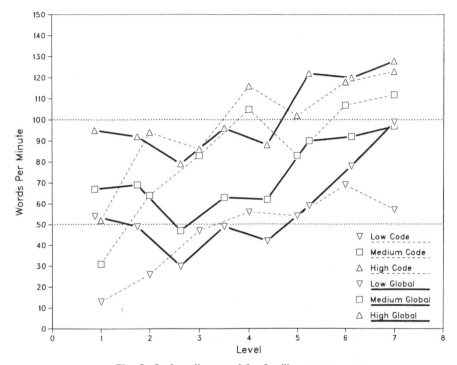

Fig. 5. Oral reading speed for familiar passages.

sages, whereas transfer in nonphonics curricula results from the accumulation (presumably rather slowly) of a broad range of specific word experiences rather than from direct acquisition of decoding rules.

6. Oral Reading Errors

There were clear ability group differences in oral reading error rates, as can be seen in Figs. 7 and 8. There were also cohort differences. In the first grade, the error rates on familiar passages in the Code cohort were higher than in the Global cohort; the mean at the first test point was almost 20%, versus 6% for the Global group. However, by second grade both cohorts were showing mean error rates on familiar passages of around 5%. Even the low-ability groups had fewer than 10% errors in the later part of the curriculum. In the Code cohort the low-ability children took longer to improve their error rates on transfer than on familiar passages. Otherwise, the pattern for transfer passages in both cohorts is similar to that for familiar, except that there is a somewhat higher error rate throughout for transfer passages.

Some interesting differences in types of errors were also noted. Qualitative error analysis data are summarized in Tables III and IV. Since no

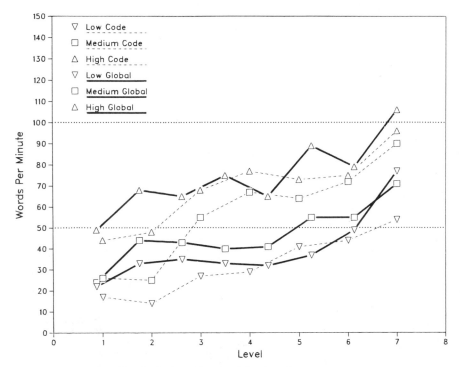

Fig. 6. Oral reading speed for transfer passages.

significant change in patterns across levels was detectable, the oral reading error data were averaged over levels for ease of interpretation. The data show ability by error type interactions. The low-skill children appeared to be intentionally passing over words that they could not recognize or decode (*intentional skip* errors), while the high-skill children seemed to be accidentally missing a few words (*accidental omit* errors). Also, the better readers tended occasionally to insert words as they read, a feature largely absent in the reading of the low-skill children. Finally, high-ability children were more likely than low-ability children to read a word correctly but with the wrong ending. All told, the only striking cohort difference is that Code Cohort children had somewhat more nonsense errors than the Global children.

E. Structural Modeling Analyses

The general pattern of the results discussed above suggests that individual word processing skill is an important component of high levels of reading achievement in the primary grades. This is in accord with previous findings

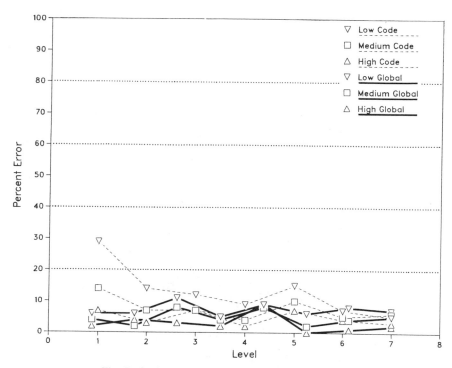

Fig. 7. Oral reading error rates for familiar passages.

TABLE III

Qualitative Analysis of Oral Reading Errors, by Skill Levels: *Code* Cohort

Error type	High skill	Medium skill	Low skill
Child stop reading for 5 seconds or more	7.6	6.8	5.6
Child *accidentally omits* a word	6.4	3.9	4.0
Child *intentionally skips* a word	2.6	5.3	9.9
Extra word inserted	4.1	2.9	1.9
Word order switched	.2	.4	.2
Letter reversals within word (*was* for *saw*)	.7	.5	1.0
Correct word with wrong ending	12.3	10.4	9.3
Wrong word with correct ending	5.1	5.4	4.3
Other word substitutions	49.9	54.9	51.1
Nonsense (nonword)	11.0	9.5	12.7

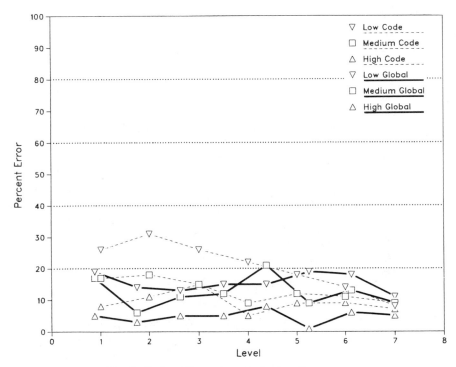

Fig. 8. Oral reading error rates for transfer passages.

TABLE IV

Qualitative Analysis of Oral Reading Errors, by Skill Levels: *Global* Cohort

Error type	High skill	Medium skill	Low skill
Child stop reading for 5 seconds or more	5.8	6.2	5.7
Child *accidentally omits* a word	13.0	5.4	5.8
Child *intentionally skips* a word	2.2	9.0	15.0
Extra word inserted	5.0	2.5	1.5
Word order switched	.1	.3	.0
Letter reversals within word (*was* for *saw*)	1.5	.6	1.0
Correct word with wrong ending	12.8	12.2	8.0
Wrong word with correct ending	6.4	5.8	5.6
Other word substitutions	46.5	49.6	51.2
Nonsense (nonword)	6.7	8.4	6.3

on the relations between word processing automaticity and reading skill reported in the literature. Our interest, however, was in closing the gap between correlational data and the causal hypotheses we would like to confirm. We knew from prior research, as well as from the data in the present study, that children with reading comprehension difficulties lack individual word skills, especially automaticity. But given only the correlations of any two measures taken at about the same time, it is unwise to draw causal conclusions. For example, we cannot decide from such data whether the word recognition facility is necessary for comprehension to succeed or whether it is the result of exercising a higher level of comprehension skill (i.e., perhaps good readers read more and thus become faster word processors).

Longitudinal data with multiple measurements on the same subjects at separate times can permit stronger tests of the hypothesis that word processing facility is an important precursor of reading facility. In examining data this way, one looks for associations between a variable measured early in the time sequence and one measured later. Since early occurring events can cause later ones, but later events cannot cause earlier ones, the causal relations between word skill and comprehension can be inferred by comparing the extent to which early word skill automaticity predicts later comprehension with the extent to which comprehension predicts later automaticity. If one of the associations is reliably greater than the other, a primary direction of causality can be inferred.[4] This is the basic logic underlying a number of longitudinal analysis methods, including cross-lag panel analysis (Campbell, 1963; Kenny, 1975) and structural equation modeling (Joreskog & Sorbom, 1978).

We originally analyzed our data using structural equations modeling procedures (Joreskog & Sorbom, 1978). For example, Lesgold and Resnick (1982) specified a model in which constructs representing word processing speed at different points in the curriculum were estimated from measures of word recognition speed and oral reading speed. For the Global cohort (the only one on which enough data were available at the time), the best fitting models of the correlations among these word processing speed measures and reading comprehension scores showed larger predictive paths from *early word processing to subsequent comprehension* than vice versa. For example, the average weighting for paths from speed to subsequent comprehension was as great as the average path from 1 year's comprehension

---

[4]If relationships in both directions are significant (or not significantly different), however, causal inferences cannot easily be made. Further, while longitudinal data can test specific causal models, only an intervention study in which the presumed causal skill is trained and the predicted effect produced can firmly validate the causal prediction.

to the next year's, while the average path from comprehension to subsequent speed measures was only one-tenth as large. Lesgold and Resnick concluded that during the first 2 years of schooling, word processing speed is an essential precursor of comprehension success.

To the extent that these results hold up over the full 3-year time period, they may be taken as implying a causal relationship between efficiency of word processing and overall comprehension competence. The present report provides a first look at the data from the entire 3-year period, for both cohorts. Basically, the data support the viewpoints taken in our earlier paper, in that word processing measures predict later reading comprehension performance better than vice versa. After considerable reflection, however, we have switched to a different method of path analysis than that used earlier. Before discussing the specifics of our findings, we will explain the reasons for this new approach.

1. Uniqueness of Predicted Variance

The structural equations approach is one in which a best overall fit of path parameters is estimated. Reliable and accurate path analyses can emerge from this modeling method only when the structure variables are relatively nonoverlapping in their sources. If two structure variables overlap in the capabilities they measure, then there will be some instability in the path weightings generated. Whichever of the two has the most unique predictive power will likely have heavy path weights to the criterion variable, even if the common predictive ability of the two is very high. Because our measures of word processing accuracy and word processing facility were known to overlap highly, we feared that the predictive capability they shared would automatically accrue to whichever of them had a slight edge in unique predictive power. In fact, this happened when we performed structural equations analyses of the final data. There was the appearance of strong differences between curricula in the relative importance of word processing *accuracy* and word processing *speed* to ultimate reading achievement.

To avoid misinterpretation of this result, we have searched for approaches that would allow us to make very clear the extent to which apparent path differences were due to shared common variance being allocated to whichever predictor had the edge in unique predictability. The approach we developed is one that is also suggested by some statisticians (e.g., Marascuilo & Levin, 1983). Specifically, we establish path weights using multiple regression techniques, and then we perform commonality analyses (Kerlinger & Pedhazur, 1973) whenever the extent to which variables share predictive power is an issue. With this approach in mind, let us turn to the analyses of our data.

2. Path Analysis Results

The basic path analysis results are shown in Figs. 9 and 10. In these analyses, we created several derived variables to use as predictors. These measures were created by converting raw measures to z-scores and then averaging over multiple measures and multiple testing periods. The *Speed* measures represent an averaging of four measures: word vocalization response speed, category judgment response speed, oral reading speed for familiar passages, and oral reading speed for transfer passages. The *Accuracy* measures represent an averaging of word vocalization and category judgment accuracies. Data were also collapsed over adjacent test points.

The *Early* measures come from Levels 1 and 2 of the Code Cohort and Levels 1 through 3 of the Global Cohort, both spanning most of the first grade. Similarly, the *Middle* measures were averaged over two levels subsuming approximately the second grade, and the *Late* measures were averaged over the last three Levels, subsuming third grade for an average student. The reading comprehension subtests of the standardized achievement tests given by the schools were also used in these analyses. Appropriate achievement test data were available only beginning in second grade for the Code cohorts, and the number of students surviving until the fourth grade test for that group was too low to include fourth-grade data (about 15 children). Finally, the vertical dimension of the figures approximately represents the passage of time over the 3 years of primary instruction.

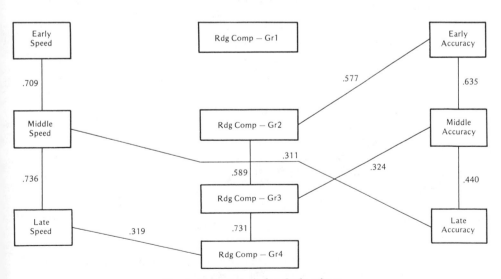

Fig. 9. Path analysis for *Code* cohort.

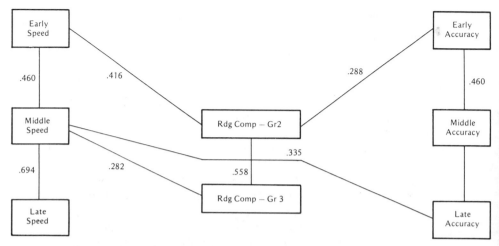

Fig. 10. Path analysis for *Global* cohort.

The results confirm our expectations that *Speed* and *Accuracy* measures would be better predictors of later reading comprehension performance than vice versa. Also, there is an interesting effect in both cohorts, with *Middle Speed* predicting *Late Accuracy* rather strongly. This may be due to the fact that the shorter words learned earlier in the curriculum contain spelling units that must be handled with facility in order to accurately process longer words that appear later. Finally, there is the appearance that progress in the Code cohorts is driven primarily by progress in word processing speed, while progress in the Global cohort seems more to be related to word processing accuracy. This apparent difference is what drove us to use commonality analyses on our data, so we turn to those analyses next.

Figures 11 and 12 show the results of commonality analyses of the regression of second-, third-, and fourth-grade reading comprehension on the Speed, Accuracy, and standardized reading comprehension test measures from the year before the predicted performance.[5] The numbers in the Venn diagram circles represent proportions of the variance of reading comprehension accounted for by each of the predictor variables uniquely and in combination with others.

A first result to note is that for the Global cohort most of the predictive power is shared. This is less marked for the Code cohort. Another differ-

[5]First-grade reading comprehension tests were not given at the same time to all Code-Group students, so we could not sensibly use first-grade reading comprehension test scores as a predictor for that cohort. We also did not retain enough fourth-grade code children to enable any regression analyses for fourth-grade Code group reading comprehension ability.

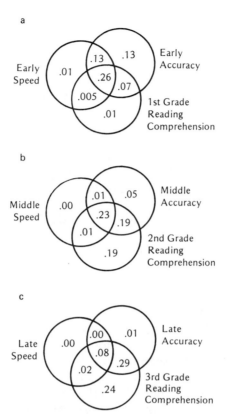

Fig. 11. Commonality analysis of Global group predictors of reading comprehension in (a) second grade, (b) third grade, and (c) fourth grade.

ence between cohorts is in the small amount of unique predictability that comes from *Speed* versus *Accuracy*. The Global cohort shows some predictive power for accuracy and none for speed, while the pattern is reversed for the Code cohort. A third important result is that the contribution of 1 year's reading comprehension to predicting the next year's increases over time, while the contribution of word-processing measures declines. This replicates an earlier study by Curtis (1980). We will say more about the decreasing importance of individual word processing measures in predicting achievement in later grades later in this article.

We also performed commonality analyses using effective reading speed as the criterion variable. Effective reading speed was computed by averaging the z-scores for oral reading speed and oral reading accuracy. The predictor measures were word vocalization efficiency (the average of the

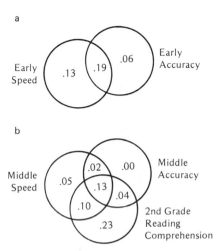

Fig. 12. Commonality analysis of Code group predictors of reading comprehension in (a) second grade and (b) third grade.

vocalization speed and accuracy z-scores) and semantic processing efficiency (the average of the category judgment latency and accuracy z-scores). Figure 13 shows the results for the Global group, while Fig. 14 shows the same results for the Code group. At both second and third grade, the prediction of effective reading speed derives from variance shared by all predictors in the case of the Global cohort while there is unique predictive variance in the Code Cohort. Another difference between the groups is in the contribution of semantic access efficiency versus word vocalization efficiency. Vocalization efficiency carries more weight in the Global cohort predictions while semantic access efficiency carries more for the Code group.

F. Summary and Implications

The longitudinal data we have gathered show a clear relationship between word recognition efficiency early in learning and reading comprehension performance later on. This is consistent with the view that efficient word recognition skill that does not require substantial allocation of limited cognitive resources is important to the overall development of reading skill. The asymmetry of the relationship—the fact that early comprehension skill is not associated with later word recognition efficiency—strongly suggests that word-level skills facilitate the acquisition of comprehension skills. While certain alternative possibilities, such as another unidentified factor that first causes word recognition and later comprehension skill, are not strictly ruled out, our findings do require that we reject the idea that word recognition

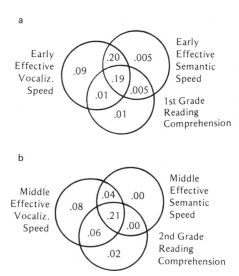

Fig. 13. Commonality analyses for predictions of Global Group effective reading speed in (a) second grade and (b) third grade.

facility develops as a direct *result* of comprehension skill. It seems, then, that developing word recognition efficiency ought to be an important goal of early reading instruction.

Our data suggest that the goal of word processing efficiency was not being

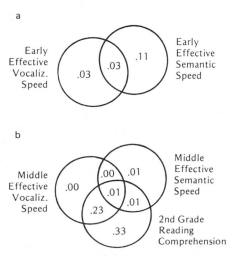

Fig. 14. Commonality analyses for predictions of Code Group effective reading speed in (a) second grade and (b) third grade.

fully achieved in either of the classrooms we studied. It is clear that a certain proportion of students (perhaps 15%) in each cohort was allowed to pass from unit to unit of the reading program without developing word processing facility. This was perhaps to be expected in the Global method classrooms, which did not have formal criteria for passing from one unit to the next. However, it is, on first consideration, surprising for the individualized Code method classrooms. There, to pass from one level to the next each child had to pass a test demonstrating ability to read words that used the spelling patterns that had been taught. How could it be that so many children who could read words accurately enough to pass these successive tests had, at the end of third grade, word recognition skills as weak as those we have documented for the low-ability group? The answer seems to lie in exactly what was tested, and therefore emphasized, in instruction. In the code program studied, children were taught a phoneme-by-phoneme decoding and blending algorithm and were encouraged to use it whenever they did not immediately recognize a word. In the tests, and in teaching, children were given as long as they needed to pronounce individual words, using the algorithm as necessary. The emphasis, in other words, was on accurate but not on automatic word recognition. Under these conditions, some children were able to pass from level to level despite very slow word recognition.[6]

The Code method's strong focus on the accuracy component of word recognition may also account for the different patterns that the two cohorts displayed in the structural equation and commonality analyses. In both cohorts, word facility developed ahead of and was related (perhaps causally) to later comprehension skill. However, in the Code cohort *speed* of word recognition carried the (slightly) greater weight in these relationships, whereas in the Global cohort *accuracy* of recognition carried the greater weight. A consideration of the teaching methods and what they imply for acquisition suggests why this difference should occur. In the Code method classrooms, some of the individual components of reading skill were separated out and given extra attention and practice. Of the many components of word recognition skill, the one that instruction emphasized was recognition accuracy. Under these conditions, accuracy could be expected to develop ahead of other components, and perhaps not be fully integrated into the child's general reading competence, at least for weaker readers. Under these conditions, accuracy of word recognition cannot be expected to index how well early reading skill was developing and would not forecast later

[6]In fact, the accuracy criterion was not all that high, either. Had a higher accuracy criterion been used, the practice needed to produce high accuracy would have forced automation of word recognition, but at the expense of less time spent on the higher level components of reading.

comprehension ability. Speed of word recognition, which was not explicitly stressed in instruction, can and does do this job.

In the Global method classrooms, by contrast, instruction was organized around the reading of successive stories. In this context, children discussed and briefly practiced various specific elements of reading: word meanings, sentence meanings, grapheme–phoneme correspondences, related "world knowledge," and the like. None of these components took precedence over any other; instead all were expected to develop simultaneously, more or less as a "package." Under these conditions, accuracy can be expected to serve as a good index of how reading skill is developing. One reason for this is that accuracy of word recognition is very easy for teachers to assess, even without formal tests. It is therefore likely to play an important role in which reading groups children are assigned to. These assignments in turn determine how much and what kind of reading exposure children are likely to have. A higher reading group means reading more different stories and thus more practice on all components of reading. Accuracy was also more reliably measured than speed in our study, since there is substantial variability in reaction time data, especially for young children. This, too, would favor the emergence of accuracy as an indicator of how general reading skill was developing.

The commonality analysis results for the two cohorts support the interpretation that development was occurring globally in one cohort and componentially in the other. For example, in the predictions of second grade reading comprehension scores for the Global cohort, the biggest source of predictive variance was common to earlier word recognition speed, accuracy, and overall reading comprehension. For the Code cohort, more of the predictive variance was unique to the individual variables or common only to pairs of the three variables. There was a similar pattern for predicting third grade reading speed. This is even more marked in predicting effective reading speed (Figs. 13 and 14). Predicting the Global cohort's third-grade effective reading speed, for example, the bulk of the explained variance was again shared (.21), while there was essentially no triply shared variance for the Code cohort (.01). A final supporting fact is that in the Global cohort, speed and accuracy of semantic category judgments improved together over time (Figs. 3 and 4), while in the Code cohort accuracy dropped as speed increased.

We also found that the two different teaching approaches resulted in substantial qualitative differences in trajectories for acquisition of some aspects of word recognition facility. The most striking difference is that in all speed measures, the Code children began more slowly, and then showed sharp increases in speed; while the Global children began faster and showed a very gradual increase over the 3 years of the study (see Figs. 1, 3, and 5).

This difference in shape of the trajectory is not surprising: the Code children were deliberately slowing down during the early units of instruction in order to use the blending algorithm. By the end of third grade, the oral reading differences had disappeared. Indeed, there is some indication that middle-ability children in the Code group may even have surpassed their Global-group peers in third grade, having started out behind them. On the isolated-word tasks, the Global group showed a small persisting advantage, ending a half second faster in word vocalization and slightly faster in the category judgment task.

It is not yet entirely clear how these cohort differences ought to be interpreted. We have collected some further data on those children in our samples who remained in the same schools into fourth and fifth grades. These data will allow us to relate the early patterns described here to overall reading competence, particularly in comprehension, later in elementary school. Analysis of these data will perhaps give a clearer sense of the meaning of the different developmental patterns that we have observed in the present study. For the moment, we can only say that there is evidence that there are indeed multiple pathways to the goal of reading fluency and that instructional programs can influence which of these pathways a child takes.

While our present findings do not give us a basis for choosing between Global and Code approaches to teaching beginning reading, they do suggest that neither approach—at least as practiced in the classrooms we studied— was providing the strongest possible support for developing word recognition efficiency. It is clear that children in the low-ability groups of both cohorts were about to leave the primary grades with reading skills inadequate to the demands likely to be placed on them in subsequent schooling. Reading speeds of 50 to 70 words per minute—the average speed on transfer passages for the low-ability groups—are so slow as to interfere with comprehension even of easy material, and are certainly unlikely to leave much memory capacity free for *developing* new comprehension abilities.

Some of this problem could probably be resolved by better management of reading instruction, in particular resisting the temptation to pass children on to higher levels in the curriculum when fundamental abilities were still poorly established. However, to hold children back in order to do more of the same kind of teaching is unlikely to produce dramatic successes. Instead, ways need to be found to build word recognition efficiency more effectively. Certainly, radical alterations of curriculum should not be proposed in the absence of direct tests of the proposed changes. However, the data in hand now suggest that combing the curriculum for opportunities to increase efficient word recognition and the ability to deal quickly with word meaning will be a worthwhile enterprise, especially if it is combined with extensive practice in reading real texts for meaning.

ACKNOWLEDGMENTS

The research we report was funded by the Learning Research and Development Center, University of Pittsburgh, through an institutional grant from the National Institute of Education. The ideas and positions in the article are wholly the authors', and no endorsement by NIE or any other government agency of the contents of this article is implied. Deborah Wijnberg, Hope Cordonier, and Carol Sharp were the primary research assistants for this project, and Mary E. Curtis participated substantially in the design of the study and the first years of implementation.

REFERENCES

Beck, I. L., & Mitroff, D. C. *The rationale and design of a primary grades reading system for an individualized classroom.* Pittsburgh, PA: University of Pittsburgh, Learning Research and Development Center, 1972/4.

Campbell, D. T. From description to experimentation: Interpreting trends as quasi experiments. In C. W. Harris (Ed.), *Problems in measuring change.* Madison: Univ. of Wisconsin Press, 1963.

Chall, J. S. *Learning to read: The great debate.* New York: McGraw-Hill, 1983.

Curtis, M. E. Development of components of reading skill. *Journal of Educational Psychology,* 1980, **72,** 656–699.

Fischer, G., Burton, R. R., & Brown, J. S. Aspects of a theory of simplification, debugging, and coaching. *Proceedings of the second national conference of the Canadian Society for Computational Studies of Intelligence.* Toronto: Univ. of Toronto Press, 1978.

Frederiksen, J. R. Sources of process interactions in reading. In A. M. Lesgold & C. A. Perfetti (Eds.), *Interactive processes in reading.* Hillsdale, New Jersey: Erlbaum, 1981.

Glaser, R. Components of a psychology of instruction. *Review of Educational Research,* 1976, **46,** 1–23.

Hood, J. Qualitative analysis of oral reading errors: The inter-judge reliability of scores. *Reading Research Quarterly,* 1975–76, **11,** 577–598.

Jackson, M. D., & McClelland, J. J. Processing determinants of reading speed. *Journal of Experimental Psychology: General,* 1979, **108**(2), 151–181.

Joreskog, K. G., & Sorbom, D. *LISREL: Analysis of linear structural relationships by the method of maximum likelihood* (User's guide, Version IV, Release 2). Chicago: International Education Services, 1978.

Kenny, D. A. Cross-lag panel correlation: A test for spuriousness. *Psychological Bulletin,* 1975, **82,** 887–903.

Kerlinger, F. N., & Pedhazur, E. J. *Multiple regression in behavioral research.* New York: Holt, 1973.

LaBerge, D., & Samuels, S. J. Toward a theory of automatic information processing in reading. *Cognitive Psychology,* 1974, **6,** 293–323.

Lesgold, A. M., & Perfetti, C. A. Interactive processes in reading comprehension. *Discourse Processes,* 1978, **1,** 323–336.

Lesgold, A. M., & Resnick, L. B. How reading disabilities develop: Perspectives from a longitudinal study. In J. P. Das, R. Mulcahy, & A. E. Wall (Eds.), *Theory and research in learning disability,* New York: Plenum, 1982.

Marascuilo, L. A., & Levin, J. R. *Multivariate statistics in the social sciences: A researcher's guide.* Monterey, California: Brooks/Cole, 1983.

Perfetti, C. A., & Lesgold, A. M. Discourse processing and sources of individual differences. In P. Carpenter & M. Just (Eds.), *Cognitive processes in comprehension.* Hillsdale, New Jersey: Erlbaum, 1977.

Perfetti, C. A., & Lesgold, A. M. Coding and comprehension in skilled reading. In L. B. Resnick & P. Weaver (Eds.), *Theory and practice of early reading.* Hillsdale, New Jersey: Erlbaum, 1979.

Resnick, L. B. Theory and practice in beginning reading instruction. In L. B. Resnick & P. A. Weaver (Eds.), *Theory and practice of early reading* (Vol. 3). Hillsdale, New Jersey: Erlbaum, 1979.

Resnick, D. P., & Resnick, L. B. The nature of literacy: An historical exploration. *Harvard Educational Review,* 1977, **47**(3), 370-385.

Shiffrin, R. M., & Schneider, W. Controlled and automatic human information processing (Vol. 2). Perceptual learning, automatic attending, and a general theory. *Psychological Review,* 1977, **84**, 127-190.

INFORMATION PROCESSING IN SKILLED READERS

GEOFFREY UNDERWOOD

Department of Psychology
University of Nottingham
Nottingham, England

I. THE NATURE OF THE TASK

Reading can be described as a transformational task for a number of reasons. Whereas it is certainly a powerful educational tool which can be used to transform minds, the transformations to be discussed here are more immediate and are necessary for the educational process to be possible. When we make sense of written language, we can be said to have transformed the marks on the page into meanings. As the written symbols change our thoughts they can be said to be acting to transform our state of mind, by the process of being themselves transformed. It is this process of understanding which is the subject of the present article, and of particular concern will be the subprocesses used by the skilled reader in the attempt to convert script into recognizable patterns and so into ideas.

The model of reading to be presented here rests upon certain assumptions concerning human information processing. Models which view humans as information processors take account of the mental operations necessary for recognition and for the derivation of new meaning, and so specify reading as a recoding process. In very general terms, the analogy describes humans as adaptive biological machines seeking to make appropriate responses to their environments by first understanding and creating representations. The processes of understanding, and the structures maintaining the representations, will vary according to the information in the environment, but the principles of information processing will be the same for verbal and nonverbal displays. For a display to be understood it must be transformed into the same code as that used to store the representation in memory. For us to perform the transformation of print to meaning, the script must be coded visually; this code must then address the mental lexicon and the recognized meaning be entered into a temporary memory. The codes of a number of words are here integrated to derive the underlying meaning of the phrase or sentence. The meaning can be said to be recognized when the recoded print accesses a representation in semantic memory, and the meaning of the phrase is recognized when the individual word meanings are used to qualify each other and to develop a schema for the underlying meaning. This process, of understanding the meaning of the writer of the words, requires us to accept assumptions of (1) the description of print as information, and (2) the recoding of the print into different forms as it is subjected to different cognitive processes. These assumptions are the subject of the following discussion.

II. INFORMATION AND SKILL

What is the information used in reading, and how can patterns of information processing be shown to change as a function of skill? This section examines the varieties of information available in printed words, concluding that skilled reading involves interactive information extraction, and examines the notion that reading can be described as a skill in the sense that some motor activities are skilled.

A. Reading as Information Processing

Information is defined technically as that which eliminates alternatives. If the appearance of each word on a page was equally probable, then our task here would be rather simple. Not only do different words convey different amounts of information, but the information which they do convey has different qualities for different readers. Factors which contribute to the variation in the information content of a word will include any factor which renders that word more predictable. Word frequency, and syntactic and semantic context are obvious factors here, but will not have constant effects for all readers. Not only will readers of varying skill provide different estimates of the predictability of words, however, but any particular word will access an internal lexicon which differs by shades from reader to reader.

Given that we must define words in terms of other words, and that meanings will be acquired personally according to unique contexts, differences between the experiences of individuals must be reflected in the interpretations which they put into words. Differences in experience would be expected to have their greatest effects with young children, as a result of their limited and selective experience. As children gain experience, so the individual differences in their word usage, and word understanding, will be minimized. Petrey (1977) presents this argument in terms of a distinction between Tulving's (1972) episodic and semantic memories. Whereas young children tend to associate word meanings with the perceived context of presentation of a word, older children associate meanings with an abstract semantic content. These differences in meaning cannot be eliminated altogether, of course, for the abstraction of meaning depends upon different episodic experience.

Words do not contain information in the same sense that a communications engineer might talk about "information transmission," for two reasons. The first is that words do not occur equally probably, so the measurement of information content is complicated. The second reason is that information is extracted from print in conjunction with the knowledge of the reader. Readers having different experiences will have different understandings of the meanings of words. Not only will individuals gain different information about meanings, but they will also use different information about the visual structure of a word to determine the identity of a word.

As Humpty-Dumpty was well aware, words will have slightly different meanings for each of us. Defining information in terms of binary alternatives is fine if we are dealing with coin-tossing, but less clear when describing the recognition of words. However, the exercise is useful in helping to identify sources of variation in word recognition which can be attributed to the cognitive abilities of individuals. This analysis forms part of a framework which identifies skilled readers as those who recognize words by using their relative predictability derived from any knowledge base available—orthographic-visual, lexical, syntactic, or semantic. The view to be represented here is that of the skilled reader who uses the most informative aspect of the word itself in conjunction with contextual predictors. Information gained from aspects of the print will be used in conjunction with other intraword information and in conjunction with knowledge-based interword information.

This is a view which emphasizes the interaction of information from various sources during word recognition, and has its base in the notions proposed by Morton (1969, 1980), Rumelhart (1977), and Stanovich (1980). As one source of information becomes less useful for the particular task in hand, so more reliance will be placed on other sources. The skilled reader has strategic flexibility, and although the analogy of a biological machine is maintained here, the predetermined flow of information is not. Individuals are of course limited by their available cognitive structures, but it is a mistake to consider readers as passive processors of the information which is presented to them. More accurate would be the view which entertains the flexibility of a processor applying to the print whichever of its cognitive structures that will break the code most effectively. This is a specific application to the description of reading skill of the notion of strategical information processing that is developed elsewhere (Underwood, 1978).

What evidence do we have then to suggest that good readers are more flexible than poor readers, and that skilled reading is not just faster reading? Most of this evidence will indicate that differences between good and poor readers are not simply quantitative, but that the differences concern the flexible use of different sources of information according to the demands of the specific reading task. The information extracted from the print is that representation which is used to contact the internal lexicon. There still exists some debate over the issue of the size of the "perceptual unit" in word recognition, and adherents to each major theoretical approach may still be found. We may recognize words as whole unit, or by first identifying each constituent letter, or by using clusters of letters as the unit of identification, but this debate will not long detain us here. The outcome of the debate will not, in principle, affect the view of reading as a skilled and interactive process. However, to clarify the description of reading as information processing, it is necessary for us to look at the alternative units of information which might be used.

One of the oldest questions about reading concerns the unit of analysis used in word identification—the letter, clusters of letters, or whole words? Part of the difficulty in providing an answer results from the nature of word recognition itself. Recognition is a flexible process, and although it has automatic components which invariably provide the reader with certain forms of information, the unit of analysis will vary according to the demands of the particular task set by the investigator. Readers can use any of these sources of information, in addition to contextual information derived from the prior sentence, and so it is not surprising that different investigators have found evidence for each of them.

Whereas Gough and Cosky (1977) found evidence of the increased processing required by increasing the number of letters in a word, using a number of tasks, additional evidence by Cosky (1976) argues against the individual letter as the unit of analysis. Words made up of either discriminable letters or less-discriminable letters did not differ in a naming task. If individual letters must first be identified, then the difficulty of identification of the letters should affect the overall difficulty of recognition of the word which is formed by them. The relationships between the letters of a word can influence their recognition, indicating that letters are not identified in contextual isolation. Thompson and Massaro (1973) used the word superiority effect with forced-choice letter identification to indicate how the context of the word can influence the decision about the letter. Partial features of letters can be used in conjunction with features of other letters to isolate alternatives. In fluent reading the same process can apply. If we come across a two-letter word (taking the simplest example) which we can identify as containing a small letter plus an ascending letter, then many alternatives are immediately excluded. If we further identify the first letter as an *o,* then the word is completely identified. Further analysis of the second letter is redundant.

Regularly occurring groups of letters might also be identified using their graphemic contexts and partial features, and so-called transgraphemic features have sometimes been cited as the units of analysis. The final candidate here is the overall shape of the word, the envelope.

By eliminating the familiar word envelope, experiments have attempted to dismiss word shape as a viable cue for identification. In their case alternation experiments, Smith (1969), Smith, Lott, and Cronnell (1969), McClelland (1976), and McConkie and Zola (1979), found no disruption in performance. Unfortunately, their tasks involved rather more processing than encoding alone, and interpretation of their data is difficult. Influences of word shape have been shown to affect word naming, when shape is manipulated by upper-case and lower-case presentations (Baron & Strawson, 1976; Coltheart & Freeman, 1974; Underwood & Bargh, 1982). Using a different procedure, Broadbent and Broadbent (1977) also found that readers do employ low-frequency information such as overall shape as well as high-frequency information such as letter-details.

Attempts to identify *the* feature used in word recognition can only fail. Any features can be used by the skilled reader, and, depending upon the task set by the experimenter, the reader will select the outputs of certain processes in preference to others. Sources of information interact during the identification of words, and the bias of one source over another will not only vary from one experimental task to another, but will also vary between readers of different ability.

The importance of spatial redundancy for word recognition has been demonstrated by Mason (1978). For the simplest case of single-letter information, the letter *O*, for instance, has a low probability of appearing in the final position of a word, and a higher probability of appearing as the second letter. If readers can make use of these probabilities when attempting to identify words, then spatial redundancy should interact with other features which are known to influence the difficulty of recognition. As identification becomes more difficult, any words with high spatial redundancy should show less of an effect than of words with low spatial redundancy. This pattern of results was found by Mason (1978, Experiment 3), in which recognition difficulty was manipulated simply by varying the number of letters. When asked to pronounce nonwords such as *ilso* and *pebloc,* adults gave slower response to the longer letter strings, and to those with low spatial redundancy. Moreover, these two factors interacted such that the effect of spatial redundancy was more apparent with the shorter rather than longer nonwords. Interestingly, this interaction was also greater for the poor reader. The same pattern of interaction was observed for the pronunciation of words, but the size of the effect was smaller. This experiment gives a good indication of the way in which information from different sources can interact in word recognition. Spatial redundancy was used to reduce the adverse effects of increasing letter length, but this was true more for the skilled reader rather than unskilled adults. It was also true more for nonwords than for words, and this is a potential problem. It could be taken that the attenuation of the effect with words is an indication that the interaction of information does not apply with materials which occur naturally in language. Only if we propose a serial model of word recognition does the objection apply, however. Let us suppose that the completion of early stages of visual processing (feature extraction) can be influenced by the activity of later processes (lexical access). The fact that the redundancy-length interaction holds best for nonwords can then be taken as support for the interaction model. How could lexical activation aid feature extraction when access is supposedly dependent upon early visual processing? As with the experiment reported by Thompson and Massaro (1973), the present question is resolved by supposing that prior to complete visual identification a number of **candidate** lexical entries are activated. When the word *card* was presented a short list of candidates might be activated according to their visual similarity to *card.* A short list including *lard, cord, card,* and *carp* could then be used to determine which visual features were present in the display. This procedure could only be used with words for which lexical entries exist, and could in this way serve to reduce the effects of encoding difficulty. The notion of a short list of candidate lexical entries is not without its difficulties, and it will not be considered at any length here. Mason's experiment indicates that spatial redundancy, one source of information available about print, can be used to reduce encoding difficulty, and that it is skilled readers who can best make use of this information. Other sources of information can be used to similar effect.

There are many reports of the interaction between visual information and context, and the locus of the contextual facilitation effect is an issue to which we shall return shortly (Section III, A). This is an important issue, for it concerns the extent to which reading is data driven (i.e., print driven) rather than conceptually driven. Current indications are that the answer depends upon the difficulty of the task and upon the skill of the reader, but for the present we shall look at a few examples of how context has been shown to interact with recognition, to establish the plausibility of the conceptually driven view.

The seminal demonstration of the influence of context is that of Tulving and Gold (1963), who asked readers to name a word which was presented tachistoscopically. The dependent measure was the exposure duration necessary for correct identification. Prior to each exposure of the word, subjects saw an incomplete sentence or part of a sentence, but the word was not always a rational continuation of the context. When it was, then its recognition was enabled at an exposure duration lower than when it was not. Increasing the amount of context increased the size of the facilitation effect for contextually appropriate words, and the size of the interference effect for inappropriate words. Results such as this led to the formulation of Morton's (1969) model of word recognition, in which information from different sources interact, and in which word information, or evidence, is collected by logogens until the specific threshold is exceeded. Subsequent demonstrations of the contextual facilitation effect include indications that the size of the effect is increased by increasing the difficulty of the target word (Stanovich & West, 1979, 1981), and that the effect can be obtained with single-word contexts (Massaro *et al.,* 1978; Meyer & Schvaneveldt, 1971; Neely, 1977). The difficulty of encoding can be attenuated by the presentation of context, again suggesting an interaction of sources of information. Using stimulus degradation and intensity reduction, respectively, Meyer, Schvaneveldt, and Ruddy (1975) and Becker and Killion (1977) found faster responses to pairs of words that were semantically related than to pairs that were unrelated. As with Mason's (1978) experiment, information stored in the internal lexicon can be used to influence the extraction of visual information from print.

Context from the preceding sentence can moderate the harmful effects of words which are difficult to decode. Effects of stimulus degradation and word frequency and length were shown to be influenced by contextual information by Stanovich and West (1979, 1981), and naming is also sensitive to a number of other manipulations.

Changing the overall shape of a word can lead to differences in the use of processing, for instance, and this manipulation interacts with the use of context. The clearest results implicating the importance of global word shape come from tasks employing cAse aLtErNaTiOn (Baron & Strawson, 1976; Coltheart & Freeman, 1974; Mason, 1978; Underwood, Parry, & Bull, 1978). In contrast to these word-naming experiments, some studies employing other tasks have reported the absence of effects, and this evidence is harmful to the notion of the importance of shape for identification. Before discussing the interactions found with this source of information, it is necessary to account for those results finding no effect.

Smith (1969) and Smith *et al.* (1969) used a task in which subjects scanned lists for target words, and found no effects of alternation, and McClelland (1976) reported that the word superiority effect in letter identification also did not depend upon consistency in the use of case. Finally, in an experiment reported by McConkie and Zola (1979) employing eye movement measures, changing a whole line of text, while it was being read, had no effect upon subsequent fixation durations, saccade length, or frequency of regressive saccades. As interesting as each of these results is, none of them pertains to encoding processes. Each of the experiments involves post-recognition processes which could act to mask any differences in the encoding of normal and alternated words. Smith used a search task which required the retention of the target words in memory, and McClelland asked his subjects for the report of a single letter. In these tasks any effects of encoding difficulty may have been attenuated by additional processing requirements. To establish whether recognition is influenced by changes in the word shape, more direct tests of recognition are required.

Evidence of the importance of word shape has recently come from a study reported by Monk and Hulme (1983) in which subjects read a passage in preparation for a comprehension test, while checking for misspellings. Mutilations of the spellings which preserved the original word envelope were detected less often than those which changed the overall shape. The shape of the word envelope is not sufficient to define the identity of each word, but it does act as a delimiter. Suppose the reader had half recognized a word, and had correctly identified the initial letters, but was unsure as to the identity of the final letters. Alternative words may be short listed as candidates, and it is here that shape information can become useful. When attempting to recognize the word *commerce,* shape information will provide minimal cues in comparison with the word *commence,* but if the choice were between *commerce* and *commends,* then shape information alone would provide a distinguishing feature. The experiments using pronunciation tasks may have been sensitive to these distinguishing features, but reading words printed with case alternation is not a well-practiced task, and may not be representative of skilled reading. Word envelopes are also removed by printing words with upper case letters, and Baron and Strawson (1976) and Coltheart and Freeman (1974) also found this manipulation to be harmful to word naming. By changing text from lower case to upper case Fisher (1975) found a 10% increase in reading time, indicating a generality to the impairment. Furthermore, case of presentation was found by Underwood and Bargh (1982) to interact with contextual information previously provided about the word. As suggested by the earlier results of Tulving and Gold (1963) and Stanovich and West (1979, 1981), pronunciation of a word presented as a completion of a sentence was aided when the word was contextually congruent with the sentence (e.g., "For protection many frightened animals stop still and" . . . "cower") rather than when the word was incongruent (e.g., "The ingredients must be carefully weighed when preparing" . . . "moan"). Although the investigation also looked at interactions with orthographic regularity, these will be discussed later (Section III, B). Underwood and Bargh (1982) found that the informative word envelope of lower case words facilitated recognition with incongruent sentences, but that when the word provided a satisfactory completion there was no reliable difference between upper case and lower case presentations. In other words, if there is useful information available about a word, then word shape has less apparent effects. If the word envelope affects recognition, and it is difficult to see how it could have its influence after recognition, then this experiment gives support to the argument of Stanovich and West (1982) that context also affects the recognition of words.

The purpose of this discussion is to indicate the varieties of information which are available about printed words, and to indicate that, for skilled readers at least, the source of information will vary according to the difficulty of encoding. If information about the shape of the word envelope is not available, then we can demonstrate more reliance upon the context in which the word is presented. If an encoding task is made more difficult, by increasing the number of letters in a nonword, then we can demonstrate more reliance upon orthographic redundancy within the word. In the following discussions we shall consider the cognitive processes which are applied to this information, again looking for differences in performances which emerge as a function of general reading skill.

B. The Nature of Skill as It Applies to Reading

As a learning curve asymptotes, the activity can be said to be skillful as a result of practice. This statement can be applied to motor activities such as tying shoelaces or riding a bicycle, and it can be applied to cognitive activities such as mental arithmetic and recognizing the meanings of words.

Before discussing reading as a skilled activity, it is first necessary to examine the nature of skill.

Skilled motor activities differ from the unskilled both qualitatively and quantitatively. They also differ phenomenologically. Skilled activities are performed faster, and are performed more smoothly, but perhaps the greatest change is in the experience of the performer. Whereas an unskilled act requires careful attention, and will be disturbed if the performer is distracted, a skilled performance is characterized by its relaxed quality and its ease of mental effort. The change from unskilled to skilled performance, during which our minds become less and less involved in the small details of the act, has been described as resulting from a change in the mode of control (Keele & Summers, 1976; Reason, 1979; Underwood, 1982). A feedback loop may be necessary in the performance of an unfamiliar action, so that errors may be corrected *during* performance. Continuous use of feedback would be described as closed-loop control (CLC), whereas a familiar action may be performed with open-loop control (OLC) in which feedback is neglected. The change from CLC to OLC mode is usually accompanied by smoother performance, as minor corrections are no longer being executed, but the experience of the performer also changes. Actions which have been overlearned to the extent that execution errors are rarely made and feedback neglected are those actions which seem to occur automatically. Returning to the language of the engineer once more, these actions seem to be **productions** which are initiated by the appearance of the **calling pattern.**

When tying my shoelaces, I do not need to inspect each stage in the process ("hold both ends firmly" . . . "pass each end to the other hand by way of passing one end around the other lace" . . . "pull both ends firmly" . . . etc.[1]) to ensure success. Alternative actions do not need to be given conscious consideration. Decisions are made within the **total** action itself, except when describing **parts** of the action, as I have attempted for the case of tying my shoelaces here. Each state of completion is the calling pattern for the next part of the action, and conscious inspection of the current state is unnecessary. Indeed, when we do start to think about the components of an action, performance may be disturbed. This does not hold only for motor actions, for having an interest in reading processes, and a curiosity about one's own processes, can serve to disrupt fluent reading unnervingly.

With words and shoelaces a recognizable calling pattern results in an overlearned action. For the production-systems engineer, the performance

---

[1]Indicating the difficulty in remembering and describing this action may be sufficient to make the point. I confess to having had to untie and tie my own laces to remind me of what the action is, in attempting to describe it here. Being able to perform an act, be it physical or mental, is independent of being able to provide a verbal report of that performance.

is subject to **condition-action rules,** whereby a defined environmental condition is itself sufficient to call a defined action without the intervention of a decision maker (see also Allport, 1980). In the case of human performance, the decision making is aided by the consideration of alternatives, and for this reason we can argue that consciousness has a purpose in the evaluation and selection of our choices (Underwood, 1978). When choices are not available, or are not necessary (as in skilled OLC performances) we are not aware of our moment-by-moment actions. Automatized actions, which I have held to be OLC actions (Underwood, 1982), are those for which direct, conscious control is unnecessary. With these overlearned actions, control comes from the environment, and our own volitional efforts are free for allocation elsewhere. The existence of a specific calling pattern is sufficient for the control of the action. Only with novel stimuli or novel actions do we need to selectively process the stimuli or selectively choose the responses.

In the case of cognitive skill, the same principles of overlearning to eliminate error, and performance without the consideration of alternatives, can be observed to apply. In the domain of retrieval from memory, we do not need to set up search hierarchies or consider our choices when asked "What is the capital city of France?" or "What is three multiplied by four?" or even "can canaries fly?" The answers are available as a product of condition-action rules. When the "problem" is understood the conditions are defined and the mental action follows. Only when the question does not have a familiar action associated with it, do choices have to be considered. Questions for which CLC may be necessary would include "What is the capital city of South Africa?," or "What is seven multiplied by thirteen?," or "do canaries have spark plugs?" Differences in the mode of performance can be seen in reading with children of different ability. The decoding of a word may be a tortuous procedure for a child looking for alternative combinations of letters, but the same word for an older child may be read aloud without effort. For this more skilled reader, the calling pattern is familiar and the condition-action rule itself dictates the decoding of visual pattern into meaning. For the unskilled reader, however, the pattern has not been categorized as a familiar event, and it must be segmented into a sequence of smaller, familiar events. These events are then recombined in different ways, the outcomes evaluated, and the best fit selected. The evaluation of outcomes corresponds to the use of feedback from the preceding action, and for the skilled reader this is unnecessary. Only when we come across new or otherwise unfamiliar words do we resort to CLC in word decoding.

For skilled readers, words are calling patterns for cognitive actions involving access of the meaning, and possibly generation of the phonological code of the word. These are actions which are well-practiced and automatized, and just as shoelaces may be tied effectively without conscious control, so it is that we do not need to attend to the activity of recognizing individual words when reading.

The increasing automaticity of word decoding skilled is a feature of the model of reading development suggested by LaBerge and Samuels (1974). This model identifies levels of processing in decoding, from letter and word recognition through to sentence comprehension, and holds that fluency in the reading skill develops because the lower level processes become automatized. When attention does not need to be directed to letter identification, it can be allocated to comprehension. The measure of automaticity is the extent to which an activity can be performed at the same time as a second activity to which attention must be directed. If performance of task A is automatic, then it can be performed at the same time as task B which involves choice and thereby requires attention. Our earlier discussion concluded that only tasks which have overlearned condition–action rules can be performed without attention, for only then do decisions not have to be made. Evidence supporting this notion of automatic decoding skills has come from a number of sources, and in Section III, B consideration will be given to the mechanisms of word recognition evident in adult, skilled readers. However, in the context of LaBerge and Samuels's (1974) views of the developing automatization of low-level processes, the remainder of this section concerns the development of decoding processes in the absence of attention.

Two methods of the investigation of automatization will be considered here. One of these infers the existence of an automatic process by its pattern of influence upon an attended task, and in the second the absence of an interaction between two sources of attended information is taken as an indication of the operation of automatization. These are methods employing Stroop-like interference tasks and word-naming in sentence contexts.

In the original form of the Stroop task, word recognition is inferred as a result of the interfering effect of an irrelevant word upon a color-naming task. The word *green*, printed in blue ink, has a slower color-naming time than a color-irrelevant word printed in blue ink. From this we may conclude that the word *green*, although irrelevant to the task as described to the subject, has been recognized and its meaning processed to a level where it can interfere with the generation of the name of the color. A number of studies have observed the extent of the interference effect in readers of different ability, but they have not always used the classic version of the color-word Stroop task. Rather than observe the effect of words upon color naming, for instance, it is possible to observe their effect upon picture naming. Whatever the primary task, color naming or picture naming, or indeed any attended activity, the reasoning is the same: if an irrelevant word is effective in changing behavior, then that word must have been recognized.

The prediction from the LaBerge and Samuels's (1974) model is that as reading skills develop, and word recognition becomes automatized, then skilled readers should show a greater interference effect than unskilled readers. For adult readers, Martin (1978) confirmed the prediction with color naming, but when skill is observed developmentally the conclusions are not so straightforward, West and Stanovich (1978, task 2—see their Fig. 2) found no increase in the amount of color-naming interference between the fourth grade (8, 9, and 10 years old) and college subjects. Another negative result was reported by Schiller (1966), who reported a decline in the extent of interference with reading age. Hicks and Jackson (1981) also found that the interference effect diminished as reading age increased, with a group of poor readers classified as "dyslexic." These results do not fit the predictions from LaBerge and Samuels's model, and may indicate an increase in the ability to attend selectively to the color naming. For the case of color naming, however, the problem with these negative results may have been the age of the subjects on testing. Stanovich, Cunningham, and West (1981) did succeed in demonstrating a developmental increase in the size of the effect, but only during the early months in the first grade. Later in the first grade the increase in interference flattens out. Encouragingly, greater interference was shown by the better readers, and Stanovich *et al.* were able to conclude in favor of the LaBerge and Samuels' model, suggesting that, for the words used in their sample, automatization of recognition had been achieved during the first months of schooling. This conclusion has been supported by an extensive study of color-naming interference by Schadler and Thissen (1981). Prereaders, and children up to the sixth grade (12 years old), were tested in this experiment, and although greater reading ability (fourth grade onward) was associated with a reduction in the interference effect, for these subjects the effect increased up to the second or fourth grade. For Schadler and Thissen (1981), automatization takes rather longer to develop than we conclude from the other studies. They also conclude that the decreasing interference with older children is a reflection of an increased ability to disregard irrelevant stimuli, accompanying a general increase in organization and processing efficiency. The decrease is a function of greater self-control over the individual's cognitive processes.

Using picture-naming tasks to observe the interfering influence of irrelevant words, Rosinski, Golinkoff, and Kukish (1975) and Golinkoff and Rosinski (1976) found no evidence of a change in the size of the effect with readers of differing ability. They tested children who had left the first grade, and Guttentag and Haith (1979) confirmed this result. We have also failed to find a reliable difference in the size of the effect between good and poor adult readers, and between good and poor young readers (Briggs & Underwood, 1982; Underwood & Briggs, 1984). When testing newcomers to the first grade, however, Guttentag and Haith found an increase in the effect during the first 6 months of schooling. Consistent with the Stanovich *et al.* (1981) result, this suggests that the interference effect is sensitive to the early development of automatized skills, but that within the first year of schooling word recognition is sufficiently automatized to show no further increase. It is not only recognition of word meaning which is recognized automatically. The picture-word interference experiment reported by Underwood and Briggs (1984) also found a sensitivity to the graphemic and phonemic characteristics of printed words. The only measure which distinguished between good and poor young readers in this experiment was the overall picture-naming time. Whereas input processes may be automatized in readers of a range of abilities, naming problems may prove to be a source of reading retardation. Such difficulties may result from not being able to retain temporary memories of what has been read.

With both color naming and picture naming, interference can be shown to be a function of reading skill. Interference increases as reading experience increases, but only during the first few months of schooling. Thereafter, it appears that word recognition skills are sufficiently automatic for the effect to appear at all ages to an equivalent extent. Differences in the abilities of readers beyond this point must therefore be a function of postrecognition processes such as explicit naming, propositional integration, and sentence comprehension.

A different source of evidence of automatized processing comes from experiments observing the effect of sentence context upon word recognition. The absence of certain patterns of influence, as reading skill increases, has been interpreted in favor of the notion of fast word recognition in conjunction with automatic contextual activation. A full description of the model of contextual interaction (Posner & Snyder, 1975) is more appropriate to Section III, B, which deals with attention and word recognition, and so only the barest details will be presented here.

The question which is addressed by this model is that of the processes by which contextual priming can affect the recognition of an item. Items which are expected, whether they are words, pictures, or simply sensory stimuli such as the flash of a light or the sounding of a buzzer, seem to be processed more easily than those which are unexpected. Posner and Snyder (1975) suggested two mechanisms by which priming can operate, and West and Stanovich (1978) interpreted developmental trends in reading performance in terms of changes in these processes. Priming can operate as a conscious, attentional process, or it can be automatic and operate without the volition of the perceiver.

If given time to generate an expectancy of the next item to be presented, then the attentional process can be said to operate because choice is involved. When given the incomplete sentence "the man kicked the dog in the," we can ponder the likely completions and perhaps select a best fit. If the perceiver had selected the word *park* and that word had then been presented, then recognition would have been facilitated by the attentional process. However, if the presented word had been *backside* then perception would have been slower. Facilitation effects in such experiments are best observed when the completion is highly predictable, as in "the accountant balanced the . . . books," and inhibition observed for words which do not provide good completions of the sentence, as with "the accountant balanced the . . . people" (Fischler & Bloom, 1979). Generation of an expectancy by the attentional process can lead to facilitation or inhibition, according to whether or not the word presented is the word expected. Posner and Synder suggest that inhibition follows from the assumption of limited capacity for attentional processes. An item called into awareness by this process will be mismatched against the item presented and the process of excluding it from awareness will cause time penalties. More mechanical views of inhibition discuss the shifting of the limited capacity process from one location in memory to another, with the inhibition resulting from the necessity to move before the presented item can be processed. So much for inhibition, which is not observed if the expectancy follows from Posner and Synder's automatic spreading activation process.

When a memory location is activated by the presentation of a word, some other locations are affected by a spread of activation. This notion has received support in the discussions of Collins and Loftus (1975) and Meyer and Schvaneveldt (1971) in particular. The locations which are indirectly affected are those which are semantically associated to the activated location. This is an automatic process in that it does not use attentional capacity, and, most importantly, it only affects semantic associates of the activated item. A further difference between these two expectancy processes is in their delay functions. Whereas the automatic process is considered to be fast acting, operation of the attentional process is slow. Much of the evidence justifying these three differences between the processes (i.e., automaticity, scope of effect, and speed) has come from experiments investigating effects of single items upon other single items, but of interest here is the way in which West and Stanovich (1978) accounted for reading skill differences with these two processes.

West and Stanovich (1978) tested readers of three ages, from fourth grade (8, 9, and 10 years old), to sixth grade (10, 11, and 12 years old) and college students (mean age 20 years old) on a sentence completion task. Subjects read aloud a word which followed an incomplete sentence, as in "the dog ran after the . . . cat,'' and the naming latency to the target word recorded. The sentence can be considered as being available for the generation of an expectancy about the identity of the target word. Three completion conditions were used, with the target following a congruous sentence or an incongruous sentence (as in "the dog ran after the . . . chair''), or following the word *the* in isolation. This third condition provides a neutral context, and allows the observation of facilitation and inhibition effects independently. The results of this experiment were quite startling. Whereas the young readers showed both inhibition and facilitation, the college readers showed facilitation only. West and Stanovich concluded that with poor readers the word identification was so slow that the conscious, attentional process was able to generate an expectancy of a likely completion, and that this accounted for their facilitation and their inhibition effects. With more skilled readers, however, word identification was so fast that only the automatic spread of activation was able to influence processing, and thus only facilitation was observed. The sixth grade readers fell some way between these extremes. The Posner and Snyder model provides a good description of the data from this experiment, and the notion of automatic (skilled) word recognition is supported. When children of the same age are tested, it should be mentioned, the results are not so unequivocal.

Briggs, Austin, and Underwood (1984) attempted to repeat the sentence context experiment with matched pairs of children. Good and poor readers, who were matched on age (9 and 10 years old) and nonverbal IQ but differed by at least 2 years on a reading test, performed a similar naming task as that described by West and Stanovich. Similar results were not obtained. Both good and poor readers gave an inhibition effect for incongruous words, suggesting the intentional generation of expectancies. Only the poor readers gave a facilitation effect with congruous words, however, a result of conflict with the prediction from the Posner and Snyder (1975) model. Inhibition-without-facilitation was observed by Fischler and Bloom (1979), and in both cases postrecognition processes are implicated. Briggs *et al.* concluded that the differences between the good and poor readers were a consequence of different reading strategies, with the poor readers showing more reliance on the context provided by the sentence. No evidence of automatic expectancy effects was found, however, and so we must leave open the question of whether context effects are the product of automatic word processing skills.

This discussion has considered reading to be a cognitive skill with similar operating properties as other skills, including motor skills. As practice increases, and the calling pattern for performance becomes more and more familiar, so the condition–action rule will operate to minimize the need for intentional initiation. Skilled readers do not ponder over the meanings of individual words, but recognize them directly. Decoding is taken care of by condition–action rules operating on the calling pattern contained in the orthographic structure. To a certain extent at least, the development of these condition-action rules can be observed in developing readers. In the following sections we shall turn to word recognition operations demonstrated by skilled adult readers.

III. AUTOMATIC INFORMATION PROCESSING IN READING

Much of what goes on when we read sentences is automatic, in the sense intended by LaBerge and Samuels (1974), and this discussion will review evidence of automaticity in skilled readers. In the previous section it was argued that automaticity is a necessary component of skilled activity, with the development of condition–action rules which respond directly when their environmental calling patterns are present. This description can apply to reading as well as to tying shoelaces, and in the following discussions words will be identified with the calling patterns used during fluent reading.

The mechanism which responds to printed words, the internal lexicon, is first outlined, and evidence of automatic word processing then reviewed. The phenomenon around which these discussions are based is one which is perhaps all-too-well known to many of us, and follows from reading without attention. If attempting to read without attending to the underlying structure of the text, it is all too easy to find oneself at the bottom of a paragraph with little idea of what the text meant. At the same time as not knowing about the meanings of the phrases and the sentences, however, the reader may have the impression that each word had been inspected and recognized. Upon looking at the paragraph a second time, a feeling of familiarity greets the eye. Each word is in its rightful place, and the individual meanings are unchanged, so why was the text not understood on the first viewing? Whenever I have this experience I can usually associate the first viewing of the paragraph with distraction—although my eyes behaved as they would have done if I had attempted to understand the schematic meaning, my thoughts would be elsewhere. Rephrasing this slightly, word recognition is automatic, but derivation of the underlying text meaning cannot be performed without attention. It is for exactly the same reason that intelligent copy-typists can transcribe individual words accurately, and correct spelling errors as they do so, but fail to grasp the meanings of the sentences. When attending to individual words, interword relationships are neglected. Given our conclusions about attention and choice, this is not surprising. Individual words are calling' patterns, and when they are recognized the appropriate cognitive actions follow directly. Their meanings are derived from condition–action rules which have unique specifications. It is only with ambiguous words that selection of the appropriate meaning may be necessary, and there exists evidence to suggest that ambiguity does impose an additional cognitive load (e.g., Foss, 1970; Foss & Jenkins, 1973; Swinney & Hakes, 1976). Whenever alternative meanings must be selected, attention will be required. Lexical ambiguity is one case where selection is necessary, but selection, and therefore attention, is demanded continuously if we are to integrate the meanings of individual words into a unique structure corresponding to the underlying text meaning. If attention is elsewhere, then words may be recognized but the underlying meanings of text will be lost.

A. Word Recognition Processes

How does the reader recover from the page the meanings of individual words? To be able to recognize word meanings we need to be able to compare the visual pattern with a memory, and our concern here is to identify the memory system which is consulted when recognizing words.

The system which contains our memories of words has been likened to an internal dictionary, and was an integral component of Treisman's (1960) model of attention. In this model words were seen to access the dictionary, in an attenuated or unattenuated form according to whether they were unattended or not, and activate "dictionary units" according to the degree of attenuation. Thus, an unattended word would have less impact upon the dictionary because the attenuation would reduce the signal-to-noise ratio of the message. Accordingly, only high frequency or highly probable words would be recognized if they were part of an unattended message. The "dictionary units" have been subsequently referred to as "lexical representations," and in the most influential model of word recognition they are called "logogens" (Morton, 1969, 1980[2]). The function of these memories remains the same, however, with evidence about a word accumulating until a threshold is reached. When the threshold level of evidence is collected, the logogen is said to be activated, and the word is said to be recognized. Morton's logogen system collects evidence from any source available, with

---

[2]In 1969 the logogens were considered to be generalized structures which collected evidence from any modality, but by 1980 the model had been extended to accommodate separate input logogens for reading and listening. This became necessary to account for evidence of an absence of an interaction between spoken and visual forms of a word (see Morton, 1969). Furthermore, Morton has regularly considered the logogen system to be separate from a semantic or cognitive system, suggesting that the lexicon is a nonassociative lexical list. In the present discussion this distinction is not used, and it is assumed that the lexicon stores meanings of words in an associative manner. This makes certain priming effects easier to understand.

visual evidence from the page and contextual evidence provided by the reader's "cognitive system" being two dominant general sources of information. Evidence is said to be used interactively, and this is a very important feature of the model, reappearing in the accounts offered by Rumelhart (1977) and Stanovich (1980). Before examining what it is that the logogens might be, and before mentioning alternative accounts of word processing, a brief diversion will be made to examine the notion of interactive processing.

Good readers can be distinguished from poor readers in their use of different types of information when reading. As mentioned in Section II, A, Mason (1978) reported that good readers can make use of orthographic knowledge to compensate for adverse treatments such as increasing word length. Perhaps the simplest demonstration of interactive effects is that reported by Meyer *et al.* (1975), however, in which stimulus degradation interacted with context. Lexical decisions to pairs of related words were less impaired by the superimposition of a dot pattern on the display than were the decisions to pairs of unrelated words. This interaction suggests that stimulus quality and simple interword context have an influence at the same stage of processing. Because stimulus quality must be effective during encoding we infer that context also affects encoding. Having recognized one word (e.g., *bread*) the second word is encoded more easily if it is an associate (e.g., *butter*) than if it is an unrelated word (e.g., *nurse*). A similar result was reported by Massaro *et al.* (1978). When encoding was increased in difficulty by turning a target word upside-down, the effectiveness of a category-prime was observed to increase. As stimulus encoding became more difficult, readers tended to rely more on the context of presentation. In the West and Stanovich (1978) experiment mentioned in the previous section, the same relationship can be seen to hold, for the poor readers (who have difficulty with stimulus encoding) relied more on the expectancy generated by the context of the preceding sentence. For their good readers, recognition was too fast for conscious expectancies to influence reading times. If one source of information is impoverished, the interaction principle says, then other sources of information will have a greater effect upon performance.

The frequencies of words in the lexicon provide a simple starting point in the analysis of its organization. Perhaps the lexicon is a list of words ordered in terms of their frequencies of usage, with the word frequency effect accountable to a strategy of searching the earliest items in the list first. The absence of an interaction with stimulus degradation leads us to question any model which gives such an early role in recognition to frequency, but the alternative has been entertained by Becker (1976) and Forster (1976). These models differ from Morton's account in the mechanisms by which decisions are made about words, and in the structural organization of the word list. Morton's early explanation of the word frequency effect was to suggest that the thresholds were set differently according to frequency, whereas Becker and Forster suggest that the effect results from the search procedure. There is as yet sparse evidence to separate these candidates, but a warning about the importance of frequency has recently been provided by Jastrzembski (1981).

In challenging the traditional view of the primacy of word frequency in recognition, Jastrzembski suggested that the research which leads us to this conclusion ignored a factor equally as potent. The same graphemic pattern is often used to indicate a number of meanings, and whereas these meanings are usually related, the number of meanings of word can confound its measured frequency. Frequency is counted in the absence of a consideration of the semantic context in which the word appears. The word *saw,* for instance, has a high frequency of occurrence, but the count would be affected by instances of *saw* as meaning "observed," "carpenter's tool," "use of that carpenter's tool," etc. Jastrzembski found that words with many meanings provided faster lexical decisions than those with few meanings, and, most importantly, that this effect was obtained when word frequency was held constant. The two factors did interact, with a greater frequency effect for words with few meanings, suggesting that these manipulations have their effect at the same stage of processing. Whereas Jastrzembski concluded that it is encoding which is affected by the number of meanings, the possibility exists that postrecognition processes such as spelling or meaning checks could account for the differences in response times. The failure of Jastrzembski to find either a main effect of orthographic redundancy or an interaction with redundancy (measured by bigram frequency totals), could be interpreted as suggesting that encoding effects did not predominate with his procedure.

The main conclusion from Jastrzembski's work is that word frequency is not the only base for lexical access. Models which suggest that the lexicon is accessed with a frequency-ordered search cannot account for his effect whereby some low-frequency words gain faster decisions than some high-frequency words. At the very least, the frequency models must be modified. Jastrzembski also lists several "benchmark" experiments in the literature of word recognition, in which frequency was controlled, but number of meanings neglected. Investigations of frequency, and experiments using sets of words matched for frequency, are meaningless unless the number of meanings of the words is taken into account.

The notion of a logogen system for word recognition is general enough to accommodate Jastrzembski's findings. Multiple meanings might be represented by multiple logogens, each with the same graphemic access code.

In the artificial conditions of the lexical decision task, in which meanings are not differentiated, access to any of the logogens with the same spelling would be sufficient to start the response. The more logogens a word has, the more likely it is that one will accumulate sufficient evidence for activation.

So far we have assumed that logogens correspond to words, but the view which is now accepted is that logogens are morphemes, or word stems. Three methods will be used here to indicate the generality of this view—priming, lexical decision, and word generation. Murrell and Morton (1974) established the case for morphemic priming (rather than semantic priming) in a task with a time interval in the order of minutes between presentations of the prime and the target. They found that the response to the word *boring* was facilitated by the prior presentation of *bore,* but not by *born.* Semantic priming was ruled out because *pained* did not facilitate *boring* over the time scales used. In the Meyer and Schvaneveldt (1971) experiment, using immediate presentation of one word after the other, semantic priming **was** observed. It is not clear why morphemic priming should occur over long intervals only, and semantic priming over short intervals only, and so this experiment alone cannot be accepted as a clear demonstration that logogens are morphemic elements. Murrell and Morton may have found an effect which is restricted to a very specific experimental procedure. When effects are derived from such essential characteristics, they should be generally observable. However, a second piece of evidence does support their position, and this comes from a lexical decision experiment concerned with responses to nonwords. Taft and Forster (1975) found that nonwords formed from morphemic stems (e.g., *semble*) were associated with longer decision times than nonwords which were not stems (e.g., *sassin*) but which are taken from the same part of the word as the real stem. (Both of these examples are created by deleting the letters *as* from words.) They took this to suggest that the morphemic stems are represented in the lexicon, and that the longer decision times resulted from false access. In related experiments, Taft and Forster also found that nonwords created by adding a prefix to a morpheme (e.g., *besist*) resulted in slower responses than those to control items containing no stem (e.g., *bescue*). The third source of evidence comes from MacKay's (1978) word generation task. Listeners were presented with verbs such as *excite* and required to generate an appropriate noun. The complexity of the conversion affected the speed and accuracy of performance, with *involve→ involvement* being easier than *exist → existence.* Nominalizations with the -*ence* suffix required a syllabic regrouping of the stem, and as complexity was increased further, with, for instance *corrode → corrosion* and further still with *inhibit → inhibition,* performance fell away. The more the stem had to be changed, so the task became more difficult.

MacKay suggested the effect depended upon retrieval of the stem and manipulation of the stem. Derivation of the noun required recovery of the stem, and identification of the appropriate suffix. Although the differences in performance here were due to postaccess processes, the underlying morphemic stem appears to be used in the derivation of related groups of words, and this gives support to the view of a lexicon containing morphemes and their modification markers.

Words with common morphemes are seen as being stored in the lexicon as morphemes plus markers, but this is not the only form of multiple representation. Jastrzembski (1981) provided evidence which can be interpreted as suggesting that words with multiple meanings are stored as separate logogens. The word *reading,* then, would be stored several times to indicate meanings such as "action of a reader," "an interpretation," "recital of a formal document," etc., and each representation would be as the morphemic stem plus the modifier. It would also be stored as a morpheme in its own right, corresponding to a town in England, but recognition here would depend upon at least the first letter being printed in upper case type. Words with multiple meanings can be derived from the same stem or, as a result of etymological accidents, they can be derived from different stems. The *saw* has two clusters of meanings, one corresponding to *see* and one corresponding to *tool.* Jastrzembski reported that the number of different clusters of meanings did not affect his basic effect of number of meanings. When meanings were associated with only one derivation, lexical decision tended to be faster, but the effect of the total number of meanings was observed independently of this. With the number of derivations held constant, increasing the number of meanings within a derivational cluster acted to produce faster decisions. On the basis of this effect Jastrzembski suggested that logogens of clustered words (i.e., of the same derivation) are connected to each other, as we might expect words of the same morphemic stem to be connected. Words of different morphemic stems are not connected to each other, because words which had either many meanings, or a single large cluster (but the same total number), were associated with faster decisions than words with either few meanings or with clusters of similar size. When a logogen becomes activated, all logogens in the cluster are activated, but logogens in other clusters are unaffected even when the logogen is graphemically identical. Although Jastrzembski considered that each meaning was associated with a unique logogen, it would be sufficient for each derivational stem to correspond to a logogen, if the number of meanings could affect the threshold setting of the logogen.

The independence of morphemic stem clusters is a principle requiring modification, according to evidence of the multiple access of lexically ambiguous words. Swinney (1979) demonstrated that multiple meanings are accessed, even for words with multiple derivations.

In an ingenious experiment to observe the effect of a disambiguating sentence context, Swinney found that two meanings of a polysemous word such as *bug* were available immediately after presentation. The effect held even when the prior context suggested only one meaning as being appropriate. Subjects heard the following:

"The man was not surprised when he found several spiders, roaches and other bugs in the corner of the room"

Immediately after hearing *bugs,* they saw a letter-string on a screen, and made a lexical decision response to it. A decision to *spy* was faster than a decision to *sew,* suggesting that an alternative meaning of *bugs* had been accessed and was able to prime the recognition of *spy.* The effect vanished if the lexical decision task was delayed for about 1 second after presentation of the polysemous word. Alternative meanings are accessed, but if the context does not sustain them, then they are ineffective, possibly as a result of a decision about the most appropriate meaning. Studies of lexical ambiguity using phoneme-monitoring tasks have suggested that polysemous words provide an extra processing load (e.g., Foss, 1970; Foss & Jenkins, 1973; Swinney & Hakes, 1976), and although such tasks have been questioned on methodological grounds there is some not contradictory evidence here of decisions, and therefore attention, being implicated.

It might reasonably be asked, about the disambiguating sentence in Swinney's delightful experiment, why it was that both meanings of the polysemous words were accessed at all. Given the general entomological context of the sentence above, why were both etymological stems accessed? This could be taken as evidence of context failing to influence the encoding of the appropriate word, and, if this is so, then we must question Morton's assumptions about logogens as collectors of evidence from multiple sources, and our general assumptions about the interaction of information in word recognition. We shall therefore conclude our discussion of the word recognition structures with a comment on the influence of context upon encoding.

West and Stanovich's (1978) fascinating data on the developmental course of contextual facilitation suggested that skilled readers recognize words too quickly for their conscious expectancies to affect recognition. In contrast, younger readers with less skilled recognition abilities tended to use context, and the evidence for this conclusion was the pattern of facilitation-with-inhibition according to the model of Posner and Snyder (1975). The automatic activation process of expectancy can facilitate the processing of expected words, but cannot affect unexpected words, whereas the conscious, strategical process can facilitate the expected, and inhibit recognition of the unexpected. Moreover, the automatic process is fast acting and the conscious process, which requires decisions, is by comparison slow acting. West and Stanovich suggested that the automatic expectancy process, which resembles the spread of activation discussed by Meyer and Schvaneveldt (1971) and Collins and Loftus (1975), was the only process to affect their skilled readers, and that the effects of context were located at word recognition. When skilled readers were put at the disadvantage of having word recognition slowed, by stimulus degradation, then they too showed both facilitation for congruous words and inhibition for incongruous words (Stanovich & West, 1979). Delaying onset of the target word, to give the conscious activation process more time to operate, also allowed inhibition to be demonstrated. As the level of difficulty of recognition of the target word increases, with "difficulty" including both frequency and word length, so the contextual facilitation effect also increases (Stanovich & West, 1981).

This pattern of results may be interpreted as an influence of context upon encoding, with logogens collecting both contextual and visual evidence in conjunction. However, recent data and arguments have brought the issue of context and encoding into question. Swinney's (1979) experiment poses an indirect problem for the interaction model, while Fischler and Bloom's (1979) experiment contradicts the facilitation/inhibition pattern altogether. Fischler and Bloom found less facilitation and more inhibition than Stanovich and West, and while the appearance of inhibition poses a problem for the Posner and Snyder two-process explanation, a number of differences between the two sets of experiments should be mentioned. Whereas Stanovich and West had their subjects reading out the context as it appeared on a screen, and then recorded the latency of the naming response to the target word, Fischler and Bloom had their subjects reading silently and providing a lexical decision response to the target. The former measure leads to questions about the reading strategies of the silent subjects, and the second measure, which was taken as a more direct investigation of lexical access without phonological processing, leads to questions of the involvement of postaccess decision processes. Performing a lexical decision to a word at the end of a sentence may have imposed specific processing demands upon their readers, and postaccess checking processes may have been involved in their experiment. Forster (1981) develops this argument and concludes that inhibition can result from postaccess message processing. Lexical decision tasks may not always be the most appropriate tools for the investigation of encoding processes, and similar remarks apply to the use of the rapid serial visual presentation (RSVP) method.

With the RSVP task, subjects read passages presented a few words at a time. If context aids recognition, we might argue, then readers should require less time to view words as they progress through the passage. Such decreases in viewing time are not observed (see Stanovich, 1980, for a review), but this could be a result of not testing encoding directly. As we progress through a passage, attempting to understand it, the cognitive load increases as more words and propositions are integrated, and this could mask any facilitatory effect upon encoding. If a direct test is provided, then encoding can be shown to be implicated. During the presentation of a passage Sharkey (1982) inserted a lexical decision task, and found that words related to the meaning of the passage gained faster responses than those which were unrelated. Forster's (1981) comments about postaccess message processing lead to doubts about the use of lexical decision measures in studies of comprehension, however.

Strong evidence exists of the influence of context in recognition from the word–word-priming experiments of Meyer and Schvaneveldt (1971), Neely (1977), and others, and so it is beyond question whether context influences encoding. What is in question is whether the expectancy generated from a sentence can influence the encoding of a word presented as a part of that sentence. Following the demonstration of an interaction between stimulus degradation and context in the experiments reported by Meyer *et al.* (1975) and by Massaro *et al.* (1978), Underwood and Bargh (1982) demonstrated a related interaction using sentence, rather than word, contexts. When encoding was disrupted by upper case presentation of a target word rather than a lower case word with a distinctive word envelope, then the effects were reduced if context provided more information.

If context influences encoding, then why did Swinney find evidence of the lexical access of both meanings of a polysemous word? Swinney's effect is by no means unique, for similar demonstrations have been reported by Conrad (1974), by Onifer and Swinney (1981), by Tanenhaus, Leiman, and Seidenberg (1979), and by Underwood (1980). Context should have influenced the encoding of the critical word and only one of the possible logogens activated. Instead, the multiple meanings were available, even if for a short time only. The model suggested by West and Stanovich (1978), based upon the two-process theory of expectancy of Posner and Snyder (1975), can only accommodate the data if we assume that word recognition is so fast with skilled readers that encoding is completed prior to automatic activation having an effect. This would seem to suggest that encoding is unaffected by context, of course, and in a recent discussion Stanovich and West (1982) seem to be suggesting just this. The automatic spread of activation should affect the recognition of *bugs,* in Swinney's experiment, as it occurs directly after

"found several spiders, roaches and other"

If automatic activation does not operate with sentences such as these, then it is difficult to imagine what purpose the process could serve when reading sentences, and yet both meanings of *bugs* were active. One possibility is that Jastrzembski's arguments about cluster isolation are wrong, and that activation of *bugs/insects* spreads to *bugs/microphones*. Some evidence in favor of this notion will be presented in the following section, which deals more directly with the question of automatic processes in word recognition. Whereas this section has focused upon the issue of what the recognition device is, we turn now to the cognitive processes which are applied to the visual pattern to convert it to a form which can access this memory system.

B. The Automatization of Word Recognition

If words are recognized so fast that expectancies do not affect their encoding, and that all meanings of polysemous words are activated, then what evidence do we have of this skilled, automatic word recognition? Swinney (1979) found that two meanings of a polysemous word were accessed, and that a disambiguating context of presentation did not prevent the unrequired meaning being effective. This supports the view expressed by West and Stanovich (1978) that word recognition occurs too quickly for contextual biases to affect encoding. Swinney used a spoken presentation of the passage, however, and so the application of his results to the analysis of reading must be undertaken with caution.

One way to establish the case that words are recognizable automatically would be to first identify the codes used in lexical access, and then demonstrate that the codes can be used without attention. However, the identification of the code has not been straightforward, and so a more direct procedure is appropriate. Such a procedure involves the demonstration of the "reading" of words while attention is not focused upon them. This section introduces evidence of unattended reading by first examining attempts to isolate the lexical access code.

The internal lexicon is a store of word meanings, and the process applied to the visual pattern of a word in order for it to access the store of meanings is the process of coding the print in a form recognizable by the store. There are two main candidates for the code, but neither can be demonstrated to be used exclusively, and it may be reasonable to conclude that both can be used in appropriate circumstances. The problem then becomes one of describing the conditions under which one code will be used in preference to the other. The alternative access codes, which themselves specify processes which must be applied to the print, involve access by phonological mediation and access by a visual code of the word. Coltheart (1978) has described both of these access routes as being available to the flexible reader, and the "dual access" model provides a good fit for the data (see also Coltheart, Davelaar, Jonasson, & Besner, 1977; Meyer *et al.*, 1974).

Evidence giving plausibility to the phonological route has been provided in abundance during the last decade, and has received extensive reviews by Coltheart (1978), McCusker, Hillinger, and Bias (1981) and others. The following description will be accordingly brief. The lexical decision task, used by Rubenstein, Lewis, and Rubenstein (1971) gave an indication of phonological coding, and it is largely as a result of this experiment that current interest prevails. This experiment demonstrated that lexical decisions about nonwords which were homophonic with real words (e.g., *burd*) were slower than decisions about nonhomophonic nonwords (e.g., *sluc*). This difference could occur only if readers were generating a phonological version of the nonwords, and if these codes were accessing the lexicon. The longer response times for the pseudohomophones could result from a spelling check occurring after access had been achieved. The model proposed by Rubenstein *et al.* suggested that access proceeds by first recoding the visual form of the letter-string, and, if a match is made between the phonological code and the phonologically based lexical entry, then a second match is attempted on the basis of orthography. Coltheart *et al.* (1977) rejected these data as evidence of the phonological coding of words, on the basis of an experiment showing no effect of homophony for words. They proposed instead that the pseudohomophone effect gave evidence of the phonological coding of nonwords in the lexical decision task, and that this process could not be assumed to be used when accessing the meanings of words. The dual access model proposes that both access codes are used when lexical decisions are attempted, and that in the case of nonwords a response time "deadline" must be set by the subject. If the deadline gives the opportunity for the slow generation of the phonological code, then evidence of phonological coding will be found. Conservative deadlines may have been responsible for the appearance of the pseudohomophone effect, but it is not only with the setting of the deadline in which flexibility can be indicated. Readers have two access routes available, according to the model, and indeed, the manipulation of materials in the experiment can encourage subjects to select one access strategy or the other. Davelaar, Coltheart, Besner, and Jonasson (1978) have reported the attenuation of a homophone effect with words by the introduction of pseudohomophonic nonwords, and McQuade (1981) has also shown that the proportions of pseudohomophones affect lexical times. When phonological coding leads to a higher probability of a false-positive error, then evidence is reported which indicates a reduced reliance upon that procedure.

The phonological basis of the pseudohomophone effect has been questioned recently (Martin, 1982; Taft, 1982), for when steps are taken to equate the graphemic familiarity of the pseudohomophones and their nonhomophonic controls used in an experiment, then the differences between them are reduced or eliminated. This finding encourages caution in the interpretation of the pseudohomophone effect in particular, and general caution in the interpretation of experiments employing nonwords.

A strong objection to the notion of exclusively phonological access concerns the recognition of words with exceptional pronunciations. Not all words may be pronounced using a generalized set of grapheme–phoneme correspondence (GPC) rules, and if recognition of the meanings of these words depended upon generation of their phonological code, then unique rules must be applied. Baron and Strawson (1976) demonstrated the importance of the generalized GPC rules in a pronunciation task, reporting that regular words were pronounced more easily than irregular words. Words such as *leaf* and *save* can be pronounced according to the GPC rules, and have faster naming times than irregular words such as *deaf* and *have,* which have specialized pronunciations. The regularity effect can be attenuated in appropriate contexts, however, and just as the pseudohomophone effect diminished when phonological coding became disadvantageous, so the regularity effect is diminished when direct visual access becomes easier. Underwood and Bargh (1982) observed an advantage for the naming of regular words presented in isolation, but only for upper-case presentations. Lower-case words have more distinctive word envelopes, and these features facilitate recognition by the direct visual route. Many of the investigations of the regularity effect appear to have used upper-case presentations (e.g. Baron & Strawson, 1976; Glushko, 1979; Parkin, 1982; Stanovich & Bauer, 1979), and in one of the experiments which have reported using lower-case words, Mason (1978) failed to find a difference. Not surprisingly perhaps, pronunciation effects are most apparent with unskilled readers. A regularity effect was found in a naming task with lower case words for 10- to 12-year-old children by Briggs and Underwood (1982), but not with adult readers who were presumably more sensitive to the visual features of words and could recognize them directly. The children in this experiment did not show different effects according to their reading ability, however, in contrast to children of similar age tested by Barron (1978). Using a lexical decision task, rather than a naming task, Barron found evidence of better readers showing more ease with phonological coding. His good readers produced a larger pseudohomophone effect than his poor readers, and the size of this effect correlated well with overall reading speed. [Note that Martin's (1982) and Taft's (1982) investigations of the possible nonphonological basis of the pseudohomophone effect suggests that this result may not be as interesting as it first seems.]

Word naming tasks do not provide the best vehicle for investigations of lexical access, however, for pronunciation latencies must be dependent upon the time taken to assemble the motor program for speech output, which could be a postaccess process. The regularity of pronunciation should be investigated in the absence of pronunciation itself, if the GPC rules are to be seen to be affecting access. When the lexical decision response was used to investigate regularity, Coltheart, Besner, Jonasson, and Davelaar (1979) and Bauer and Stanovich (1980) found no difference between regular and irregular words. Underwood and Bargh (1982) also demonstrated that even with a naming task, regularity effects can be attenuated by the presentation of additional sources of information about the word.

These experiments suggest that phonological encoding is used for access on some occasions, but not on others. The lexical environment of the word will affect the choice of access strategy, as will the availability of other information about the word, and the extent of reading experience of the subjects. When good visual cues are available to the skilled reader, then evidence of phonological processing will not be readily available.

If word recognition is automatic, then we have to accommodate evidence that it can be modified by the demands of the task, and that the strategical manipulation of information will vary according to the experimental situation. The phonological code, in particular, makes an appearance in word naming and in lexical decision task, but is not always in evidence. Young readers, especially skilled young readers, show differences indicative of their use of this code, but adults show such differences only when the encoding conditions do not encourage a reliance upon visual features. Effects of irregularity tend to be reduced with the lexical decision task, in which post-access phonology is eliminated, and the strong evidence of the pseudohom-ophone effect is restricted to the case of processing letter-strings without lexical entries. If coding is flexible, then how can we entertain the notion of automatic processing? Several possibilities occur: operation of one access route may be automatic, and use of the other optional, or operation of both routes may be automatic, with the flexibility showing its effects after access has been achieved. In naming tasks, in particular, generation of the speech output code could lead to a reliance upon a phonological code after access. Postaccess coding of this form will be referred to here as phono-logical recoding, to distinguish it from phonological encoding, which is the use of phonology to gain lexical access. The following examination of the notion of automatic word recognition concludes that recognition of the meanings of words is a process which is automatic, and that generation of the phonological code also occurs without attention.

West and Stanovich (1978) concluded that they had observed automatic word recognition in their skilled readers, because the recognition of incongruous words was not impeded. The Posner and Snyder (1975) two-process view of expectancy considers that the conscious anticipation of a stimulus is generated slowly, and that by the time it is completed, recognition of the stimulus may have been achieved. The automatic activation process is, by contrast, a faster process, and can aid stimulus recognition. The observation of facilitation-without-inhibition, for congruous items, depends upon the automatic process being faster than the conscious process. Whereas data from the West and Stanovich (1978) experiment, and from an experiment which observed the priming effects of one word upon another (Neely, 1977), are all in agreement with the predictions of the two-process model, this is indirect evidence of automatic word recognition. The words to be recognized were those to which the response was to be made, and so were those to gain conscious scrutiny at some point. More direct evidence of the automaticity of processing may be gained by observing the effects of unattended messages.

Lewis (1970) used unattended words in a dichotic listening study to establish the effects of semantically related words upon words heard at the same time and which were to be shadowed. The appearance of an effect of a semantic relationship indicates that the unattended word is processed for meaning. It also indicates that recognition of the meaning is not necessarily accompanied by awareness of that recognition. Subjects do not have to be aware of the unattended words for these effects to occur. Although the experiments reported by Lewis (1970) and others demonstrate an effect of automatic word recognition for **spoken** words (see also Corteen & Wood, 1972; MacKay, 1973; Smith & Groen, 1974; Treisman, Squire, & Green, 1974; Underwood, 1977), they do set a general precedent, and can be shown to extend to the visual modality. Before considering the visual presentation of words, however, two results in particular should be mentioned, as they relate to the general issue of the role of attention in language processing.

The position being presented in this article is that word recognition is a process for which specific condition–action rules can be applied to the calling patterns in the orthography, and that when these rules are learned recognition becomes automatic. In contrast, the comprehension of sentences cannot become automatic because the calling patterns are mostly unique, or, at best infrequent. No condition–action rules can be developed unless the same sentences are encountered regularly. MacKay (1973) and Underwood (1977) reported experiments investigating the role of attention in the integration of the word meanings in spoken sentences. In MacKay's experiment the ambiguity of attended sentences was resolved, by the presentation of unattended words, only when the ambiguity was lexical in nature. After hearing and shadowing a sentence such as "They threw stones towards the bank yesterday," subjects selected alternative meanings. When an unattended word appeared at the same time as the polysemous word *bank,* it served to provide a small but noticeable shift in the interpretation. If the unattended word had been *river* or *money,* subjects would tend to select appropriate sentence meanings. However, if the resolution of ambiguity required the integration of word meanings, then no shift in interpretation was observable. With the sentence "They thought the shooting of the hunters was dreadful," the presentation of the unattended words "sportsmen slain" was ineffective. Individual words in the attended message were affected by unattended words, but the analysis of the deep structure was unaffected. The integration of word meanings is not influenced by the recognition of unattended words, possibly because the deep structure of those words must first be derived, and because this is a process itself which requires attention.

West and Stanovich (1978) demonstrated the facilitatory effect of prior context upon word processing, for the case of visual presentations, and similar effects can be shown with spoken sentences (Marslen-Wilson, 1973; Morton & Long, 1976). In a development of this procedure, I observed the effect of unattended spoken context upon a target word (Underwood, 1977). Subjects shadowed a sentence or a randomly selected set of words, and their shadowing latency to the final word gained a faster response when it was presented as part of a sentence. When random words were used to replace part of the sentence, then the fewer replacements there were, the greater was the shadowing facilitation. On some occasions, words from the beginning of the sentence were replaced with randomly selected words with similar numbers of syllables. This part of the experiment observed an increasing facilitation effect with increasing amounts of shadowed context. The second part of the experiment observed the influence of increasing amounts of unshadowed context. While the subjects shadowed lists of randomly selected words, terminating with the same target word as above, the sentence context was presented to their unattended ears. When the context was just a couple of words immediately prior to the target, a facilitation effect emerged, but increasing the amount of context did not act to increase the amount of facilitation. One interpretation of this result assumes that attention is required for the integration of word meanings in the appreciation of context, and that the failure to find an effect of increasing the amount of context results from attention not being directed to the context. The small, constant, facilitation effect from the unattended context could have resulted from lexical priming by the spreading activation process suggested by Meyer and Schvaneveldt (1971) and Collins and Loftus (1975).

The evidence from studies of spoken language suggests that attention is not required for the recognition of the meanings of individual words, but that it is necessary for the integration of those word meanings when sentences need to be understood. What evidence there is from studies of reading tends to support this view.

In the studies of auditory attention mentioned above, we inferred that lexical processing of the unattended message had occurred, by observing the influence of that message upon the response to the attended message. The same inferential method will be used here. In Bradshaw's (1974) experiment subjects looked at a 120 msec presentation of a polysemous word (e.g., *palm*), and offered an interpretation. Their responses tended to be biased by the presence of a second word in the same presentation. A few degrees to the right of the fixated word was a disambiguating word (e.g., *hand*), and subjects were influenced by this second word even when they could not report its presence. MacKay's (1973) subjects had shown similar effects of lexical ambiguity in his shadowing experiment. The effect of unattended printed words upon fixated stimuli can be observed with a number of response tasks. When subjects name a line drawing of a simple objects, their naming latencies are inhibited by the presence of a semantically associated word printed to the side (Underwood, 1976). The response to a drawing of a cat was slower when the picture was accompanied by the word *cream* than the word *cloud*. Both picture and word were printed on the same card, and shown for 60 msec. Attention was directed to the picture-naming task in this experiment, and the word described as a distractor which was to be ignored. As in Lewis's (1970) shadowing experiment, the naming latency was affected by the meaning of an unattended stimulus presented at the same time.

Similar effects can be demonstrated for the effect of an unattended word upon an attended word, and one such effect will be mentioned here because it concerns the identification of the code used in the lexical access process. Underwood and Thwaites (1982) and Underwood, Rusted, and Thwaites (1983) used a lexical decision task in demonstration of the influence of an unattended word upon an attended word. Both words were presented at the same time, and exposed for 50 msec. The unattended words were forward and backward masked by a visual noise pattern, and subjects reported themselves as being unable to identify the unattended stimuli. As with the previous experiments, the response latency to a word such as *rubbish* was adversely affected by the presence of an associated word such as *waste,* again indicating that the meanings of unattended words are recognized. The interesting feature of these experiments, however, was the effect of words such as *waist,* which sound as if they are related to the attended word. The effect of *waist* upon *rubbish* was indistinguishable from the effect of *waste,* and so it must be concluded that not only had the lexical meaning of the unattended word been accessed, but that its phonological code had also been generated. It is not clear from these experiments whether generation of the phonological code was responsible for lexical access of the unattended word, however, and so the issue of phonological encoding vs recoding is not resolved. What the experiments do indicate is that skilled readers recognize meanings automatically and also phonologically code words automatically.

The phonological coding of a word can aid in the processing of a subsequent word of similar phonology, and this could be taken as evidence of the use of phonological encoding. Hillinger (1980) and Tanenhaus, Flanigan, and Seidenberg (1980) demonstrated an effect of the phonological code of one word upon nonphonological responses to a second word. Hillinger's experiment looked at sequential effects with lexical decision responses, and found that if the word *eight* was followed with the word *mate,* then a faster response was obtained than if the first word had been dissimilar. Tanenhaus *et al.* used a rather more complex procedure to demonstrate an influence of automatic phonological encoding, but as with the Underwood and Thwaites (1982) and Underwood *et al.* (1983) experiments, the phonological code serves as a distraction to the main task. Subjects first saw a priming word such as *rude,* which was attended and presented for 300 msec, and after a delay of 200 msec they saw a colored word such as *food.* The task was to name the color of ink of this second word. As with many of the Stroop experiments, an irrelevant relationship inhibited the color-naming response. The experiment of Tanenhaus *et al.* indicates that the phonological code of the color word had been generated, even though it was not an essential part of the subjects' task.

These effects of irrelevant stimuli indicate that attention is not required for the recognition of the meaning of words or for the generation of the phonological code of words. Perhaps this should not be surprising, given the amount of practice which adult skilled readers have given to the tasks of understanding words and generating a speech code for them. Demonstrations of the failed recognition of the deep structure, of unattended words, are not readily available for us to complete the argument, but one result is appropriate and can be presented as supporting evidence.

In the case of spoken language, MacKay (1973) and Underwood (1977) demonstrated that unattended words are not integrated with the deep structure of the attended sentence and that the deep structure of an unattended message cannot be used to anticipate a subsequently presented word. In a study of speech recoding Kleiman (1975) had subjects shadow lists of digits while making decisions about visually presented words. Their attention was thereby occupied by the shadowing, but not entirely, because they were able to make responses about the graphemic or phonemic similarity of pairs of words, and make judgments about category memberships. The phonemic similarity task was severely impeded by the requirement to shadow at the same time as judging, without involvement of phonological encoding. This conclusion is cautious because the articulatory suppression tasks used by Kleiman and others do not necessarily exclude phonological encoding so much as articulatory recoding. It may be that the first can take place in the absence of the second. However, the interesting result from Kleiman's experiment, from the point of view of this discussion of attention and language processing, concerns a fourth condition, in which "sentence acceptability" judgments were made. In this condition subjects shadowed digits while attempting to judge whether sentences of the form "Pizzas have been eating Jerry" made any sense. The presence of the shadowing task, which is a task requiring attention, had a very considerable effect upon the speed of these judgments. When asked to integrate the meanings of the words in a sentence and derive a deep structure, then the diversion of attention away from the sentence inhibited processing. This is not a direct test of the hypothesis of attention during reading, because studies of the cross-modal division of attention yield slightly different results to within-mode studies, but Kleiman's experiment does give the hypothesis some support.

By investigating the effects of unattended words we have been able to demonstrate that they are encoded automatically, that their meanings interact with the meanings of attended words automatically, and that their phonological codes are generated automatically. When attention is diverted away from language processing, then the integration of word meanings is inhibited. Word recognition is a flexible, strategical process, and the skilled reader can adapt his behavior to accommodate to the sources of information available, but once learned, the automatic processes will also be in evidence whether they are useful to the task or not. In many of the experiments mentioned above, we have observed the effects of automatic processing in tasks in which it is irrelevant to the main task, and occasionally harmful to the main task. Subjects could not inhibit these effects, and the influence of unattended words must be taken as evidence of automatic processing. As part of the summary of the main points of this article, the next section will examine the possible uses of these automatic processes during skilled reading.

IV. A SUMMARY AND SOME IMPLICATIONS

Reading is an information-processing task which changes according to the skills possessed by the reader. There are a number of sources of information available about the printed word, and the developing reader first makes use of many sources while grappling with word decoding. This compensatory stage has been demonstrated by observing the greater use of sentence context in word naming (West & Stanovich, 1978), by observing a greater number of contextually congruent and graphically independent errors during oral reading (Biemiller, 1970; Juel, 1980), and by observing that "typing errors" were more likely to be read as being contextually congruent in developing readers (Allington & Strange, 1977). The compensatory model detailed by Stanovich (1980) proposes that young readers use whatever information they do have available to compensate for their poor word-decoding skills. As word recognition becomes easier, reliance upon contextual information is less evident, and recognition is described as being automatic.

This is not to say that only one source of information is used, however, for as reading becomes a skilled activity, interactions between different sources of information continue to aid recognition. Recognition of word meanings can be shown to be automatic (Bradshaw, 1974; Swinney, 1979; Underwood, 1976), and generation of the phonological code can also occur without attention (Underwood & Thwaites, 1982; Underwood et al., 1983). In addition to these automatic effects of recognizing the meanings of words, a very large number of studies have indicated that the skilled reader is able to place different reliance upon one source of information or another, depending upon the specific manipulation of the experimental procedure. If visual information is degraded, then more use of contextual information will be indicated (e.g., Meyer et al., 1975; Stanovich & West, 1979), and if the visual route to the lexicon is impeded by an impoverished word envelope, then evidence of the phonological route will be apparent (Underwood & Bargh, 1982). For the skilled reader with a number of automatic processing routes available, the manipulations of psychologists require only route changes. With a beginning reader, reliance upon contextual information may be necessary because recognition is so slow, but with a skilled reader we need to manipulate the speed of recognition in order to observe the greater use of other information.

It is not a contradiction to suggest that a skilled reader has automatic yet flexible processes available, because it is not the processes themselves which are flexible, so much as the **use** of them. When words are seen, all available automatic processes will be applied to them because they are calling patterns for specific condition–action rules. Some of these rules concern lexical access and some concern the generation of the phonological code. Once the processes which are determined by the rules have been completed, then the reader can strategically select which output to use according to the demands of the task. It is partly as a consequence of having automatic processes available that reading can be flexible.

As part of the discussion of automatic word recognition in the previous section, experiments were introduced in which unattended words affected fixated words. The article will conclude with a brief exploration of the possibility that unattended words can be of use in fluent reading. The experiments described by Bradshaw (1974) and Underwood and Thwaites (1982) showed an effect upon a fixated word of a second word printed a few degrees of visual angle to the right. Unattended words have a robust effect upon attended words when printed in the part of the visual field which would normally attract the next fixation if the subject had been reading fluently. The question then arises: do words ahead of fixation have an effect upon the processing of the fixated words? If they do, then the effect may be observed upon any of a variety of processes. One possibility is that non-fixated, unattended words affect the comprehension of the fixated material, and a second is that nonfixated words which are associated with fixated words have their effect in the selection of the next eye-fixation location. These possibilities will be examined separately here, but they are by no means mutually exclusive.

Evidence exists to show the effect of the meaning of one word upon the processing of an attended, fixated word. This is our starting point. Bradshaw (1974) demonstrated that the meaning of the attended word could be biased by the meaning of the unattended word. Furthermore, it is possible to show that an unattended word, ahead of fixation as it were, can be integrated with the meaning of prior words to affect the processing of a fixated word. In a modification of the sentence context experiment (e.g., West & Stanovich, 1978) subjects heard an incomplete sentence, and then read out a word presented to fixation (Underwood, Whitfield, & Winfield, 1982). Congruous words gained faster responses than incongruous words, of course, but an interesting effect occurred with the incongruous attended words. An unattended word printed to the right could be either congruous with the sentence, or another incongruous word unrelated to either the sentence or the fixated word. When it was a satisfactory completion, the naming response to the fixated word was impeded, indicating that the relationship between the spoken sentence and the nonfixated word had been appreciated. This indicates that nonfixated words can be integrated with linguistic material presented prior to fixation, but a more startling demonstration of the influence of unattended words upon sentence processing is that reported by Willows and MacKinnon (1973). In this experiment, subjects read alternate lines of a passage, missing out lines of unattended words. The results of a comprehension test, administered at the end of the passage, indicated that the unattended words had affected their understanding of the sentences. It is not clear whether the effect was lexical or deep structural, however. In a subsequent experiment using the same procedure, Willows (1974) observed differences in the effectiveness of the unattended words in good and poor readers (11, 12, and 13 years old). As expected, the unattended words had a greater distracting effect upon the reading times of the poor readers, but it was the good readers who were more affected by the meanings of the unattended words. The better readers were more able to ignore the presence of these words on one measure (speed) but less able to prevent the words affecting their interpretation of the passage, using the comprehension test as a measure. These experiments give plausibility to the hypothesis that nonfixated words affect our understanding of what we are reading.

Using measures of eye-fixation duration, however, Rayner (1978) found little evidence of an appreciation of the meanings of nonfixated words. The amount of time spent fixating a word is not affected by its semantic relationship with a word which previously occupied that part of the visual field. However, when measures of the location of fixations are taken into account, then it is possible to show sensitivity to the meanings of words ahead of fixation. This takes us to the second of the possible effects of nonfixated words.

Even if the meanings of nonfixated words cannot be used to influence the comprehension of what is being read (and there exists evidence to suggest that they can), there is a second way in which these words can be useful during reading. If we do not plan a sequence of eye-fixations across a page in advance of looking at the page, and Rayner (1978) concludes that this does not occur, then the locations of fixations are determined by what we see. There is a problem here, however, for how can we choose what we look at, on the basis of what we see, **until** we have seen it? The circularity can be avoided by the suggestion that nonfixated words attract future eye-fixations, that we move our eyes to parts of the text which preattentive processing has marked as being of relevance to our reading goals. If this is the case, then evidence should exist which suggests that informative parts of texts are fixated more often than less informative parts. Only if we knew that they were informative **before** fixating them, could this pattern emerge. Such evidence does exist. Rayner (1977) reported that the main verb of a sentence received more fixations than other parts of the sentence, and O'Regan (1979) reported that longer saccadic eye movements were produced when the eye was approaching the word *the* than when approaching three-letter verbs. Additionally, the frequency of the verb interacted with this effect, with words such as *had* being missed less often than words such as *ate*. O'Regan suggested that nonfixated information can be used to influence saccade length and the locations of fixations. Kennedy (1978) also demonstrated an effect of lexical knowledge upon the locations of fixations, in an investigation of the effects of the associative frequencies of words. When a strong association existed between two words in a short passage, fixations upon the second word occurred sooner and more often than when it was a weaker associate of the first word. Consistent with Rayner's (1978) summary, Kennedy found no effect upon the duration of the fixation upon the second word in his experiment. Eye-fixation behavior can be modified by words ahead of fixation, and so the hypothesis of fixation–attraction is still available.

Words which do not receive attention do not have their effects upon the lexicon prevented, and the possibility exists that this is more than a demonstration of automatic word recognition, and that nonfixated words can influence comprehension and eye-fixation behavior during fluent reading. Lexical effects can certainly be demonstrated in comprehension, as can effects upon the location of fixations. It seems less likely that nonfixated words can affect the comprehension of the deep structure of a sentence, or affect the duration of an eye-fixation.

ACKNOWLEDGMENTS

Preparation of this article was supported by project grant GR/C/02259 from the Science and Engineering Research Council, and project grant G/8127736N from the Medical Research Council. I am very grateful to Donald E. Broadbent and to Keith E. Stanovich for their extensive comments on an earlier draft.

REFERENCES

Allington, R. L., & Strange, M. Effects of grapheme substitutions in connected text upon reading behaviour. *Visible Language,* 1977, **11,** 285–297.

Allport, D. A. Attention and performance. In G. Claxton (Ed.), *Cognitive psychology: New directions.* London: Routledge & Kegan Paul, 1980.

Baron, J., & Strawson, C. Use of orthographic and word specific knowledge in reading words aloud. *Journal of Experimental Psychology: Human Perception and Performance,* 1976, **2,** 386–393.

Barron, R. W. Reading skill and phonological coding in lexical access. In M. M. Gruneberg, P. E. Morris, & R. N. Sykes (Eds.), *Practical aspects of memory.* New York: Academic Press, 1978.

Bauer, D. W., & Stanovich, K. E. Lexical access and the spelling-to-sound regularity effect. *Memory & Cognition,* 1980, **8,** 424–432.

Becker, C. A. Allocation of attention during visual word recognition. *Journal of Experimental Psychology: Human Perception and Performance,* 1976, **2,** 556–566.

Becker, C. A., & Killion, T. H. Interaction of visual and cognitive effects in word recognition. *Journal of Experimental Psychology: Human Perception and Performance,* 1977, **3,** 389–401.

Biemiller, A. The development of the use of graphic and contextual information as children learn to read. *Reading Research Quarterly,* 1970, **6,** 75–96.

Bradshaw, J. L. Peripherally presented and unreported words may bias the perceived meaning of a centrally fixated homograph. *Journal of Experimental Psychology,* 1974, **103,** 1200–1202.

Briggs, P., Austin, S., & Underwood, G. The effects of sentence context in good and poor readers: A test of Stanovich's interactive-compensatory model. *Reading Research Quarterly,* 1984, in press.

Briggs, P., & Underwood, G. Phonological coding in good and poor readers. *Journal of Experimental Child Psychology,* 1982, **34,** 93–112.

Broadbent, D. E., & Broadbent, M. H. P. General shape and local detail in word perception.

In S. Dornic (Ed.), *Attention and performance* (Vol. 6). Hillsdale, New Jersey: Erlbaum, 1977.

Collins, A. M., & Loftus, E. F. A spreading-activation theory of semantic processing. *Psychological Review,* 1975, **83**, 407–428.

Coltheart, M. Lexical access in simple reading tasks. In: G. Underwood (ed.) *Strategies of Information Processing.* New York: Academic Press, 1978.

Coltheart, M., Besner, D., Jonasson, J. T., & Davelaar, E. Phonological encoding in the lexical decision task. *Quarterly Journal of Experimental Psychology,* 1979, **31**, 489–507.

Coltheart, M., Davelaar, E., Jonasson, J. T., & Besner, D. Access to the internal lexicon. In S. Dornic (Ed.), *Attention and performance* (Vol. 6). Hillsdale, New Jersey: Erlbaum, 1977.

Coltheart, M., & Freeman, R. Case alternation impairs word identification. *Bulletin of the Psychonomic Society,* 1974, **3**, 102–104.

Conrad, C. Context effects in sentence comprehension: A study of the subjective lexicon. *Memory & Cognition,* 1974, **2**, 130–138.

Corteen, R. S., & Wood, B. Autonomic responses to shock associated words in an unattended channel. *Journal of Experimental Psychology,* 1972, **94**, 308–313.

Cosky, M. J. The role of letter recognition in word recognition. *Memory & Cognition,* 1976, **4**, 207–214.

Davelaar, E., Coltheart, M., Besner, D., & Jonasson, J. T. Phonological recoding and lexical access. *Memory & Cognition,* 1978, **6**, 391–402.

Fisher, D. F. Reading and visual search. *Memory & Cognition,* 1975, **3**, 188–196.

Fischler, I., & Bloom, P. A. Automatic and attentional processes in the effects of sentence contexts on word recognition. *Journal of Verbal Learning and Verbal Behaviour,* 1979, **19**, 1–20.

Forster, K. I. Accessing the mental lexicon. In R. J. Wales & E. Walker (Eds.), *New approaches to language mechanisms.* Amsterdam: North Holland Publ., 1976.

Forster, K. T. Priming and the effects of sentence and lexical contexts on naming time: Evidence of autonomous lexical processing. *Quarterly Journal of Experimental Psychology,* 1981, **33A**, 465–495.

Foss, D. J. Some effects of ambiguity upon sentence comprehension. *Journal of Verbal Learning and Verbal Behavior,* 1970, **9**, 699–706.

Foss, D. J., & Jenkins, C. Some effects of context on the comprehension of ambiguous sentences. *Journal of Verbal Learning and Verbal Behavior,* 1973, **12**, 577–589.

Glushko, R. The organization and activation of orthographic knowledge in reading aloud. *Journal of Experimental Psychology: Human Perception and Performance,* 1979, **5**, 674–691.

Golinkoff, R. M., & Rosinski, R. R. Decoding, semantic processing and reading comprehension skill. *Child Development,* 1976, **47**, 252–258.

Gough, P. B., & Cosky, M. J. One second of reading again. In N. J. Castellan, D. B. Pisoni, & G. R. Potts (Eds.), *Cognitive Theory* (Vol. 2). Hillsdale, New Jersey: Erlbaum, 1977.

Guttentag, R. E., & Haith, M. M. A developmental study of automatic word processing in a picture classification task. *Child Development,* 1979, **50**, 894–896.

Hicks, C., & Jackson, P. A study of the relationship between the Stroop effect and reading age in dyslexic subjects. *Journal of Research in Reading,* 1981, **4**, 29–33.

Hillinger, M. L. Priming effects with phonemically similar words: The encoding bias hypothesis reconsidered. *Memory & Cognition,* 1980, **8**, 115–123.

Jastrzembski, J. E. Multiple meanings, number of related meanings, frequency of occurrence, and the lexicon. *Cognitive Psychology,* 1981, **13**, 278–305.

Juel, C. Comparison of word identification strategies with varying context, word type and reader skill. *Reading Research Quarterly,* 1980, **15**, 358–376.

Keele, S. W., & Summers, J. The structure of motor programs. In G. E. Stelmach (Ed.), *Motor control: Issues and trends.* New York: Academic Press, 1976.

Kennedy, R. A. Reading sentences: Some observations on the control of eye movements. In G. Underwood (Ed.), *Strategies of Information Processing.* New York: Academic Press, 1978.

Kleiman, G. M. Speech recoding in reading. *Journal of Verbal Learning and Verbal Behavior,* 1975, **14**, 323–339.

LaBerge, D., & Samuels, S. J. Toward a theory of automatic information processing in reading. *Cognitive Psychology,* 1974, **6**, 293–323.

Lewis, J. L. Semantic processing of unattended messages using dichotic listening. *Journal of Experimental Psychology,* 1970, **85**, 225–228.

MacKay, D. G. Aspects of the theory of comprehension, memory and attention. *Quarterly Journal of Experimental Psychology,* 1973, **25**, 22–40.

MacKay, D. G. Derivational rules and the internal lexicon. *Journal of Verbal Learning and Verbal Behavior,* 1978, **17**, 61–71.

McClelland, J. L. Preliminary letter identification in the perception of words and non-words. *Journal of Experimental Psychology: Human Perception and Performance,* 1976, **2**, 80–91.

McConkie, G. W., & Zola, D. Is visual information integrated across successive fixations? *Perception & Psychophysics,* 1974, **25**, 221–224.

McCusker, L. X., Hillinger, M. L., & Bias, R. G. Phonological recoding and reading. *Psychological Bulletin,* 1981, **89**, 217–245.

McQuade, D. V. Variable reliance on phonological information in visual word recognition. *Language and Speech,* 1981, **24**, 99–109.

Marslen-Wilson, W. D. Linguistic structure and speech shadowing at very short latencies. *Nature,* (London), 1973, **244**, 522–523.

Martin, M. Speech recoding in silent reading. *Memory & Cognition,* 1978, **6**, 108–114.

Martin, R. C. The pseudohomophone effect: The role of visual similarity in non-word decisions. *Quarterly Journal of Experimental Psychology,* 1982, **34A**, 395–409.

Mason, M. From print to sound in mature readers as a function of reader ability and two forms of orthographic regularity. *Memory & Cognition,* 1978, **6**, 568–581.

Massaro, D. W., Jones, R. D., Lipscomb, C., & Scholz, R. Role of prior knowledge on naming and lexical decisions with good and poor stimulus information. *Journal of Experimental Psychology: Human Learning and Memory,* 1978, **4**, 498–512.

Meyer, D. E., & Schvaneveldt, R. W. Facilitation in recognizing pairs of words: Evidence of a dependence between retrieval operations. *Journal of Experimental Psychology,* 1971, **90**, 227–234.

Meyer, D. E., Schvaneveldt, R. W., & Ruddy, M. G. Functions of graphemic and phonemic codes in visual word recognition. *Memory & Cognition,* 1974, **2**, 309–321.

Meyer, D. E., Schvaneveldt, R. W., & Ruddy, M. G. Loci of contextual effects in visual word recognition. In P. M. A. Rabbitt & S. Dornic (Eds.), *Attention and performance* (Vol. 5). New York: Academic Press, 1975.

Mitchell, D. C. *The process of reading.* New York: Wiley, 1982.

Monk, A. F., & Hulme, C. Errors in proof-reading: Evidence for the use of word shape in word recognition. *Memory & Cognition,* 1983, **11**, 16–23.

Morton, J. Interaction of information in word recognition. *Psychological Review,* 1969, **76**, 165–178.

Morton, J. The logogen model and orthographic structure. In U. Frith (Ed.), *Cognitive processes in spelling.* New York: Academic Press, 1980.

Morton, J., & Long, J. Effect of transition probability on phoneme identification. *Journal of Verbal Learning and Verbal Behavior,* 1976, **15**, 43–51.

Murrell, G. A., & Morton, J. Word recognition and morphemic structure. *Journal of Experimental Psychology,* 1974, **102,** 963-968.

Neely, J. H. Semantic priming and retrieval from lexical memory: Roles of inhibitionless spreading activation and limited-capacity attention. *Journal of Experimental Psychology: General,* 1977, **105,** 226-254.

Onifer, W., & Swinney, D. A. Accessing lexical ambiguities during sentence comprehension: Effects of frequency of meaning and contextual bias. *Memory & Cognition,* 1981, **9,** 225-236.

O'Regan, K. Saccade size in reading: Evidence for the linguistic control hypothesis. *Perception & Psychophysics,* 1979, **25,** 501-509.

Parkin, A. J. Phonological recoding in lexical decision: Effects of spelling-to-sound regularity depend upon how regularity is defined. *Memory & Cognition,* 1982, **10,** 43-53.

Petrey, S. Word associations and the development of lexical memory. *Cognition,* 1977, **5,** 57-71.

Posner, M. I., & Snyder, C. R. R. Attention and cognitive control. In R. Solso (Ed.), *Information processing and cognition: The Loyola symposium.* Hillsdale, New Jersey: Erlbaum, 1975.

Rayner, K. Visual attention in reading: Eye movements reflect cognitive processes. *Memory & Cognition,* 1977, **5,** 443-448.

Rayner, K. Eye movements in reading and information processing. *Psychological Bulletin,* 1978, **85,** 618-660.

Reason, J. Actions not as planned: The price of automatization. In G. Underwood & R. Stevens (Eds.), *Aspects of consciousness* (Vol. 1). New York: Academic Press, 1979.

Rosinski, R. R., Golinkoff, R. M., & Kukish, K. Automatic semantic processing in a picture-word interference task. *Child Development,* 1975, **46,** 247-253.

Rubenstein, H., Lewis, S. S., & Rubenstein, M. A. Evidence for phonemic recoding in visual word recognition. *Journal of Verbal Learning and Verbal Behavior,* 1971, **10,** 645-657.

Rumelhart, D. E. Toward an interactive model of reading. In S. Dornic (Ed.), *Attention and performance* (Vol. 6). Hillsdale, New Jersey: Erlbaum, 1977.

Schadler, M., & Thissen, D. M. The development of automatic word recognition and reading skill. *Memory & Cognition,* 1981, **9,** 132-141.

Schiller, P. H. Developmental study of color-word interference. *Journal of Experimental Psychology,* 1966, **72,** 105-108.

Sharkey, N. Unpublished manuscript, University of Exeter. (Cited in Mitchell, 1982.)

Smith, F. Familiarity of configuration *versus* discriminability of features in the visual identification of words. *Psychonomic Science,* 1969, **14,** 261-262.

Smith, F., Lott, D., & Cronnell, B. The effect of type size and case alternation on word identification. *American Journal of Psychology,* 1969, **82,** 248-253.

Smith, M. C., & Groen, M. Evidence for semantic analysis of unattended verbal items. *Journal of Experimental Psychology,* 1974, **102,** 595-603.

Stanovich, K. E. Toward an interactive–compensatory model of individual differences in the development of reading fluency. *Reading Research Quarterly,* 1980, **16,** 32-71.

Stanovich, K. E., & Bauer, D. W. Experiments on the spelling to sound regularity effect in word recognition. *Memory & Cognition,* 1979, **6,** 410-415.

Stanovich, K. E., Cunningham, A. E., & West, R. F. A longitudinal study of the development of automatic recognition skills in first graders. *Journal of Reading Behavior,* 1981, **13,** 57-74.

Stanovich, K. E., & West, R. F. Mechanisms of sentence context effects in reading: Automatic activation and conscious attention. *Memory & Cognition,* 1979, **7,** 77-85.

Stanovich, K. E., & West, R. F. The effect of sentence context on ongoing word recognition:

Tests of a two-process theory. *Journal of Experimental Psychology: Human Perception and Performance,* 1981, **7**, 658–672.

Stanovich, K. E., & West, R. F. On priming by a sentence context. *Journal of Experimental Psychology: General,* 1983, **112**, 1–35.

Swinney, D. A. Lexical access during sentence comprehension: (Re)consideration of sentence effects. *Journal of Verbal Learning and Verbal Behavior,* 1979, **18**, 645–659.

Swinney, D., & Hakes, D. Effects of prior context upon lexical access during sentence comprehension. *Journal of Verbal Learning and Verbal Behavior,* 1976, **15**, 681–689.

Taft, M. An alternative to grapheme-phoneme conversion rules? *Memory & Cognition,* 1982, **10**, 465–474.

Taft, M., & Forster, K. I. Lexical storage and retrieval of prefixed words. *Journal of Verbal Learning and Verbal Behavior,* 1975, **14**, 638–647.

Tanenhaus, M. K., Flanigan, H. P., & Seidenberg, M. S. Orthographic and phonological activation in auditory and visual word recognition. *Memory & Cognition,* 1980, **8**, 513–520.

Tanenhaus, M. K., Leiman, J. M., & Seidenberg, M. S. Evidence for multiple stages in the processing of ambiguous on syntactic contexts. *Journal of Verbal Learning and Verbal Behavior,* 1979, **18**, 427–440.

Thompson, M. C., & Massaro, D. W. The role of visual information and redundancy in reading. *Journal of Experimental Psychology,* 1973, **98**, 49–54.

Treisman, A. M. Contextual cues in selective listening. *Quarterly Journal of Experimental Psychology,* 1960, **12**, 242–248.

Treisman, A., Squire, R., & Green, J. Semantic processing in dichotic listening?: A replication. *Memory & Cognition,* 1974, **2**, 641–646.

Tulving, E. Episodic and semantic memory. In E. Tulving, E. & W. Donaldson (Eds.), *Organization of memory.* New York: Academic Press, 1972.

Tulving, E., & Gold, C. Stimulus information and contextual information as determinants of tachistoscopic recognition of words. *Journal of Experimental Psychology,* 1963, **66**, 319–327.

Underwood, G. Semantic interference from unattended printed words. *British Journal of Psychology,* 1976, **67**, 327–338.

Underwood, G. Contextual facilitation from attended and unattended messages. *Journal of Verbal Learning and Verbal Behavior,* 1977, **16**, 99–106.

Underwood, G. Attentional selectivity and behavioural control. In G. Underwood (Ed.), *Strategies of information processing.* New York: Academic Press, 1978.

Underwood, G. Attention and the nonselective lexical access of ambiguous words. *Canadian Journal of Psychology,* 1980, **34**, 72–76.

Underwood, G. Attention and awareness in cognitive and motor skills. In G. Underwood (Ed.), *Aspects of consciousness* (Vol. 3). New York: Academic Press, 1982.

Underwood, G., & Bargh, K. Word shape, orthographic regularity, and contextual interactions in a reading task. *Cognition,* 1982, **12**, 197–209.

Underwood, G., and Briggs, P. The development of word recognition processes. *British Journal of Psychology,* 1984, **75**, 243–255.

Underwood, G., Parry, R. S., & Bull, L. A. Simple reading tasks are affected by unattended context. In M. M. Gruneberg, P. E. Morris, & R. N. Sykes (Eds.), *Practical aspects of memory.* New York: Academic Press, 1978.

Underwood, G., Rusted, J., & Thwaites, S. Parafoveal words are effective in both hemifields: Preattentive processing of semantic and phonological codes. *Perception,* 1983, **12**, 213–221.

Underwood, G., & Thwaites, S. Automatic phonological coding of unattended printed words. *Memory & Cognition,* 1982, **10**, 434–442.

Underwood, G., Whitfield, A., & Winfield, J. Effects of contextual constraints and non-fixated words in a simple reading task. *Journal of Research in Reading,* 1982, **5,** 89–100.

West, R. F., & Stanovich, K. F. Automatic contextual facilitation in readers of three ages. *Child Development,* 1978, **49,** 717–727.

Willows, D. M. Reading between the lines: Selective attention in good and poor readers. *Child Development,* 1974, **45,** 408–415.

Willows, D. M., & MacKinnon, G. E. Selective reading: Attention to the "unattended" lines. *Canadian Journal of Psychology,* 1973, **27,** 292–304.

RAPID READING PROCESSES
AND SKILLS

MICHAEL E. J. MASSON

Department of Psychology
University of Victoria
Victoria, British Columbia, Canada

I. OVERVIEW

The general domain of rapid reading of text is explored in this article, with an emphasis on the issues of how reading processes change as reading rate increases and on the nature of the trade-off between reading speed and quality of comprehension. The ability to double or triple one's reading rate highlights the degree of flexibility in the reading process and it is important to know under which conditions or for which sets of goals a reader is willing

183

to adopt various types of rapid reading strategies. In addition, there are a number of practical issues associated with rapid reading: the utility of various mechanical and natural methods of increasing reading speed and the extent to which limitations of the human information processing system constrain potential rapid reading skills.

The organization of the article is as follows. I begin with a consideration of the normal reading process and have adopted the view that reading is best considered as a set of interactive processes or subskills. Next, differences between naturally fast and slow readers are examined and related to possible consequences of speeding up the reading process. In addition, research related to improvement of various reading subskills as a means of achieving faster reading rates is reviewed. The remainder of the article is devoted to a discussion of the relatively recent empirical and theoretical work on methods of rapid reading. Three specific methods are considered: skimming, rapid sequential visual presentation (successive, brief presentation of individual words of a text), and speed reading. Theory-based research on these forms of speeded reading has not enjoyed a very long history, but recent efforts have proven to be very promising. Advances include the development of an artificial intelligence program for skimming newspaper stories, analyses of eye movements during skimming and speed reading, and rather detailed assessment of text comprehension and memory associated with all three methods of rapid reading.

II. READING AS AN INTERACTIVE PROCESS

One of the fundamental conclusions that can be drawn from much of cognitive research on reading is that the process of reading should be characterized as an interaction between visually processed print and activation of existing knowledge. In fact, the use of general knowledge in speeded reading tasks is critically important, and so it is necessary to understand how knowledge is used during reading if we are to come to grips with the issue of rapid reading comprehension. In this section of the article I consider the influence of general world knowledge on comprehension and discuss how a number of reading models account for this influence.

A. Conceptually and Data Driven Processes

Interpretation of graphemic information during reading appears to depend not only on the quality of visual data extracted from the page, but also on expectations and knowledge about what is being read. Bobrow and Norman (1975) have termed these two types of process *data driven* and *conceptually driven,* respectively. Data driven processes are affected by the quality of viewing conditions and primarily are responsible for coding printed information in the visual system, while conceptually driven processes are involved in the recognition and interpretation of the words and concepts expressed in a printed message. In addition, there is ample evidence to suggest that recognition of words, syntactic structures, and even ideas is made more efficient when a reader is able to use existing knowledge to aid the recognition process (Rumelhart, 1977). Consequently, reading has been conceptualized as a set of subskills that *interact* with one another to produce comprehension.

One example of the facilitation of comprehension through conceptually driven processes that is particularly relevant to rapid reading was provided by Marcel (1974). He found that increasing contextual constraint on sentences by using successive approximations to English produced larger effective visual fields during reading. Increased contextual constraint permitted reduced sampling of visual information for word recognition, thereby allowing more capacity for processing information in the periphery. As a second example, we can take Ehrlich and Rayner's (1981) demonstration that fixation durations and detection of spelling errors associated with highly predictable words were much lower than for less predictable words.

Since conceptually driven processes appear to increase the efficiency of reading, one might predict that fluent readers make more use of such processes than less skilled readers and that this difference would help to account for reading skill differences. It has been shown, however, that this is not necessarily the case. Using context to aid word recognition, for example, appears to be common among less skilled as well as fluent readers (Perfetti, Goldman, & Hogaboam, 1979; West & Stanovich, 1978). This fact has led to an interesting interpretation of the possible uses to which conceptually driven processes may be put during reading. Stanovich (1981) and Perfetti and Roth (1981) have suggested that the use of context among less skilled readers might be a compensatory strategy for slow word recognition processes.

Conceptually driven processes also play a role in the comprehension of ideas or propositions during reading. The topic or title of a passage provides information about the general knowledge the reader should use in comprehending the passage. In fact, if the reader has difficulty determining the passage's topic, comprehension difficulties will occur and will be manifest by long reading times and inaccurate identification of the main idea of the passage (Kieras, 1978, 1981). In extreme cases comprehension may break down completely if the reader is unable to determine how the passage content relates to knowledge he or she already possesses (Bransford & McCarrell, 1974). Evidence for a more subtle influence of a passage's title was

obtained by Kozminsky (1977) who found that the set of propositions recalled after reading a passage was strongly affected by changes in the passage's title. Comprehension and encoding operations seemed to be focused
on propositions that were relevant to the passage's title and, probably, to
the associated general knowledge invoked by the reader during comprehension.

Conceptually driven processes may also be involved in generating expectations about upcoming topics or events in a passage (Meijsing, 1980). These
expectations may facilitate comprehension and would consequently contribute to reading speed. Furthermore, readers are able to use their general
knowledge to make inferences that help maintain the coherence of the text
by establishing relationships between explicitly stated propositions (Kintsch
& van Dijk, 1978; Lesgold, Roth, & Curtis, 1979). Plausible inferences may
also be drawn which elaborate on the ideas explicitly stated in a text and
which are consistent with knowledge relevant to the text topic (Reder, 1979).
It is argued below that these types of inferential processes are crucial to the
success of many types of rapid reading.

B. Models of Reading

A number of models of normal reading processes have been developed
which incorporate some of the attributes of interactive processing discussed
above. Two general classes of models will be considered here, each of which
makes important contributions to current understanding of rapid reading
processes. The first class of reading models has been developed to account
for comprehension and recall of text. One of the most detailed models has
been developed by Kintsch and his colleagues (Kintsch & van Dijk, 1978;
Kintsch & Vipond, 1979; Miller & Kintsch, 1980). In this model it is assumed
that a group of propositions from a text are coded in working memory and
added to a hierarchically organized text base in long-term memory. Important propositions (primarily those which share arguments with a number
of succeeding propositions) occupy the higher levels. One group of propositions is processed in a single cycle, then the next few propositions in the
text are coded into working memory. In order to maintain coherence a small
number of important propositions from the previous cycle will be held over
in working memory for use in the current cycle. These propositions often
form the basis for the development of the macrostructure or gist representation of the passage, are highly likely to be included in a passage summary,
and are well recalled.

Additional evidence supporting the model has been provided by experiments on reading time. Cirilo and Foss (1980) showed that sentences representing high level text information took longer to read than lower level

sentences, partly because of the greater density of new information (recall that high level propositions often contain the first mention of particular arguments or concepts). This result supports Kintsch's model as well as the notion that expected information can more quickly be incorporated into the comprehension process. In further support of this latter idea, Cirilo and Foss found consistently shorter reading times for sentences occurring later in passages.

A second class of reading models has emphasized patterns of eye movements during reading. Under normal reading conditions readers move their eyes in a series of saccades punctuated by fixations that last an average of 250 msec (Rayner, 1978). There is ample evidence that eye movement patterns, especially duration of fixations, are indicative of concurrent comprehension processes. Carpenter and Just (1977a, b) and Shebilske, Reid, and Wright (1977) have demonstrated that fixations are longer in duration at those points when subjects are performing particularly complex mental operations such as inference making. More recently, Carpenter and Daneman (1981) have shown that words that disambiguate the interpretation of previous words receive particularly long fixation durations. In fact, Just and Carpenter (1980; Thibadeau, Just, & Carpenter, 1982) have developed a detailed comprehension model to account for patterns of gaze durations (total time spent on a word, collapsed across consecutive fixations on that word) during reading. They assumed that a significant amount of the processing carried out on a word occurs while it is fixated, and were able to account for gaze durations using a model based on this assumption. In accordance with the model extra processing time was associated with difficult (e.g., unfamiliar) words, with segments of text that required integration of important clauses, and with inference making at the ends of sentences.

Aspects of both classes of models will be used in a number of ways to help interpret the results of empirical work on rapid reading that will be reviewed below. In addition, it is possible to use the models to predict what should happen to reading processes when they are speeded. In turn, attempting to use these reading models to account for the results of rapid reading experiments provides a strong test of the validity and extensibility of the models.

III. SPEEDING UP THE READING PROCESS

There are a number of different components of reading comprehension that are likely to be affected when a reader increases his or her text processing speed. Two different methods of identifying these components will be explored in this section. One method simply involves asking questions about subskill differences between naturally fast and slow readers. The second method consists of an examination of research on programs aimed at improving the reading speed of normal readers. These sources of converging evidence yield some tentative conclusions concerning limitations of reading speed which will be evaluated in the remaining parts of the article when theory-based research on rapid reading comprehension is considered.

A. Characteristics of Naturally Fast Readers

It is clear that there are wide individual differences among readers with respect to preferred reading speed and it is equally clear that free reading rate is not consistently correlated with comprehension performance (e.g., Gibson & Levin, 1975). This implies that different readers operate at different points on some sort of speed-accuracy trade-off curve, and that this curve is different for different individuals. That is, two readers operating at a particular rate of speed may differ widely in degree of comprehension of the passage in question. A hypothetical and highly oversimplified example of this situation is shown in Fig. 1 in the form of speed-accuracy trade-off curves for two readers of different ability. Reader A is the better reader and attains much higher comprehension than Reader B when they both operate at 350 words/minute. Reader B must slow to about 200 words/minute to reach Reader A's 350-word/minute level of comprehension. Four components of the reading process that may contribute to speed-accuracy trade-off curve differences among readers will be considered here.

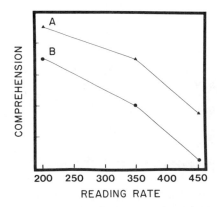

Fig. 1. Hypothetical speed-accuracy trade-off curves for a fast comprehender (A) and a slow comprehender (B).

1. Visual Span of Perception

Rayner and McConkie (1977) have carried out a careful study of eye movements during reading and have mapped the effective span of perception. On the average, readers are able to extract enough visual information from words within 12 characters to the right and four to the left of fixation to produce a semantic interpretation of the words. Information about word shape and extreme letters up to about 18 characters to the right of fixation is used to guide eye movements. Therefore, the average reader is able to determine the meaning of about two words at each fixation. There are, however, differences among readers with respect to their perceptual spans and it has been known for some time that size of perceptual span is directly related to reading speed (Buswell, 1957; Gilbert, 1959).

More recently, Jackson and McClelland (1975) identified fast and slow readers and tested them on a variety of tasks including perceptual span. Reading speed groups were determined by combining reading rate and performance on a comprehension test so that fast readers could be characterized as reading relatively quickly while maintaining good comprehension. They found that fast readers were able to report more words from a briefly presented sentence followed by a mask than slower readers. A similar result was obtained when strings of unrelated consonants were used, implying that fast readers might have a generally larger perceptual span. If this were true, then fast readers would be able to make fewer fixations while reading since they should be able to interpret more information at each fixation, thereby reducing the time required to read a passage.

2. Speed of Access to Memory Codes

A second advantage enjoyed by fast readers appears to be speed of accessing memory codes represented in long-term memory (e.g., Hunt, Lunneborg, & Lewis, 1975). This advantage has a number of important implications. First, it offers a nonperceptual explanation for the relationship between perceptual span and reading speed. Jackson and McClelland (1979) pointed out that report of information from briefly available visual displays is critically dependent on speed of identification of the elements in the displays. Thus, faster readers may have larger perceptual spans because they can identify visual patterns more quickly than slower readers, enabling them to report more information before the sensory representation of the display has badly deteriorated. Second, faster access to overlearned memory codes for letters or words should enable the reader to execute various sentence comprehension operations more efficiently by ensuring that appropriate long-term memory information is activated when needed (cf. Perfetti & Lesgold, 1977).

It could be argued, however, that differences between fast and slow readers on speed of accessing letter codes are a by-product of reading skill differences rather than a contributing cause. For example, fast readers might read more and consequently might have more practice at accessing memory codes for letters and words than would slower readers. This argument does not appear credible in light of results reported by Jackson (1980). As in his earlier work, Jackson identified groups of fast and slow readers. In addition, he developed two sets of novel characters which are shown in Fig. 2.

Using one set of the characters subjects performed a physical matching task in which a pair of items was shown and subjects responded as rapidly as possible in deciding whether the two items were physically identical. Using the other set of characters subjects learned to associate a novel three-letter name with each of two characters. Then subjects were shown pairs of these characters and were to indicate as rapidly as possible whether or not the two items had the same name. Physically different characters were used on all trials, but on positive trials two items with the same name were used.

If faster readers have a natural advantage over slow readers with respect to accessing memory codes associated with visual patterns, they should be faster in responding on the name matching task. Moreover, if this advantage has nothing to do with perceptual factors in terms of visual coding of features, the two types of readers should not differ in speed of performance of the physical matching task. The speed and accuracy data obtained by Jackson are shown in Table I, and it can be seen that these expectations were confirmed, even over two sessions of the name matching task. These results suggest that fast readers generally are able to access memory codes associated with visual patterns more rapidly than slow readers and that this

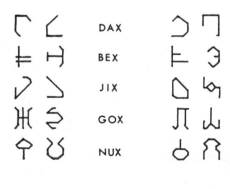

1   2

Fig. 2. Two sets of novel characters and names used in character matching tasks. From Jackson (1980).

TABLE I

Mean Reaction Times (msec) and Accuracy (d') for Skilled and Less Skilled Readers
for the Character Matching Tasks[a]

Matching task	Skilled		Less Skilled	
	M	SD	M	SD
Physical				
Reaction time	404	41.2	406	29.6
Accuracy	1.95	.30	2.05	.47
Name				
Session 1				
Reaction time	1023	122.6	1134	216.1
Accuracy	1.74	1.01	2.13	.86
Session 2				
Reaction time	835	72.3	925	76.2
Accuracy	2.18	.96	2.23	.80

[a]From Jackson (1980).

difference is not due to different amounts of practice with specific material.
It is very likely, therefore, that speed of accessing memory codes is a causal
factor in reading speed differences.

Posner and McLeod (1982, p. 503), however, have recently pointed out
a result that is not immediately accommodated by this conclusion. In a
study by Hunt, Davidson, and Lansman (1981) readers of varying skill were
tested on a number of speeded memory access tasks. They found that although speed of memory access was correlated with scores on the timed
Nelson–Denny reading comprehension test, it was not correlated with the
reading speed measure obtained using that test. The most plausible explanation of this pattern of results emphasizes the manner in which the "reading speed" scores were calculated. In the Nelson–Denny test such scores
are determined by having subjects mark their location in the passage they
are reading after the first minute of working on the comprehension test. In
addition to potential reliability problems (reading rate rarely correlated with
anything in the whole experiment), it is clear that this measure of reading
takes into account only one of the two dimensions of a reader's speed-
accuracy trade-off curve for reading comprehension. That is, it is quite possible that a less skilled reader may have been reading relatively quickly and
not comprehending very well. Only the reading comprehension test takes
steps to account for such cases. The fact that correlations between free reading speed and comprehension are not strong or consistent suggests that the
number of cases of this type may be rather high. Consequently, the reader
may be moving his or her eyes rapidly but may not be *comprehending* rapidly.

3. Working Memory

Included in a number of models of reading is the assumption that working memory plays an important role in integrating text information during reading (e.g., Just & Carpenter, 1980; Kintsch & van Dijk, 1978; Lesgold & Perfetti, 1978). Given this assumption, we might expect that efficiency of processing information in working memory would be related to reading skill and, in particular, the speed with which text can be read while maintaining comprehension. But experiments using memory span tests to assess the storage capacity of working memory have not shown any strong relationship between capacity and reading skill (Hunt, Frost, & Lunneborg, 1973; Perfetti & Goldman, 1976).

A more recent approach has been to assess other characteristics of working memory and their relationships to reading skill. Daneman and Carpenter (1980) focused on the role of working memory in the storage *and processing* of text. Arguing that working memory is responsible for more than storage of text information, they claimed that a reader's ability to perform operations on information in working memory and to coordinate these operations with the storage function should be related to reading skill. This is because a reader must be able to maintain propositions in working memory while new information is read in from the next segment of text. In Kintsch and van Dijk's model, for example, it is claimed that readers hold over in working memory a few propositions from the previous processing cycle so that newly encountered propositions can be integrated in a coherent fashion with what has already been comprehended. This process is central to Kintsch and van Dijk's theory of how coherence is maintained during text comprehension, and skill at executing this process should be closely related to efficiency of reading comprehension.

The trade-off between maintaining information in working memory and encoding new text information was assessed in Daneman and Carpenter's study by using what they have called a *reading span* test. The test required both comprehension of sentences and concurrent maintenance of information in working memory. Subjects read a set of unrelated sentences then reported the last word of each sentence. On successive trials of the test, the number of sentences was incremented and reading span was defined as the maximum number of sentences the subject could read while still being able to recall all sentence ending words. Their subjects' reading spans ranged from two to five and this measure was positively correlated with scores on the Verbal Scholastic Achievement Test (VSAT), accuracy in answering factual questions from a passage, and ability to determine the source of pronominal references. The latter correlation was an impressive .90! Moreover, a word span test included as a measure of the storage function of working memory did not significantly correlate with any of the reading skill measures.

These results indicate that coordination of storage and processing functions of working memory are significantly related to reading skill, and that these functions may play a very important role in comprehension. With respect to rapid reading in particular, VSAT scores are based partly on timed reading comprehension tests. Furthermore, in a recent replication and extension of Daneman and Carpenter's study it has been shown that the reading span test correlates reliably with performance on the speeded comprehension subtest of the Nelson–Denny reading ability test (Masson & Miller, 1983). Consequently, we can conclude that fast and accurate readers are especially efficient at coordinating the storage and process functions of working memory.

4. General Language Comprehension Ability

Aside from the requirements of recognizing visual symbols and coding their interpretations in working memory, reading comprehension depends on the efficient operation of language and "idea understanding" skills. These skills should be common to other language comprehension tasks such as listening. In fact, there is recent evidence that some general language manipulation skills are important for both listening and reading. Jackson (1980) and Jackson and McClelland (1979) have shown that comprehension of orally presented passages is significantly related to reading comprehension and efficiency (reading speed times comprehension score). This common variance is not related to speed of access to memory codes from visual patterns since the listening comprehension test was not correlated with memory access speed. In addition, Daneman and Carpenter (1980) developed a listening span test (an auditory analog of their reading span test) and found that it was strongly correlated with reading and listening comprehension measures.

A number of studies have obtained data that suggest possible types of language processing skill that might be involved in accurate rapid reading. Aaronson and Scarborough (1977) had subjects read sentences that were presented word by word. The subjects initiated presentation of successive words by pressing a button, and time between button presses was taken as a measure of processing time spent on each word. To account for these reading times Aaronson and Scarborough developed a model that included components corresponding to reading time for individual words, time required for organization of words in the current phrase when a phrase boundary is encountered, and time for integrating the current phrase with all preceding words in the sentence. Reading time profiles across words in a sentence were characterized by peaks or particularly long reading times that often corresponded to words that occurred at phrase boundaries.

The model was used to account for peak reading times in the following way. Peak reading times were linearly related to number of words in the currect phrase (i.e., the organization process) and to number of words in preceding phrases (i.e., the integration process), increasing with number of words in both cases. These linear functions produced two sets of slope and intercept parameters, one for organization and one for integration, in which slopes represented rate of execution of these processes and intercepts represented individual word reading and motor response time. Of particular interest here was the comparison of the organization and integration parameters for fast and slow readers. First, slow readers had larger intercepts, indicating that individual word reading time and motor response time is longer for slower readers. [Jackson and McClelland's (1979) results suggest that the difference primarily is associated with recognition of individual words rather than motor response speed.] More important was the finding that the slope of the function for organization processes (relating peak reading time to number of words in the current phrase) was much steeper for slow (84.3 msec/word) than for fast (30.5 msec/word) readers. This suggests that slow readers required more time to organize words into a phrase unit. The slopes for the function relating peak reading times and number of words in preceding phrases, however, were the same for the two types of readers (17.5 msec/word). Thus, slower readers seem to have difficulty organizing words into a coherent phrase unit, but do not seem to have problems with higher order integration processes.

A similar result was obtained by Graesser, Hoffman, and Clark (1980) working with a slightly different empirical paradigm and modeling approach. They had subjects read complete stories in a sentence by sentence fashion, pressing a button to see successive sentences. Reading times for whole sentences were recorded and submitted to multiple regression analyses. Among the predictor variables they selected were six that are of interest here. Three were classified as related to microstructure processing (cf. Kintsch & van Dijk, 1978), which generally corresponds to subprocesses executed within individual sentences. The other three were classified as macrostructure processing variables, which are responsible for interrelating sentences and organizing the passage as a whole. The microstructure variables were number of words in the sentence, syntactic complexity of the sentence, and the number of propositions in the sentence. Macrostructure variables were the number of new nouns (concepts) introduced by the sentence (i.e., these new concepts were not mentioned in any previous sentence in the passage), familiarity with the topic of the passage in which the sentence occurred, and the degree to which the passage could be classified as narrative in style.

Reading times for each sentence of the 12 passages used were submitted to a multiple regression analysis and it was found that macrostructure variables accounted for most of the reading time variability but that significant contributions were also made by the microstructure variables. In addition, Graesser *et al.* divided their subjects into two groups according to reading speed. For each subject they determined the slope of the best fitting regression line relating reading time to each of the six variables of interest. The mean slopes for the fast and slow readers on each of the six variables were compared. As in Aaronson and Scarborough's (1977) study, steep slopes indicated longer reading time and, therefore, difficulty handling the type of processing associated with the variable. The fast and slow subjects of Graesser *et al.* did not differ with respect to the slopes for any of the three macrostructure variables, but the slow readers had significantly steeper slopes for all three of the microstructure variables. Graesser *et al.* concluded, like Aarsonson and Scarborough, that slower readers took longer to execute microstructure analyses, but were as adept as faster readers at performing macrostructure operations that integrated information from different sentences.

A rather different conclusion was reached by Vipond (1980), however, in his work with readers of varying levels of skill. Unlike the two studies described above, Vipond defined his groups of readers not simply on the basis of speed, but on the basis of a combination of speed and comprehension accuracy. Given the earlier discussion of the importance of considering the differences between readers' speed-accuracy trade-off curves, Vipond's results carry heavy weight relative to cases that consider only reading speed. Vipond identified a set of microprocessing and macroprocessing variables, the former associated with propositions explicitly stated in a passage and the latter associated with integration of information across propositions and sentences. He used these as predictor variables in multiple regression analyses where the dependent variable was based on average time taken to read a passage (when presented one paragraph at a time) divided by the average amount of the passage that was later recalled by the subjects. This measure of comprehension efficiency takes into account both reading speed and the degree to which subjects were able to comprehend and encode into memory the passage's content. Two forms of comprehension efficiency were used, one based on microcomprehension (recall scored for reproduction of explicitly stated propositions) and one based on macrocomprehension (recall scored for accurate reconstructions or inferences as well as reproduction of the original propositions).

Regression analyses were carried out separately for the two types of comprehension efficiency (micro and macro) and the two groups of readers (low and high ability according to the Davis Reading Test, a timed reading comprehension test). In each of these four cases, one regression analysis was done by entering the microcomprehension variables first and one was done by entering the macrocomprehension variables first. The percentages of variance accounted for by the two types of variables in each of the eight regression analyses are shown in Table II. It is clear that in all versions low ability readers' comprehension efficiency primarily was determined by microprocessing variables, which is quite consistent with Aaronson and Scarborough and Graesser *et al.* On the other hand, high ability readers were much more sensitive to macroprocessing variables than low ability readers.

Thus, when both reading speed and comprehension are used to define reading ability (i.e., reading speed measures are constrained by the requirement of accurate comprehension) and when comprehension efficiency (not just viewing time) is measured, a different set of conclusions about differences between fast and slow readers emerges. Specifically, it appears that slower comprehenders focus their processing at the microprocessing level (a result found in all three studies), and that readers who can comprehend at higher speeds focus their processing at the macrostructure level. This conclusion is consistent with Stanovich's (1981) observation that skilled and less skilled readers can be distinguished on the basis of general comprehension strategies.

B. Improvement of Reading Subskills

Four characteristics that distinguish fast and slow comprehenders have been discussed at length, and I will now turn to a consideration of what might be done to improve the performance of less efficient readers. First,

TABLE II
Summary of Multiple Regressions for Low and High Ability Readers[a,b]

Amount of variance explained (R^2) by	Microvariables first, macrovariables second dependent measure		Macrovariables first, microvariables second dependent measure	
	Microcomp.	Macrocomp.	Microcomp.	Macrocomp.
Low-ability readers				
First set	42%	41	0	18
Second set	0	27	42	42
(Total)	(42)	(68)	(42)	(60)
High-ability readers				
First set	0	19	35	49
Second set	35	59	16	23
(Total)	(35)	(78)	(51)	(72)

[a]Vipond (1980).

[b]A variable enters the equation only if its regression coefficient is statistically significant.

it is reasonable to conclude that differences in perceptual span are closely related to differences in speed of access to memory codes from visual symbols. Large perceptual spans and rapid memory access are both associated with fast comprehenders, and ability to report large amounts of information from a briefly exposed visual array depends on rapid identification of the elements in the array. Under the assumptions that these two factors are interdependent and that they may be related to stable physiological differences (cf. Jackson & McClelland, 1979), it would be predicted that attempts to increase perceptual span or speed of memory access should be of little value.

Indeed, Jackson (1980) has shown that differences in memory access speed are not due to practice and that such differences appear even when newly learned codes are tested. It should not be surprising, then, to find that studies attempting to improve reading speed by increasing perceptual span have met with very little success. Although subjects seem to be willing to increase their reading speed after practice at extracting information from peripheral vision, comprehension suffers accordingly (Brim, 1968; Sailor & Ball, 1975). It is as if subjects were simply shifting along their speed-accuracy trade-off curves, rather than actually changing the curves.

The other characteristics associated with fast readers may be more susceptible to practice effects. Efficiency at processing text in working memory and focusing attention at the level of macroprocessing rather than microprocessing might both be skills that can be improved through training. Unfortunately, very little is known concerning how to go about teaching these skills. One can see early attempts in the context of work with children who have difficulty learning to read. Some researchers in this area recently have turned to the concept of metacognition and children's ability to monitor their comprehension processes (e.g., Brown, 1980). In the context of adult readers, it might be expected that comprehension efficiency could be improved through training that emphasized reading goals and styles. For example, Rothkopf and Fisher (1981) have found wide individual differences in the extent to which readers are willing to alter their reading styles when presented with different goals (e.g., read for full comprehension, read to find the answer to a predesignated question). Some readers do not speed up even in cases where comprehension of only a very small part of a passage is required. It is as if these readers were locked into a particular mode of reading that depends on very careful analysis of all aspects of a passage. Many reading goals do not require such a careful analysis and it might be possible to train readers to be more flexible in their comprehension strategies. Programs such as speed reading courses attempt to do just that and we will examine the nature of the changes such courses seem to induce later in this article (Section VI). To get a better idea of how important flexible comprehension strategies are likely to be for rapid reading, however, we need to consider the range of possible consequences of increasing the rate at which a reader processes text.

C. What Happens When Reading Rate Increases?

When readers try to comprehend text at rates that extend beyond those used when reading for full comprehension, a number of characteristics of the reading process may change and the particular set of changes that is implemented can drastically affect the quality of comprehension. Three facets of reading that are likely to be affected by increased rate will be considered here.

1. Limitations on Eye Movements

Reviewing the constraints on patterns of eye movements and fixations that are in effect during reading will help establish general boundary conditions on reading speed and gross number of words that can enter the system per unit time. First, there are physical limits on how fast the eyes can execute a series of controlled (accurately placed) fixations (Arnold & Tinker, 1939; Salthouse & Ellis, 1980; Tinker, 1958). Second, fixation durations must be long enough for sufficient visual processing to occur so that words will be recognized. Finally, there are rather strict constraints on the number of words that can be recognized in a single fixation during normal reading—about one or two (Rayner, 1978). Taking these facts into consideration produces a maximum reading rate of about 800–900 words/minute if all words are to be processed. Reading a passage at rates exceeding 1000 words/minute (as in speed reading) very likely involves missing a significant proportion of the text.

2. Limitations on the Rate of Comprehension

It is quite probable that even when reading at a rate about equal to the general boundary of 800 words/minute readers are skipping many of the printed words. This is because if a passage was read at that speed the average fixation duration would be only about half the average normal reading fixation of 250 msec, assuming virtually no regressions. Why should this be a problem? The answer seems to be that there are limits on how fast comprehension processes (including lexical access from visual patterns, organization of words into propositions, and integration of propositions) can be executed. Three sources of evidence concerning limitations on the rate of comprehension can be identified. First, at an intuitive level, it is noteworthy that average normal reading rates are only about 200–300 words/minute even for college students. This rate is far less than what could be accomplished if eye movements were pushed to their limits, suggesting that some process other than oculomotor control is responsible for determining preferred normal reading rates. It is reasonable to suppose that this determining factor is associated with comprehension and/or encoding of text information into memory.

Second, Just and Carpenter's (1980) model of eye movement patterns during reading offers some clues regarding the length of time subjects seem to require for processing each word while comprehending a text. Their data clearly show that subjects generally spend varying amounts of time on words as a function of such variables as the frequency of the word's occurrence in the English language, its grammatical role in the sentence that contains it, and so on. Thus, processes such as lexical access and parsing do not seem to occur instantaneously but require measurable amounts of time. In fact, the average gaze duration (total time spent on a word, aggregated across all forward fixations on that word) in Just and Carpenter's work with technical passages was 239 msec. Individual words' gaze durations modulated around this value in meaningful ways, as indicated by their multiple regression model—subjects did not randomly vary the duration of their eye fixations. For example, the occurrence of a novel word added an average of 802 msec to the gaze duration for that word, and integration of clauses was indicated by an average of 71 msec added to the gaze duration of a word occurring at the end of a sentence. The accuracy of comprehension could well depend on the freedom to allocate sufficient fixation time to parts of a text that are particularly demanding.

Finally, a few studies that have evaluated the effects of speeded text presentation on quality of comprehension should be noted. Kieras (1974) had subjects read sets of related sentences either at their own rates or at a rapidly paced rate. Recognition of the sentences in a later test was lower for those subjects who were forced to read at a fast pace, and Kieras suggested that the increased rate of presentation caused sentence information to be represented in a less complete and less accessible form in memory. Sticht (1977) has presented a theory of reading literacy in which he has claimed that the optimal level of reading that one can achieve is related to speech understanding ability. He has found that even subjects with the most efficient decoding processes have reading comprehension rates that are limited by their speech comprehension rates. This view of the relationship between reading and speech comprehension hints at some fundamental constraint on speed of language processing.

It is not surprising, therefore, to find that many attempts to improve reading speed have succeeded and at the same time failed to maintain the level of comprehension achieved under normal reading conditions. Training methods such as learning to scan paperbacks (Berger, 1972), listening to time compressed speech (Thames & Rossiter, 1972), and rapidly paced text presentation (Himelstein & Greenberg, 1974; Maxwell & Mueller, 1967; Poulton, 1961) have failed to produce reasonable increases in reading rate without comprehension loss. In cases where comprehension at least remained constant, increases in reading speed were no greater than what could be expected from increased motivation (cf. Tinker, 1967). In one case, however, Carpenter and Jones (1975) taught subjects to improve reading rate by seeking main ideas, and an average speed of 515 words/minute was achieved with improved comprehension on the Nelson–Denny test. But it is quite possible that the subjects had learned an effective scanning strategy that allowed them to preview the comprehension questions (which are printed beside the relevant passage) then locate appropriate answers in the passages. Although comprehension of segments of text associated with specific questions may have been achieved, the fate of the rest of the passage content is unknown.

3. Consequences of Skipping Information While Reading

If readers are to process text at speeds that exceed normal comprehension rates it is quite likely that this will be accomplished by sampling parts of a passage while skipping (failing to look at) other parts. This is because truncating the processing time of words that are viewed probably is constrained by a reader's tolerance for uncertainty. For example, reducing the average gaze duration on each word by 50% or so would about double reading rate. But under these conditions the reader is not able to achieve the level of comprehension that results from spending sufficient time on words to be reasonably sure of their identity and their role in the passage. Rather than risking inaccurate interpretation of all or most of the passage, a better strategy might be to trade-off certain parts of a passage, missing them completely, while spending enough time on other sections to ensure that they are comprehended at least moderately well. This trade-off is typical of what we would call *skimming,* and it has predictable consequences for quality of comprehension.

The nature of the information that the reader skips will be a powerful determinant of concomitant comprehension deficits. For example, if a reader is fortunate enough to be able to skip only redundant or unimportant words he or she may be able to comprehend the whole passage. This expectation, however, relies on the assumption that the unimportant words play only an optional role in mediating comprehension (i.e., that comprehension can proceed at usual speed without having to encode such words). This turns out not to be the case. Bassin and Martin (1976) simulated the optimal text sampling strategy by deleting from passages words that were judged to be unimportant. Subjects who read these passages performed as well on a comprehension test as subjects who read the complete version of the passages. But in order to reach this level of performance subjects who read the mutilated passages required about the same reading time as those who read the complete passages, so that reading rate as measured in words/minute was considerably slower in the former case.

Naturally occurring selection strategies, moreover, are not likely as accurate as Bassin and Martin's deletion scheme. Instead, whole phrases or even sentences might be skipped, producing potential problems with respect to maintaining coherence among propositions in a passage. If key propositions are missed the reader might fail to understand the major idea or theme of a passage. On the other hand, if less important ones are skipped coherence may be maintained through inference making (cf. Kintsch & van Dijk, 1978) although the reader will fail to comprehend and encode some of the passage's details. Exploring these issues in greater depth will require consideration of research on rapid reading techniques, and the remainder of the article is devoted to this task.

IV. SKIMMING

When reading certain types of material or when reading with particular goals in mind, we are not always concerned with fully comprehending every detail of a passage. Often we might be reading for a specific kind of information or trying to get the passage's gist, while "ignoring" irrelevant segments of the text. In these cases a reader is able to move swiftly through the text, but at the same time probably relies rather heavily on conceptually driven processes to help provide coherence between propositions and to complete partially read propositions. The key to successfully skimming for desired information is twofold. The skimmer must be able to visually sample or select from the text information that is appropriate for his or her task, and the skimmer must also be able to form a coherent representation of the selected text segments. In this section I will consider strategies that may be used to accomplish these goals and will review experiments that illustrate how characteristics of the human information processing system constrain the success of this enterprise. Finally, an artificial intelligence program that has avoided many of these constraints and that successfully "skims" newspaper stories will be described.

A. Purposes and Strategies

Rothkopf and Fisher (1981) have identified a number of reading goals that would be relevant to skimming, such as searching a passage for the answer to a specific question. One would expect that a good strategy in this case would be to scan the passage for words relevant to the question or to sample phrases to check for associations with the critical question. When pertinent information is located the reader should slow down and more carefully process the text so that the full answer can be found and accurately comprehended. Using eye movement records Rothkopf and Fisher discovered that most readers follow this basic pattern, although others show very little variation in reading speed when relevant and irrelevant text segments are viewed. This description of how readers skim for specific information implies that they may comprehend little of the text that is not relevant to the question at hand, and there is evidence that this is in fact the case (Anderson & Biddle, 1975).

Another common goal in skimming a passage is to understand its gist or main points. Intuitively, this is accomplished by reading what appear to be the important words or phrases while skipping details. When asked to describe how they skim, college students mention a number of strategies that are consistent with this intuition and that depend on passage structure (Masson, 1982). For example, a frequently mentioned strategy was to read the first sentence of each paragraph. This approach assumes that the passage conforms to certain rules of organization. It has been shown that readers are not accustomed to having these rules violated and they react badly when infractions occur. If the paragraph's topic concept does not occur early or does not serve as surface subject of sentences, readers take longer to read the passage and find it difficult to accurately identify the passage topic (Kieras, 1981). The consequences of failing to maintain conventions of passage organization would be amplified during skimming, particularly with respect to comprehension of the main topic of the passage. Strategies for visually sampling parts of the text surely would go awry causing inappropriate information to be selected and potentially critical propositions to be skipped.

Patterns of visual processing of text are not the only characteristics of reading that are altered by adoption of various reading goals. Some evidence for alteration of macroprocessing of text as a function of changes in reading goals has been provided by Graesser et al. (1980). They assigned subjects one of two goals while normally reading passages. The goals were to be able to take either an essay or a multiple choice test on the passages. The goal of reading to prepare for an essay exam requires that the reader form an especially coherent macrostructure of the passage so that written answers will be meaningful, logically consistent, and retrievable from memory. Graesser et al. found that subjects who read in preparation for an essay test were more sensitive to macrostructure variables than subjects whose goal was to take a multiple choice test. That is, in the multiple regression equation for predicting reading times the macrostructure predictor variables of narrativity, familiarity, and number of new argument nouns had greater slopes when reading time data from subjects in the essay group were considered. No such effect was observed when microstructure variables such as number of words and propositions were considered. Reading goals clearly have an effect on the conceptual processing that readers apply to passage content during normal reading, and they should also affect conceptual processing while skimming.

B. Limitations of Skimming

Perhaps because intuitions about and apparent success with skimming have been taken for granted, very little research has been directed toward the issue of how accurate skimmers are in their selective processing of text. A distinction can be drawn between two aspects of selective processing that appear to be critically involved in skimming. At the *perceptual* level a reader may be able to use physical cues present in the layout and structure of the passage (e.g., first sentence of each paragraph, italicized words) to guide his or her gaze to goal-relevant areas of the passage. Propositions that are visually sampled are then submitted to *conceptual* processing and this is the second level at which selectivity may operate. Depending on the relevance of a proposition or sentence for the reader's goal, the reader may process the information only superficially or completely (Spiro, 1980), deciding whether to make inferences to connect constituent propositions and whether to include the information in the macrostructure of the passage (Bower, Black, & Turner, 1979; Kintsch & van Dijk, 1978).

1. Conceptual vs Perceptual Selectivity

The utility of conceptually and perceptually selective processing will depend on the reader's goal in skimming. For example, if we consider the goal of understanding the main idea or gist of a passage, it is most important for the skimmer to perceptually select important statements and to conceptually organize them into a macrostructure. Unfortunately, there are few guides to use in perceptual selection of gist-relevant passage segments. The important information is not always in the first sentence of each paragraph and it is probably rarely possible to tell if a word is important until it and its context have been read. It is more probable that conceptually selective processing is the key to skimming for gist, rather than accurate perceptual selection of important text elements. When skimming for gist, for instance, a reader should concentrate on propositions that are important to the main topic of the passage (e.g., those that describe critical actions or their results), rather than those that represent elaborative details (e.g., description of scenery).

In a series of experiments using narrative and newspaper stories I was able to demonstrate the importance of conceptually selective processing (Masson, 1982). Subjects were allotted reading time that was equivalent to rates of 225, 375, or 600 words/minute. They were told that they could distribute their reading time over a passage in any way they wanted as long as they completed the whole passage in the time allowed. This procedure provided uniform reading times while leaving subjects free to adopt their own skimming strategies. To check the validity of the procedure a similar experiment was conducted in which subjects were allowed to read normally or skim at their own rates. The pattern of results from that experiment was exactly the same as that obtained in the experiment where reading time was restricted. After reading the passages subjects were given a recognition test that consisted of three types of true and false statements. Macro- and microstatements were based on information explicitly stated in a story, with the former type rated as more important or relevant to the story's gist. False versions of these types of statements were created by changing a few words in the original statements so that the meaning was significantly altered. Inferences were not explicitly stated in the passages, but represented important information that could be inferred. False inferences were produced by rewriting otherwise true inferences in the manner used to create false explicit statements.

If readers are able to perceptually select important information while skimming, they should do particularly well at verifying test statements that are relevant to the passage's gist and should be less accurate when given unimportant statements to verify. Moreover, this effect might be stronger when subjects read at especially fast skimming rates, so that as reading rate increases, performance on macrostatements and inferences should decline only slightly and performance on microstatements should fall off dramatically. This should occur since hypothetically the skimmers are skipping the unimportant information and so these details do not have much chance of being encoded into memory. On the other hand, if perceptual selectivity is not accurate but arbitrary, the skimmer must rely on conceptually selective processing to highlight sampled text information that is relevant to the passage's gist. What sort of recognition performance would be predicted for the different statement types in this case? Assuming that skimmers are about equally likely to visually sample important and unimportant statements, recognition accuracy on an immediate test should be about equal across levels of importance (cf. Caccamise & Kintsch, 1978; Yekovich & Thorndyke, 1981). For example, Thorndyke and Yekovich (1980) have shown that for normal readers statements at different levels of importance in passages did not differ in recognition probability, even though clear differences were apparent in recall probability as shown in Fig. 3.

In the experiments I carried out (Masson, 1982) there was no evidence at

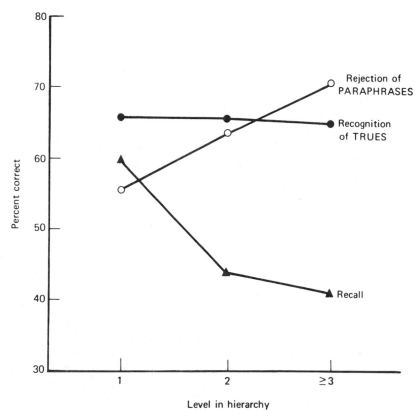

Fig. 3. Recall and recognition of propositions from different hierarchical levels in a narrative text. From Thorndyke and Yekovich (1980).

any of the reading rates that macrostatements were preferentially sampled during reading. The recognition accuracy differences among the statement types were consistent across reading rate and were no greater than the differences that were obtained when subjects attempted to verify the statements without having read the passages. Thus, had a priori plausibility of the different statement types been equated, no recognition accuracy differences due to statement type would have appeared. This result provides a forceful argument against the hypothesis that skimmers are able to perceptually select important information and ignore details.

The experiments on skimming did, however, offer two sources of evidence for conceptually selective processing when reading for gist. First, when verification *latencies* were analyzed a very interesting effect emerged. Subjects were faster at verifying macro- as opposed to microstatements, and this effect was stronger at higher reading speeds. This indicates that gist-relevant propositions were favored in the formation of memory representations of the passages, especially when readers skimmed the stories. Second, when asked to recall one paragraph of each passage after reading or skimming it, subjects were much more likely to recall propositions related to the passage's gist. In fact, recall protocols from all reading rate conditions (225–600 words/minute) were accurately accounted for by Miller and Kintsch's (1980) version of the Kintsch and van Dijk (1978) text processing model. Only one of the model's parameters had to be changed to provide close fits to the observed recall probabilities for each proposition. That parameter represented the probability of encoding a proposition into long-term memory during a processing cycle in working memory. As might be expected, this parameter decreased as reading rate increased. This probably reflects the fact that some propositions were skipped entirely when skimming and also implies that even when propositions were included in a working memory processing cycle, encoding processes were truncated or not as elaborate relative to the normal reading case. Parameters of the model that were responsible for determining the relative importance of propositions in the formation of a macrostructure could be held constant across reading rate without greatly changing the quality of the model's fit to the data. According to the text processing model, then, skimming involved application of usual reading comprehension processes (including preferential conceptual processing of gist relevant propositions) to an impoverished selection of propositions that perhaps were encoded into long-term memory less reliably than when reading normally.

One of the experiments on skimming did not require subjects to focus on gist relevant information, but instead on content that was relevant to a specific perspective that was assigned prior to reading each passage. For example, in reading a passage about a tropical island's environment readers were directed to focus attention on information in the passage that would be relevant either to a shipwrecked sailor or to the activities of seagulls that were frolicking about the island. Earlier work has shown that reading such passages at normal rates with a given perspective in mind produces patterns of recall that favor information relevant to the assigned perspective (e.g., Fass & Schumacher, 1981; Kozminsky, 1977; Pichert & Anderson, 1977). In this type of skimming task it might be reasonable to expect a reader to be able to perceptually select information that is relevant to a given perspective. When reading about the island's environment from the perspective of a shipwrecked sailor, for example, the reader should be especially sensitive to information relevant to food, fresh water, and shelter. If key words belonging to these categories are spotted the reader should slow down and more carefully read the phrases containing the key words. Readers are quite adept at detecting categorically defined targets under conditions of rapid scanning (Friedrich, Schadler, & Juola, 1979; Juola, Ward, & McNamara, 1982). Statements that were particularly relevant to only one of the possible perspectives from which a story could be read were chosen and used in a recognition test. Subjects read passages from predesignated perspectives at rates ranging from 225 to 600 words/minute, then were given the recognition test. If readers are able to selectively process perspective-relevant information, recognition performance should be more accurate on statements that are associated with the assigned perspective. The results showed this effect, although it was not very strong and did not increase with reading speed. That is, skimmers were not able to focus their reading almost exclusively on goal-relevant information.

These experiments converge on the suggestion that it is difficult for skimmers to accurately sample from a passage information that is relevant to their goal while spending superficial amounts of reading time on irrelevant information. Only when there are rather obvious perceptual clues to relevant information can perceptually selective processing be effective. In the case of newspaper stories, for example, had the subjects been more aware of the structure of these stories, in which the most important information appears early (cf. Thorndyke, 1979), they might have concentrated reading time on the first part of the story enabling them to be especially accurate at verification of important statements. Without obvious perceptual cues skimmers run a high risk of missing information that represents an important part of the passage content in which they are interested. Despite the lack of effective perceptual selectivity, however, readers are able to selectively devote conceptual processing to sampled text information that seems related to their objective.

2. Comprehension Efficiency and Skimming Ability

A second type of limitation on skimming effectiveness is general comprehension efficiency: the speed with which propositions can be understood and integrated. Since standardized reading tests use timed reading comprehension tasks, it is reasonable to hypothesize that subjects who do well on such tests are rather efficient comprehenders and so should be more adept skimmers as well. Moreover, if general comprehension efficiency underlies the advantage enjoyed by skilled readers, the difference in skimming performance of skilled and less skilled readers should be a general one, encompassing all levels of information in a passage. But if the critical difference between readers is that skilled readers are better able to selectively process goal-relevant information, we might expect them to have an especially large advantage over less skilled readers when information of that type is considered.

In a recent experiment on this issue (Masson, 1984) undergraduates were given the reading comprehension subtest of the Nelson–Denny and a median split of scores on this test was used to divide subjects into two reading ability groups. The skilled group's Nelson–Denny percentile scores ranged from 62 to 97 with a median of 86, and the range for the less skilled group was 19 to 54 with a median of 34. Half of the subjects in each of the ability groups read a set of narrative and newspaper stories at a controlled rate of 250 words/minute, using the procedure that was described earlier (Section IV,B,1). The other half of the subjects read the same passages at a controlled rate of 500 words/minute and were told to skim the passages for their gist. After reading each passage subjects provided a brief summary then answered 10 questions about the passage. Each question required a single word or phrase for an answer and half of the questions inquired about gist-relevant information while the other half queried specific details.

I will focus on the question answering data here since they were more clear-cut and reliable than the data based on the summaries. As would be expected, question answering scores were higher among readers in the slower reading rate condition than in the skimming condition and they were also higher for the more skilled readers. A striking result, however, was a powerful interaction between these two variables that indicated that skilled and less skilled readers did not differ when reading normally (63 vs 62% correct) but did differ when skimming (46 vs 32% correct favoring skilled readers). In addition, gist questions were more accurately answered than detailed questions and this difference reliably exceeded the difference found among control subjects who attempted to answer the questions without having read the passages. Reading skill did not interact with any variable other than reading rate, and an identical pattern of results was obtained when only the 10 most skilled and 10 least skilled readers in each rate condition were considered.

The interaction between reading ability and rate implies that reading skill differences that appear on timed reading comprehension tests may reflect something other than ability to comprehend text when reading at normal speeds. Subjects with markedly different scores on the Nelson–Denny test did not reliably differ when answering comprehension questions about passages that were read under very little time pressure. But when skimming passages at a moderately fast speed, reading skill differences became apparent suggesting that tests such as the Nelson–Denny may reflect a form of speeded comprehension *efficiency*. Moreover, these comprehension efficiency differences appear to be general since the skilled readers' advantage over the less skilled readers when skimming extended to detailed as well as gist-relevant information. The less skilled readers seemed able to focus their processing on important content to about the same extent as skilled readers, but were able to comprehend and encode less information overall. These results, however, do not mean that skill at conceptually selective processing of goal-relevant information is not an important part of rapid reading ability as we shall see when speed reading skills are explored (Section VI).

C. FRUMP: A Computer Program That Skims Stories

An important method of sharpening theories of reading and testing their validity involves the development of working models or simulations that are based on the theory at hand. A branch of artificial intelligence (which in turn is a branch of computer science) is devoted to this enterprise. One project that has particular significance for the problem of rapid reading consists of a computer program called the Fast Reading Understanding and Memory Program (FRUMP) which was developed by DeJong (1979). The program was designed to skim newspaper stories *in real time* (i.e., in about the same amount of time required by a human reader) and to provide a brief summary of the story. FRUMP's mechanisms reveal some important parallels to human skimming processes.

FUMP's success depends on a special approach to the problem of parsing sentences and forming conceptual representations of their content and context. DeJong integrated the system's parser with the rest of the system so that the parser could benefit from predictions made and topic-relevant knowledge possessed by higher levels of the system. Predictions about upcoming text content can then be used to solve difficult problems such as resolving pronominal referents and lexical ambiguities. Two major components comprise FRUMP, the *substantiator* and the *predictor*. The substantiator is responsible for parsing the text and providing conceptual representations to the predictor. This information is used to verify, reject, or flesh out predictions generated by the predictor, thereby refining the interpretation of the passage's content. The predictor uses knowledge about the topic of the story to generate predictions and, more specifically, seeks out only the most important information on the topic.

Knowledge specific to a domain is represented in what DeJong refers to as *sketchy scripts*. These are scaled down scripts (cf. Schank & Abelson, 1977) that represent the most important elements of a domain. In the case of earthquakes, for example, the sketchy script has slots for information such as the location, amount of damage, and size of the quake on the Richter scale. When skimming a story that it realizes is about an earthquake, FRUMP will instantiate the appropriate sketchy script, will seek information directly relevant to these aspects of earthquakes, and will use only this set of information in the development of a summary. In this sense FRUMP operates in a conceptually driven manner once the story topic has been established. Here is an example of a news story for which FRUMP produced a summary:

Teheran, Iran, March 20 (UPI)—The Shah of Iran today formally took control of the
country's multibillion dollar oil industry from foreign operators.

Shah Mohammed Reza Pahlavi announced nationalization of the industry in his
broadcast Persian New Year message. He declared the take-over gave Iran "full and
real control" of all oil operations.

The order places under control of the national Iranian Oil Company the largest oil-
field, the largest refinery, the largest export terminal and the largest man-made island
in the world. The facilities had been operated by a consortium of British, American,
French, and Dutch concerns. The nationalization came after the group refused to double
Iranian oil production to eight million barrels per day. (DeJong, 1979, pp. 263–264)

From this 110-word story FRUMP generated the summary "Iran has na-
tionalized its oil industry" using less than four seconds of CPU time. To
do this, the program had to recognize that the story was about nationalization of industry and invoke its relevant sketchy script which requested
information about the country and type of industry involved. These two
characteristics are among the most important in the program's knowledge
about nationalization.

The degree of success achieved by FRUMP may seem to reflect an overly
optimistic model (although it was not necessarily intended as a model at
all) of how rapid reading is accomplished among humans, given the inef-
ficiencies exhibited by subjects in the experiments described above (Section
IV,B). But two important points should be noted. First, FRUMP relies
heavily on conceptually selective processing of text content in order to produce efficient and representative summaries. It has already been argued that
this is the same skill that effective skimmers require. Second, FRUMP has
a major advantage that human skimmers often do not have: it is expected
to find a very specific set of facts when reading a passage, whereas humans
often work with far more vaguely defined goals. In other words, the program has a very powerful heuristic for determining which parts of a passage
deserve conceptually selective processing. Were we to give readers more precisely defined goals by targeting particular types of information we might
find that in that case FRUMP provides an accurate approximation to human skimming strategies (see Section V,B).

V. RAPID SEQUENTIAL VISUAL PRESENTATION

We have seen that a major disadvantage of skimming as a form of rapid
reading is that it forces readers to skip a significant amount of a passage's
content, thereby risking serious comprehension failure particularly in cases
where goal-relevant information is not clearly indicated by visual cues. A
different approach to rapid reading is offered by a mechanical text presentation technique known as rapid sequential visual presentation (RSVP). The

method involves presenting a passage one word at a time, each at a fixed location. When one word's presentation duration has expired it disappears and is replaced by the next word. Using the RSVP procedure ensures, therefore, that the reader will be exposed to all information in a passage, which makes RSVP a viable method of rapid reading if one subscribes to the assumption that the primary factor limiting rapid reading comprehension is time required to plan and execute eye movements (e.g., Juola et al., 1982). This is a reasonable argument since a significant part of the average fixation duration is consumed by oculomotor control processes (Salthouse & Ellis, 1980).

It is also possible, however, that immediate comprehension processes such as lexical access and integration of words into propositions contribute to fixation duration (e.g., Just & Carpenter, 1980). These operations may, in part, occur in parallel with and take as much time as oculomotor programming (Rayner & Pollatsek, 1981; Salthouse, Ellis, Diener, & Somberg, 1981). If this is the case, using RSVP to truncate the processing time for each word should produce comprehension difficulties.

The rapid sequential reading technique offers an opportunity to assess these claims about oculomotor and conceptual processing constraints on eye movements in reading. Rapid sequential reading should represent an ideal method of speeded reading if oculomotor processes are the primary determinant of fixation duration during normal reading, since no eye movements are required. But one might argue that RSVP with short durations results in masking effects that would reduce the utility of rapid sequential reading. This argument loses much of its force given Rayner, Inhoff, Morrison, Slowiaczek, and Bertera's (1981) finding that readers can extract the visual information necessary for reading within the first 50 msec of a fixation. In addition, subjects shown single RSVP sentences with a presentation duration of 50 msec/word were about 90% accurate at determining whether a sentence contained a word that represented a predesignated semantic category (Juola et al., 1982).

Two general RSVP paradigms will be discussed here. One involves the presentation of individual sentences and the other involves longer passages. Implications of the results obtained using these paradigms span a range of levels of text comprehension from word recognition to intersentence integration.

A. Sentence Processing during RSVP

If comprehension processes operate during RSVP in much the same way as they do during normal reading, it should be possible to demonstrate that characteristics of sentences that make normal comprehension difficult also make comprehension of RSVP sentences difficult. Forster (1970) provided evidence of this sort by presenting six-word RSVP sentences that varied in syntactic complexity. Complex sentences consisted of more than one clause, for example, *They persuaded him to work harder,* while simple sentences consisted of one clause, such as, *The young boy was very hungry.* In addition, Forster used scrambled versions of these sentences that were formed by randomly ordering the words in each. Sentences were presented at the rate of 16 words/second (about 63 msec/word) using the RSVP method and after each sentence the subjects were required to recall as many of the words as possible. If subjects were able to parse the sentences accurately, they should have encoded the simple ones more readily and so recalled them more accurately. Complex sentences would be harder to parse but would still have an advantage over randomly ordered word strings with respect to comprehension and encoding. These were precisely the results that Forster obtained, indicating that subjects were indeed trying to parse, with some success, the grammatical word strings even under a very rapid presentation rate.

It has been argued (e.g., Mitchell, 1979) that Forster's findings could be interpreted as the result of memory retrieval and reorganization processes that took place after sentence presentation rather than as the result of immediate comprehension processes. But Potter, Kroll, and Harris (1980) recently reported results that argue in favor of the idea that words are integrated into a growing comprehension structure as they occur in an RSVP sentence. They replaced a concrete noun in some RSVP sentences with a picture of the object. Since pictures are conceptually understood at least as quickly as words, but take at least an extra 200 msec to name (e.g., Potter & Faulconer, 1975; Smith & Magee, 1980), Potter *et al.* argued the following. If subjects code words from an RSVP sentence in short-term memory until the sentence has been completely presented and then process its meaning, the presence of a picture should be disruptive at RSVP rates like 12 words/second (83 msec/word) since it takes so long to verbally code a picture. But if each element of the sentence is conceptually processed as it occurs the presence of a picture should not be detrimental. In both recall and plausibility judgment tasks subjects handled sentences with and without pictures equally well, supporting the claim that the words and pictures were understood immediately.

An additional piece of evidence favoring the notion that some form of activation of semantic memory occurs as RSVP sentences are displayed was provided by Fischler and Bloom (1980). They earlier had established that presentation of a sentence context prior to a letter string used in a lexical decision task facilitated responses to words that were highly likely sentence completions and inhibited responses to words that were anomalous completions (Fischler & Bloom, 1979). Working from this result they presented sentence contexts in the RSVP format. If subjects are able to comprehend an RSVP sentence as it is presented, facilitative and inhibitory effects should occur when the sentence final word is part of a lexical decision task.

Fischler and Bloom found that facilitative effects were present only at very slow RSVP rates (e.g., 4 words/second), but that inhibitory effects appeared even at 28 words/second (36 msec/word). At the higher rates, the inhibitory effect was most apparent for syntactically simple sentence contexts (cf. Forster, 1970), implying that the limits of the comprehension process had been reached. Why should the inhibitory but not the facilitative effects appear at the faster speeds? Fischler and Bloom argued that the context effects were the result of an attentional process and that with regard to activation of areas of semantic memory attentional inhibition develops more rapidly than attentional facilitation (cf. Neely, 1977). These results imply that some form of semantic interpretation of an RSVP sentence develops very rapidly (but with little conscious comprehension since facilitative effects were not seen and since subjects rarely reported being able to comprehend the sentences at the faster rates), keeping up with each new word, and this interpretation can be used to direct attention to generally appropriate areas of semantic memory.

B. Text Processing during RSVP and Skimming

Although some comprehension processes may be able to keep pace with rapid sequential presentations of single sentences, it is unclear whether the level of comprehension achieved by Fischler and Bloom's (1980) subjects is sufficient to induce comprehension of multisentence passages. Some of the more successful models of text comprehension include the assumption that a critical part of comprehension is the maintenance of coherence through establishing links between successive propositions. Integrative and inferential processes of this type are claimed to often be time consuming (e.g., Just & Carpenter, 1980; Kintsch & van Dijk, 1978) and play a critical role in the formation of macrostructure representations of text content. The presentation of passages using the RSVP technique, which involves a reduction in the time available to process each word, might be detrimental to readers' integrative text processing.

If one assumes that comprehension processes are executed immediately upon presentation of each word, however, there is no reason why RSVP of text should be any more detrimental than skimming. After all, when readers skim passages they typically miss a good deal of the content and come away with impoverished representations. Potter *et al.* (1980) tested this idea by comparing rapid reading performance associated with RSVP and skimming. They used passages similar to those used by Bransford and Johnson (1972) and by Dooling and Lachman (1971). The texts were grammatically correct but semantically ambiguous in that the topic of the passage was not clear unless a special topic word was mentioned. One passage, for example, contained the sentence *Elastic fibers developed, attaching it to the rest* without ever mentioning the referent that corresponded to *it*. But if the passage contained the word *pizza* it was quite easy to understand. Potter *et al.* manipulated whether and where the critical word occurred in each passage and presented the texts to subjects in RSVP or whole passage format for rapid reading. Rates as high as 720 words/minute were tested in each format condition. In the case of skimming whole passages, each text was visible for a time period equivalent to the total time required to present that text in RSVP. Subjects were required to recall the content of each passage immediately after reading it, and two aspects of the recall protocols were assessed: percentage of content recalled and mention of the topic word. Recall of the second half of each passage's content was higher in the RSVP condition, especially at rapid reading rates and when the topic word appeared late in the passage. The report of the topic word was particularly common in the RSVP condition and did not suffer much as reading rate increased. In keeping with the immediate comprehension hypothesis it was concluded that comprehension (as assessed by mention of the topic word) kept pace with rapid sequential presentation although subjects were not able to incorporate all the information into long-term memory (content recall declined markedly as rate increased even in the RSVP condition).

A number of aspects of the study of Potter *et al.* may have been responsible for placing the RSVP technique at a special advantage. First, the passages were not comprehensible without exposure to the topic word and only in the RSVP condition was such exposure guaranteed. This was particularly true in the case of very rapid presentation when skimmers must skip a good deal of the passage content. Without being exposed to the topic word passages of this type are extremely difficult to recall (e.g., Dooling & Lachman, 1971). In addition, report of the topic word might not have been an accurate gauge of the comprehension of the passage as a whole, and would favor a presentation technique such as RSVP that ensured exposure to all words in a passage.

A series of experiments was designed to test the validity of this line of reasoning, in which normal passages were used (Masson, 1983). Text comprehension and long-term memory integration were measured by having subjects answer questions or summarize passages after reading them under skimming or RSVP conditions. A consistent advantage for the skimming condition was observed, supporting the argument that truncating the processing time for words during reading reduces the quality of conceptual processing. Another form of question answering task was used to assess comprehension more directly, without relying on the ability of subjects to encode as much text information as possible into long-term memory. Subjects were given a single question before reading each passage and were required only to find the answer to that question while reading the passage. To the extent that subjects are able to comprehend the propositions in the passage and their significance in the context of prior knowledge concerning the question at hand, subjects should be able to answer the questions very accurately. The task of skimming to find the answer to a predesignated question is very similar to what the artificial intelligence program FRUMP is required to do. In fact, the skimmer has an additional advantage over FRUMP in that before reading begins he or she has an idea of the passage's topic and is primed to comprehend information relevant to the question at hand. When performing search tasks such as this it is quite probable that FRUMP's mechanisms represent a reasonable parallel to human performance and the success enjoyed by FRUMP leads to the prediction that skimmers should do well on this task.

Answering predesignated questions also should be done accurately during RSVP if readers are able to comprehend a text and integrate its propositions as each new word is presented. But it turned out that subjects did a far better job of answering predesignated questions when skimming than when reading under RSVP, especially when the very rapid rate of 700 words/minute was used. This result indicates that immediate comprehension as well as long-term memory encoding may suffer when processing of individual words is truncated.

Despite the fact that text comprehension and memory consistently suffered during rapid sequential reading, relative to skimming, there is evidence to suggest that it may be possible to change the format of RSVP to produce much better performance. Specifically, if processing of individual words is abbreviated by short presentation durations, it may be possible to postpone the completion of processing until an appropriate opportunity arises. This could be accomplished if the reader is able to hold information relevant to a series of words in a type of memory buffer. At appropriate intervals information in the buffer might be processed and new items may then be added to it. This is precisely the type of reading model proposed by Green, Mitchell, and Hammond (1981).

This sort of buffering process may take place to some extent during normal reading, according to evidence from sentence coding experiments in which subjects seem to segment sentences at clause boundaries (Aaronson & Scarborough, 1977; Jarvella, 1979). Although these effects are more obvious when subjects attempt to code sentences for a memory test, Mitchell and Green (1978) have shown that when subjects read consecutive three-word segments of a passage under comprehension instructions they spend extra time on segments that represent the ends of sentences (see Fig. 4).

If readers are able to buffer information during RSVP when conceptual processing is severely constrained by time limits, it should be possible to produce improved RSVP performance by providing readers an opportunity to process buffered information. This was attempted in recent experiments by inserting pauses of 500 or 1000 msec between each sentence of a passage (Masson, 1983). Consequently, there no longer was an advantage of skimming over RSVP on a question answering task, and ability to answer pre-designated questions in an RSVP condition was significantly improved by introducing pauses.

It is also possible that other versions of RSVP that use units of presentation that are more consonant with buffering strategies might produce more reliable comprehension than single word presentation (cf. Ward & Juola,

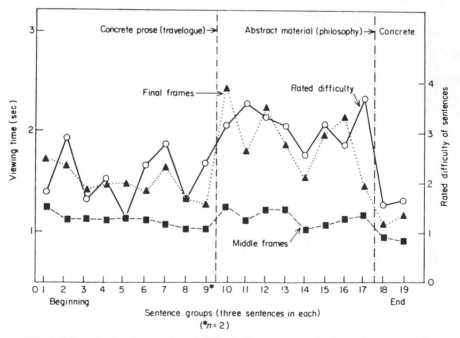

Fig. 4. Mean viewing times and rated difficulty for middle (prefinal) word groups and final (end of sentence) word groups of sentences in concrete and abstract passages. From Mitchell and Green (1978).

1982). An additional alternative would be to use RSVP durations that are similar to the average eye fixation duration of 250 msec. Juola *et al.* (1982) accomplished this by presenting windows of text averaging 15 characters each (one to three words) for 200 msec. In addition, pauses were inserted between sentences. This technique should lead to comprehension and memory results that parallel skimming performance since it approximates the pattern of visual information seen by skimmers (see Section VI,B). Question answering accuracy under this version of RSVP was indeed as accurate as that obtained by subjects when they skimmed normally presented passages.

Taken together, the results of experiments on comprehension of individual sentences and passages presented in the RSVP format imply that there are serious limits on the level of comprehension that can be expected when the duration of presentation of each word is extremely short. In the case of rapid serial presentation of single sentences there is evidence that certain areas of semantic memory relevant to the presented sentence are activated. But this degree of "comprehension" does not seem to be sufficient to build a coherent macrostructure representation of consecutively presented propositions. Both on-line comprehension and incorporation of propositions into long-term memory are severely limited when processing of individual words is truncated as in RSVP and when no opportunities are available for buffering small segments of text. Thus, it appears that immediate processing of words as they appear in rapid succession is not adequate for the form of comprehension that provides conscious awareness of the relationship between prior knowledge and propositions in a new text base. It is this level of comprehension that usually is required for the formation of lasting and useful long-term memory representations of text information.

VI. SPEED READING

It has often been claimed by proponents of speed reading (e.g., McLaughlin, 1969; Wood, 1960) that courses in speed reading teach new skills that ordinary readers do not possess and that allow the trained reader to comprehend text at incredibly fast rates. The studies reviewed earlier, however, provide ample reason for skepticism, given the amounts of text content that must be skipped when reading over 1000 words/minute and given the constraints on the acuity of peripheral vision. In this part of the article I will examine the nature of the special skill that speed readers appear to acquire. Recent empirical evidence will be reviewed that supports the resulting claim that speed readers are particularly skilled at determining the gist of passages based on familiar topics.

A. A Special Reading Skill

Studies that have found evidence for reasonably good comprehension after speed reading a passage, and many speed reading courses themselves, usually rely on multiple choice tests of comprehension. It is becoming clear, however, that this method of evaluation is inadequate. For example, Liddle (1965) showed that at least for one type of material with which he was working speed readers could read at three times the rate of normal readers and still obtain a comprehension score of 68%. But Carver (1971) found that comparable untrained subjects were able to score 57% on the same test without having read the material at all. A more informative approach was taken by Hansen (1975), who collected recall protocols from normal and speed readers after reading passages for a fixed period of time. The speed readers naturally viewed more of the passage content since they worked at a much faster speed, but the nature of the recall protocols was suggestive of the consequences for comprehension. Speed readers recalled more "idea clusters" than normal readers, but recalled less about each cluster.

The recall protocols of Hansen's speed readers are very much like what would be called the gist of a passage, implying that speed readers do indeed miss some amount of text content but are able to focus on the more important parts of the passage. In a more direct investigation of this possibility Barrus, Brown, and Inouye (1978) found that after reading at about 1800 words/minute trained speed readers could produce outlines of passages that were judged to be as accurate as those produced by normal readers who covered the material at about 320 words/minute. It turns out, however, that this study suffers from a number of potential problems, the most important of which is associated with selection of subjects. Although their subjects had reasonably similar undergraduate grade point averages, there is no guarantee that the speed reading subjects (selected as particularly successful trainees) did not differ from the control subjects with respect to reading ability before taking the speed reading course. Also, the outline comprehension test was biased in favor of the speed readers who had been specially trained in forming outlines of the sort required in the experiment.

Despite these criticisms, it appears that speed readers may learn a skill that enables them to more efficiently extract the gist of passages. When skimming research was reviewed (Section IV) it was pointed out that untrained skimmers are not spectacular in their ability to focus on the important content of a passage. If speed readers learn to improve this skill there probably are two means by which this may be accomplished. First, speed readers may possess highly developed skill at conceptually selective processing of gist relevant information that they sample from a text. In support of this idea speed readers often reveal a good deal of reconstructive recall (McLaughlin, 1969), indicating that they make heavy use of general knowledge to piece together bits of information from the printed page (cf. Thorndyke & Hayes-Roth, 1979). A striking example of the extent of this skill was provided by Ehrlich (1963) who tested speed readers on a specially constructed passage. Ehrlich wrote out two lines at a time from two different articles and alternated the pairs of lines to form the final (rather incoherent) text. The speed readers read the text three times for an overall speed of 1700 words/minute and were satisfied that they had understood it, not noticing that the passage was, in effect, incomprehensible. So it is possible that speed readers learn to enhance their ability to draw inferences about the gist of a passage based on sampled text content and prior general knowledge.

A second potential advantage that speed readers may possess involves their pattern of eye movements. Speed reading proponents have claimed that speed readers do not skim (i.e., miss large chunks of text), but distribute their fixations across a text in a uniform manner and are able to see different sentences at each fixation. The research by Rayner and McConkie (1977) immediately calls into question the second part of this claim. Printed text that appears beyond the fovea is not seen clearly enough for a reader to extract a semantic interpretation of it. Moreover, studies of eye movement protocols have found that speed readers use patterns of fixations that skip over a significant proportion of a text.

For example, Taylor (1962) monitored the eye movements of a group of speed readers who had an average rate of about 2000 words/minute and found that in general some lines were skipped completely while others received a few fixations. The scan paths could be described as small, arhythmic left to right saccades occurring while scanning down the page. A pattern that has been observed among even faster speed readers involved scanning down the middle of the left hand page and back up the middle of the right hand page, while skipping a number of lines between saccades (Llewellyn-Thomas, 1962; McLaughlin, 1969).

These patterns are quite unlike normal reading where left to right saccades are made across the full width of the page before moving down to the next line. Eye movement studies of this sort, however, have not provided any evidence concerning the nature of the information that speed readers happen to sample. It might be, for instance, that (unlike untrained skimmers) speed readers are able to perceptually select key words or important information and thereby place themselves at a special advantage with respect to comprehending the gist of a passage. Nor is it known whether speed readers learn to make efficient use of information outside the foveal area.

B. Comprehension and Eye Fixation Patterns

A recent study of speed readers, skimmers, and normal readers has provided a good deal of evidence concerning the nature of the special skills associated with speed reading. One part of the study focused on the speeded comprehension skills that are developed when ordinary readers are trained in a commercial speed reading course (Masson, Carpenter, & Just, 1982). From the evidence reviewed above, it could be concluded that speed readers are particularly adept at extracting gist-relevant information from passages. Given the difficulty of perceptually selective processing of important parts of a passage, it is quite possible that speed readers sample arbitrary portions of text. Working with such text samples they may rely on conceptually selective processing to ensure comprehension of a passage's gist. The ability to concentrate conceptual processing on gist information is a skill that may be more highly developed among speed readers than among untrained skimmers.

A number of tests of this conceptual processing hypothesis were included in the experiments reported by Masson *et al.* In the first experiment three groups of subjects were involved. One group had recently completed a 7-week commercial speed reading course and were asked to speed read a set of passages using their newly acquired technique. The other subjects had received no such training and half were asked to read normally and half were asked to skim at speeds that were similar to those of the speed readers. To determine whether speed readers were especially adept at comprehending gist information, two sets of short-answer comprehension questions were developed for each passage. One set queried gist-relevant information while the other set asked about specific details. If the conceptual selectivity hypothesis is correct, speed readers should show particularly good performance on the gist-relevant questions.

A second test of the hypothesis was generated by using two types of passages. According to the conceptually selective processing hypothesis, concentration of comprehension processes on important information depends on the availability of a large amount of background knowledge concerning the passage topic. Only if the reader has some knowledge about what sorts of information constitute the core of a topic area will he or she be able to organize a macrostructure around that information. Therefore, one set of passages was taken from *Reader's Digest* stories that dealt with familiar topics such as the American cowboy and the exploits of Alexander Graham Bell. A second set of passages was based on *Scientific American* articles dealing with less familiar technical domains such as the terrain of Mars and how bacteria stick to surfaces. The conceptual selectivity hypothesis predicts that speed readers should be at an advantage only when passages based on familiar topics are considered.

Subjects in the experiment were allowed to read at their own speed, although they were instructed to read in a manner that corresponded to the condition to which they had been assigned. The normal reading subjects read at an average speed of about 240 words/minute while the skimmers reached a rate of 600 words/minute and the speed readers averaged 700 words/minute. In order to take variability in reading rate into account, especially when comparing the two rapid reading groups, a measure that combined comprehension and speed was used. A subject's reading rate was multiplied by his or her proportion of correctly answered questions to arrive at that subject's *effective reading rate,* a measure similar to that used by Miller and Kintsch (1980) and Vipond (1980). The results clearly indicated that the only significant advantage enjoyed by the speed readers was in answering gist-relevant questions about familiar topics discussed in *Reader's Digest* passages. Moreover, when question answering scores alone were considered the normal reading group was superior to the speed readers. A very similar pattern of results was obtained when the data from three of the speed readers who had taken part in pretest sessions (prior to taking the course) were analyzed in pre- vs posttest comparisons.

In a second experiment designed to test the conceptual selectivity hypothesis, these three speed readers were asked in pre- and posttest sessions to read and answer questions about isolated paragraphs taken from *Reader's Digest* stories. The important aspect of this experiment was that the paragraphs were presented in a special way. Half of the words were deleted from each passage according to some sampling scheme. For half of the passages the scheme was random while for the remaining passages only the less important (e.g., function) words were removed. These two schemes represent two different approaches to visually sampling information from text while reading rapidly. If speed readers depend primarily on conceptual processing skills, they probably learn to deal with randomly sampled text segments rather than segments that are selected for their importance. Consequently, pre- vs posttest question answering improvement should be more apparent for the random deletion passages than for the systematic deletion passages. The results supported this prediction as only the random deletion passages were associated with significantly improved performance on the posttest.

A more direct source of evidence that speed reading skill is not associated with special text sampling schemes is eye movement data. The second part of the speed reading study involved collection of eye movement protocols from subjects while they read the *Reader's Digest* and *Scientific American* passages used in the comprehension experiment (Just, Carpenter, & Masson, 1982). Three issues of interest here were addressed by the eye movement data. One has to do with the general patterns of eye movements of skimmers and speed readers. The data, which were consistent for both types of passages, indicated that speed readers and skimmers fixated only about one-third of the words in a passage while normal readers fixated almost two-thirds. Normal readers also spent longer on each word they fixated than did the rapid readers (about 330 msec compared to 220 msec). Moreover, the rapid readers differed in their sampling schemes. The skimmers tended to skip larger chunks of text (sometimes 10 to 50 words) than speed readers (not more than 20 words) who were more uniform or consistent in their sampling.

The second issue was whether speed readers were more selective in their sampling of text than skimmers. One method of assessing selective sampling was to determine the relative probability of sampling content as opposed to function words. To control for word length effects, Just *et al.* examined the data for three-letter content and function words. Unlike normal readers who showed a reliably higher probability of sampling the content words, both groups of rapid readers were about equally likely to sample three-letter content and function words. A second method of assessing selective sampling is to monitor changes in reading rate (i.e., sampling density) as the reader moves from one section of a passage to the next. When the relevant data were considered in our study, it was found that all three groups of readers were sensitive to the same changing characteristics of text content. That is, as can be seen in Fig. 5, certain segments of a passage were associated with particularly fast reading rates while others were associated with slow rates. Interestingly, these changes were not predicted by changes in rated importance of text segments, but rather by local comprehension difficulty brought about by unusual syntactic, lexical, or grammatical properties (e.g., the unfamiliar phrase, taken from a passage about a mountain man, "Moon of the popping trees" as a description of a cold winter month). When difficult constructions are encountered, the reader probably increases sampling density to be sure of the information's relation to the gist being extracted from the passage as a whole. This process is common to all three reading groups, although the normal readers (who are able to maintain a more accurate macrostructure of the passage) are less affected than rapid readers.

The third issue regarding the eye movement patterns of speed readers is related to the claim that speed readers are able to process more text information at each fixation than normal readers. To test this possibility, we selected a set of comprehension questions about facts that were mentioned

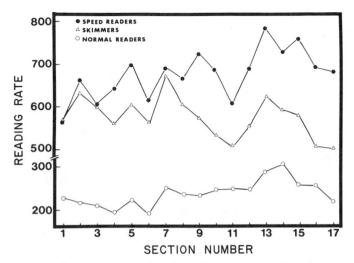

Fig. 5. Mean reading rate for normal readers, skimmers, and speed readers on consecutive sections of a narrative passage.

in only one place in a passage and determined whether speed readers were able to answer the relevant question without having fixated the fact. There were 30 cases in which speed readers did not look at or within three letters of the answer, and only once was the correct answer produced (the year of the Viking Lander touchdown on Mars—1976). Given the rather strict criterion of three letter spaces, this result strongly suggests that speed reading courses do not develop larger perceptual spans for semantic processing.

The results of our analyses of the comprehension and eye movement patterns of speed readers and skimmers point to some rather definite conclusions concerning the nature of the skill that newly trained speed readers acquire. Speed readers appear to extend the conceptually selective processing skills used by untrained skimmers. Repeated practice at making extended inferences from an impoverished data base is an important part of speed reading and it is necessary to execute these operations very rapidly to make use of a quickly accumulating set of new information (recall the reduction in gaze durations, for example). The lack of selective sampling of text information indicates that speed readers do not use cognitive resources for special guidance of eye fixations, but are content to sample text rather uniformly, slowing down when difficult to understand segments are encountered. This reading strategy is different from that espoused by and observed among many untrained skimmers who attempt (but usually fail) to intelligently target their fixations. The speed reader saves the cognitive effort required for this exercise and instead can devote it to the task of making coherent connections between arbitrarily sampled text segments. The fact remains, however, that the reader who operates at normal speed will acquire a more accurate understanding of the passage than will the speed reader.

VII. SUMMARY AND CONCLUSIONS

In this article a number of perspectives on rapid reading skills and processes have been offered. First, the reading process was conceptualized as interactive, depending on interplay between conceptually driven and data driven processes. A consideration of naturally fast comprehenders provided some evidence concerning the importance of certain aspects of conceptually and data driven processes of reading. It was noted that readers who are fast and accurate can more efficiently access memory codes from visual symbols, providing the potential for greater comprehension speed and for wider effective perceptual span. In addition, fast comprehenders are able to store and process information in working memory more efficiently than slower readers. Finally, fast comprehenders seem to focus their efforts on macroprocessing operations associated with integrating information across propositions while slower readers seem to concentrate on and have difficulty with lower level microprocessing operations.

A second perspective on rapid reading was provided by consideration of research on three different methods of speeded reading. Experiments on skimming indicated that readers typically skip significant portions of text content and are unable to effectively select important information while omitting the irrelevant parts. Therefore, when skimming for gist readers seem to rely on conceptually selective processing of important information to form a macrostructure representation of a text. Rapid sequential visual presentation of text can lead to comprehension deficits if the presentation technique does not allow for periodic buffering of information. For example, insertion of pauses between sentences reliably increased comprehension performance during RSVP. The advantage of free reading tasks such as skimming a whole text is that readers do not have to cope with truncated processing of individual words and so do not have to heavily rely on buffering of information. Abbreviated processing of individual words during RSVP likely is particularly devastating to readers who have rather slow access to memory codes from visual symbols. It was also shown that readers can learn to be particularly efficient in conceptually selective processing of text when the goal is to understand the gist of a passage. In this regard, speed readers are capable of extended inference making that provides them with a relatively coherent representation of the important information in a passage. This is not accomplished by an ability to perceptually select relevant text segments but by uniformly sampling the text and by using background knowledge of the passage topic to integrate sampled information. For this process to work, however, the reader must be able to make very rapid and efficient use of whatever is sampled from the passage.

Although I have tried to present a reasonably coherent and believable story concerning rapid reading processes and skills, it is no doubt apparent that many questions remain unanswered or only partially explained. A number of issues have not even been considered here, such as long-term memory for rapidly read text and optimal methods for improvement of reading efficiency. But fortunately the literature on rapid reading is currently enjoying an expansion on two fronts. From a theoretical perspective there is much we can learn about how reading comprehension is achieved by conducting experiments on speeded comprehension tasks. Interest in this approach has been stimulated by models of reading developed by researchers who are willing to accept the challenge of accounting for a wider range of reading strategies and goals. From a practical point of view there is much room for improvement in reading efficiency given the optimal speed of eye movements and the availability of mechanized presentation systems. Meeting this objective probably will depend on the development of presentation techniques and reading strategies that are sensitive to the fundamental, but often subtle, limitations on comprehension processes about which we are beginning to learn a great deal.

ACKNOWLEDGMENT

Preparation of this report was supported in part by Grant A7910 from the Natural Sciences and Engineering Research Council of Canada.

REFERENCES

Aaronson, D., & Scarborough, H. S. Performance theories for sentence coding: Some quantitative models. *Journal of Verbal Learning and Verbal Behavior*, 1977, **16**, 277–303.

Anderson, R. C., & Biddle, W. B. On asking people questions about what they are reading. In G. H. Bower (Ed.), *The psychology of learning and motivation* (Vol. 9). New York: Academic Press, 1975.

Arnold, D. C., & Tinker, M. A. The fixational pause of the eyes. *Journal of Experimental Psychology*, 1939, **25**, 271–280.

Barrus, K., Brown, B. L., & Inouye, D. *Rapid reading reconsidered*. Paper presented at the meeting of the Psychonomic Society, San Antonio, Texas, November 1978.

Bassin, C. B., & Martin, C. J. Effect of three types of redundancy reduction on comprehension, reading rate, and reading time of English prose. *Journal of Educational Psychology*, 1976, **68**, 649–652.

Berger, A. Increasing reading rate with paperbacks. *Reading Improvement*, 1972, **9**, 78–84.

Bobrow, D. G., & Norman, D. A. Some principles of memory schemata. In D. G. Bobrow & A. Collins (Eds.), *Representation and understanding*. New York: Academic Press, 1975.

Bower, G. H., Black, J. B., & Turner, T. J. Scripts in memory for text. *Cognitive Psychology*, 1979, **11**, 177–220.

Bransford, J. D., & Johnson, M. K. Contextual prerequisites for understanding: Some investigations of comprehension and recall. *Journal of Verbal Learning and Verbal Behavior*, 1972, **11**, 717–726.

Bransford, J. D., & McCarrell, N. S. A sketch of a cognitive approach to comprehension: Some thoughts about understanding what it means to comprehend. In W. B. Weimer & D. S. Palermo (Eds.), *Cognition and the symbolic processes*. Hillsdale, New Jersey: Erlbaum, 1974.

Brim, B. J. Impact of a reading improvement program. *Journal of Educational Research*, 1968, **62**, 177–182.

Brown, A. L. Metacognitive development and reading. In R. J. Spiro, B. C. Bruce, & W. F. Brewer (Eds.), *Theoretical issues in reading comprehension*. Hillsdale, New Jersey: Erlbaum, 1980.

Buswell, G. T. The relationship between perceptual and intellectual processes in reading. *California Journal of Educational Research*, 1957, **8**, 99–103.

Caccamise, D. J., & Kintsch, W. Recognition of important and unimportant statements from stories. *American Journal of Psychology*, 1978, **91**, 651–657.

Carpenter, P. A., & Daneman, M. Lexical retrieval and error recovery in reading: A model based on eye fixations. *Journal of Verbal Learning and Verbal Behavior*, 1981, **20**, 137–160.

Carpenter, P. A., & Just, M. A. Integrative processes in comprehension. In D. LaBerge & S. J. Samuels (Eds.), *Basic processes in reading: Perception and comprehension*. Hillsdale, New Jersey: Erlbaum, 1977. (a).

Carpenter, P. A., & Just, M. A. Reading comprehension as eyes see it. In M. A. Just & P. A. Carpenter (Eds.), *Cognitive processes in comprehension*. Hillsdale, New Jersey: Erlbaum, 1977. (b).

Carpenter, T. W., & Jones, Y. Improving comprehension and rate gain at the college level. *Journal of Reading*, 1975, **19**, 223–225.

Carver, R. P. *Sense and nonsense in speed reading*. Silver Spring, Maryland: Revrac, 1971.

Cirilo, R. K., & Foss, D. J. Text structure and reading time for sentences. *Journal of Verbal Learning and Verbal Behavior*, 1980, **19**, 96–109.

Daneman, M., & Carpenter, P. A. Individual differences in working memory and reading. *Journal of Verbal Learning and Verbal Behavior*, 1980, **19**, 450–466.

DeJong, G. Prediction and substantiation: A new approach to natural language processing. *Cognitive Science*, 1979, **3**, 251–273.

Dooling, D. J., & Lachman, R. Effects of comprehension on retention of prose. *Journal of Experimental Psychology*, 1971, **88**, 216–222.

Ehrlich, E. Opinions differ on speed reading. *NEA Journal*, 1963, **52**, 45–46.

Ehrlich, S. F., & Rayner, K. Contextual effects on word perception and eye movements during reading. *Journal of Verbal Learning and Verbal Behavior*, 1981, **20**, 641–655.

Fass, W., & Schumacher, G. M. Schema theory and prose retention: Boundary conditions for encoding and retrieval effects. *Discourse Processes*, 1981, **4**, 17–26.

Fischler, I., & Bloom, P. A. Automatic and attentional processes in the effects of sentence contexts on word recognition. *Journal of Verbal Learning and Verbal Behavior*, 1979, **18**, 1–20.

Fischler, I., & Bloom, P. A. Rapid processing of the meaning of sentences. *Memory & Cognition*, 1980, **8**, 216–225.

Forster, K. I. Visual perception of rapidly presented sentences of varying complexity. *Perception & Psychophysics*, 1970, **8**, 215–221.

Friedrich, F. J., Schadler, M., & Juola, J. F. Developmental changes in units of processing in reading. *Journal of Experimental Child Psychology*, 1979, **28**, 344–358.

Gibson, E. J., & Levin, H. *The psychology of reading.* Cambridge, Mass.: MIT Press, 1975.

Gilbert, L. C. Speed of processing visual stimuli and its relation to reading. *Journal of Educational Psychology*, 1959, **50**, 8–14.

Graesser, A. C., Hoffman, N. L., & Clark, L. F. Structural components of reading time. *Journal of Verbal Learning and Verbal Behavior*, 1980, **19**, 135–151.

Green, D. W., Mitchell, D. C., & Hammond, E. J. The scheduling of text integration processes in reading. *Quarterly Journal of Experimental Psychology*, 1981, **33A**, 455–464.

Hansen, D. M. *A discourse structure analysis of the comprehension of rapid readers.* Doctoral dissertation, Brigham Young University, 1975.

Himelstein, H. C., & Greenberg, G. The effect of increasing reading rate on comprehension. *Journal of Psychology*, 1974, **86**, 251–259.

Hunt, E., Davidson, J., & Lansman, M. Individual differences in long-term memory access. *Memory & Cognition*, 1981, **9**, 599–608.

Hunt, E., Frost, N., & Lunneborg, C. Individual differences in cognition: A new approach to intelligence. In G. H. Bower (Ed.), *The psychology of learning and motivation* (Vol. 7). New York: Academic Press, 1973.

Hunt, E., Lunneborg, C., & Lewis, J. What does it mean to be high verbal? *Cognitive Psychology*, 1975, **7**, 194–227.

Jackson, M. D. Further evidence for a relationship between memory access and reading ability. *Journal of Verbal Learning and Verbal Behavior*, 1980, **19**, 683–694.

Jackson, M. D., & McClelland, J. Sensory and cognitive determinants of reading speed. *Journal of Verbal Learning and Verbal Behavior*, 1975, **14**, 565–574.

Jackson, M. D., & McClelland, J. Processing determinants of reading speed. *Journal of Experimental Psychology: General*, 1979, **108**, 151–181.

Jarvella, R. J. Immediate memory and discourse processing. In G. H. Bower (Ed.), *The psychology of learning and motivation* (Vol. 13). New York: Academic Press, 1979.

Juola, J. F., Ward, N., & McNamara, T. Visual search and reading rapid, serial presentations of letter strings, words, and text. *Journal of Experimental Psychology: General*, 1982, **111**, 208–227.

Just, M. A., & Carpenter, P. A. A theory of reading: From eye fixations to comprehension. *Psychological Review*, 1980, **87**, 329–354.

Just, M. A., Carpenter, P. A., & Masson, M. E. J. *What eye fixations tell us about speed reading and skimming.* Unpublished manuscript, Carnegie-Mellon University, 1982.

Kieras, D. E. *Analysis of the effects of word properties and limited reading time in a sentence comprehension and verification task.* Doctoral dissertation, University of Michigan, 1974.

Kieras, D. E. Good and bad structure in simple paragraphs: Effects on apparent theme, reading time, and recall. *Journal of Verbal Learning and Verbal Behavior*, 1978, **17**, 13–28.

Kieras, D. E. The role of major referents and sentence topics in the construction of passage macrostructure. *Discourse Processes*, 1981, **4**, 1–15.

Kintsch, W., & van Dijk, T. A. Toward a model of text comprehension and production. *Psychological Review*, 1978, **85**, 363–394.

Kintsch, W., & Vipond, D. Reading comprehension and readability in educational practice and psychological theory. In L. G. Nilsson (Ed.), *Perspectives on memory research.* Hillsdale, New Jersey: Erlbaum, 1979.

Kozminsky, E. Altering comprehension: The effect of biasing titles on text comprehension. *Memory & Cognition*, 1977, **5**, 482–490.

Lesgold, A. M., & Perfetti, C. A. Interactive processes in reading comprehension. *Discourse Processes*, 1978, **1**, 323–336.

Lesgold, A. M., Roth, S. F., & Curtis, M. E. Foregrounding effects in discourse comprehension. *Journal of Verbal Learning and Verbal Behavior*, 1979, **18**, 291–308.

Liddle, W. *An investigation of the Wood reading dynamics method.* Doctoral dissertation, University of Delaware, 1965.

Llewellyn-Thomas, E. Eye movements in speed reading. In R. G. Stauffer (Ed.), *Speed reading: Practices and procedures.* Newark, Delaware: Univ. of Deleware Reading Center, 1962.

McLaughlin, G. H. Reading at "impossible" speeds. *Journal of Reading*, 1969, **12**, 449–454; 502–510.

Marcel, T. The effective visual field and the use of context in fast and slow readers of two ages. *British Journal of Psychology*, 1974, **65**, 479–492.

Masson, M. E. J. Cognitive processes in skimming stories. *Journal of Experimental Psychology: Learning, Memory, and Cognition*, 1982, **8**, 400–417.

Masson, M. E. J. Conceptual processing of text during skimming and rapid sequential reading. *Memory & Cognition*, 1983, **11**, 262–274.

Masson, M. E. J. *Individual differences in rapid reading ability.* Manuscript in preparation, 1984.

Masson, M. E. J., Carpenter, P. A., & Just, M. A. *Comprehension of gist and details in speed reading, skimming, and normal reading.* Unpublished manuscript, University of Victoria, 1982.

Masson, M. E. J., & Miller, J. A. Working memory and individual differences in comprehension and memory of text. *Journal of Educational Psychology,* 1983, **75**, 314–318.

Maxwell, M. J., & Mueller, A. C. Relative effectiveness of techniques and placebo conditions in changing reading rates. *Journal of Reading*, 1967, **11**, 184–191.

Meijsing, M. Expectations in understanding complex stories. *Poetics*, 1980, **9**, 213–221.

Miller, J. R., & Kintsch, W. Readability and recall of short prose passages: A theoretical analysis. *Journal of Experimental Psychology: Human Learning and Memory*, 1980, **6**, 335–354.

Mitchell, D. C. The locus of the experimental effects in the rapid serial visual presentation (RSVP) task. *Perception & Psychophysics*, 1979, **25**, 143–149.

Mitchell, D. C., & Green, D. W. The effects of context and content on immediate processing in reading. *Quarterly Journal of Experimental Psychology*, 1978, **30**, 609–636.

Neely, J. H. Semantic priming and retrieval from lexical memory: Roles of inhibitionless spreading activation and limited-capacity attention. *Journal of Experimental Psychology: General*, 1977, **106**, 226–254.

Perfetti, C. A., & Goldman, S. R. Discourse memory and reading comprehension skill. *Journal of Verbal Learning and Verbal Behavior*, 1976, **14**, 33–42.

Perfetti, C. A., Goldman, S. R., & Hogaboam, T. W. Reading skill and the identification of words in discourse context. *Memory & Cognition*, 1979, **7**, 273–282.

Perfetti, C. A., & Lesgold, A. M. Discourse comprehension and sources of individual differences. In M. A. Just & P. A. Carpenter (Eds.), *Cognitive processes in comprehension.* Hillsdale, New Jersey: Erlbaum, 1977.

Perfetti, C. A., & Roth, S. F. Some of the interactive processes in reading and their role in reading skill. In A. M. Lesgold & C. A. Perfetti (Eds.), *Interactive processes in reading.* Hillsdale, New Jersey: Erlbaum, 1981.

Pichert, J. W., & Anderson, R. C. Taking different perspectives on a story. *Journal of Educational Psychology*, 1977, **69**, 309–315.

Posner, M. I., & McLeod, P. Information processing models—In search of elementary operations. *Annual Review of Psychology*, 1982, **33**, 477–514.

Potter, M. C., & Faulconer, B. A. Time to understand pictures and words. *Nature (London)*, 1975, **253**, 437–438.

Potter, M. C., Kroll, J. F., & Harris, C. Comprehension and memory in rapid sequential reading. In R. S. Nickerson (Ed.), *Attention and performance VIII*. Hillsdale, New Jersey: Erlbaum, 1980.

Poulton, E. C. British courses for adults on effective reading. *British Journal of Educational Psychology*, 1961, **31**, 128–137.

Rayner, K. Eye movements in reading and information processing. *Psychological Bulletin*, 1978, **85**, 618–660.

Rayner, K., Inhoff, A. W., Morrison, R. E., Slowiaczek, M. L., & Bertera, J. H. Masking of foveal and parafoveal vision during eye fixations in reading. *Journal of Experimental Psychology: Human Perception and Performance*, 1981, **7**, 167–179.

Rayner, K., & McConkie, G. W. Perceptual processes in reading: The perceptual spans. In A. S. Reber & D. L. Scarborough (Eds.), *Toward a psychology of reading*. Hillsdale, New Jersey: Erlbaum, 1977.

Rayner, K., & Pollatsek, A. Eye movement control during reading: Evidence for direct control. *Quarterly Journal of Experimental Psychology*, 1981, **33A**, 351–373.

Reder, L. M. The role of elaboration in memory for prose. *Cognitive Psychology*, 1979, **11**, 221–234.

Rothkopf, E. Z., & Fisher, D. G. *Evidence for individual reading styles: A challenge for general models of reading*. Paper presented at the meeting of the Psychonomic Society, Philadelphia, November 1981.

Rumelhart, D. E. Toward an interactive model of reading. In S. Dornic (Ed.), *Attention and performance VI*. New York: Academic Press, 1977.

Sailor, A. L., & Ball, S. E. Peripheral vision training in reading speed and comprehension. *Perceptual and Motor Skills*, 1975, **41**, 761–762.

Salthouse, T. A., & Ellis, C. L. Determinants of eye-fixation duration. *American Journal of Psychology*, 1980, **93**, 207–234.

Salthouse, T. A., Ellis, C. L., Diener, D. C., & Somberg, B. L. Stimulus processing during eye fixations. *Journal of Experimental Psychology: Human Perception and Performance*, 1981, **7**, 611–623.

Schank, R. C., & Abelson, R. P. *Scripts, plans, goals and understanding*. Hillsdale, New Jersey: Erlbaum, 1977.

Shebilske, W. L., Reid, L. S., & Wright, C. E. *Toward the analysis of comprehension processes during reading*. Paper presented at the meeting of the Psychonomic Society, Washington, D. C., November 1977.

Smith, M. C., & Magee, L. E. Tracing the time course of picture-word processing. *Journal of Experimental Psychology: General*, 1980, **109**, 373–392.

Spiro, R. J. Prior knowledge and story processing: Integration, selection and variation. *Poetics*, 1980, **9**, 313–327.

Stanovich, K. E. Attentional and automatic context effects in reading. In A. M. Lesgold & C. A. Perfetti (Eds.), *Interactive processes in reading*. Hillsdale, New Jersey: Erlbaum, 1981.

Sticht, T. G. Comprehending reading at work. In M. A. Just & P. A. Carpenter (Eds.), *Cognitive processes in comprehension*. Hillsdale, New Jersey: Erlbaum, 1977.

Taylor, S. E. An evaluation of forty-one trainees who had recently completed the "reading dynamics" program. *Eleventh Yearbook of the National Reading Conference*, 1962, 41–55.

Thames, K. H., & Rossiter, C. M. The effects of reading practice with compressed speech on reading rate and listening comprehension. *AV Communication Review*, 1972, **20**, 35–42.

Thibadeau, R., Just, M. A., & Carpenter, P. A. A model of the time course and content of reading. *Cognitive Science*, 1982, **6**, 157–203.

Thorndyke, P. W. Knowledge acquisition from newspaper stories. *Discourse Processes*, 1979, **2**, 95–112.

Thorndyke, P. W., & Hayes-Roth, B. The use of schemata in the acquisition and transfer of knowledge. *Cognitive Psychology*, 1979, **11**, 82–106.

Thorndyke, P. W., & Yekovich, F. R. A critique of schema-based theories of human story memory. *Poetics*, 1980, **9**, 23–49.

Tinker, M. A. Recent studies of eye movements in reading. *Psychological Bulletin*, 1958, **55**, 215–231.

Tinker, M. A. Devices to improve speed of reading. *Reading Teacher*, 1967, **20**, 605–609.

Vipond, D. Micro- and macroprocesses in text comprehension. *Journal of Verbal Learning and Verbal Behavior*, 1980, **19**, 276–296.

Ward, N. J., & Juola, J. F. Reading with and without eye movements: A reply to Just, Carpenter, and Wooley. *Journal of Experimental Psychology: General*, 1982, **111**, 239–241.

West, R. F., & Stanovich, K. E. Automatic contextual facilitation in readers of three ages. *Child Development*, 1978, **49**, 717–727.

Wood, E. N. A breakthrough in reading. *Reading Teacher*, 1960, **14**, 115–117.

Yekovich, F. R., & Thorndyke, P. W. An evaluation of alternative functional models of narrative schemata. *Journal of Verbal Learning and Verbal Behavior*, 1981, **20**, 454–469.

ACQUIRED DYSLEXIA: IMPLICATIONS FOR MODELS OF READING

ELEANOR M. SAFFRAN

Department of Neurology
Temple University School of Medicine
Philadelphia, Pennsylvania

I. INTRODUCTION

The *acquired* (as distinct from *developmental*) *dyslexias* are reading disturbances that result from brain damage in formerly literate individuals. Until recently, neurologically based reading disorders were primarily studied with neuroanatomical questions in mind (e.g., Benson, 1981). However, as neuropsychologists have become increasingly oriented toward cognitive issues in the past decade, interest in the acquired dyslexias has shifted toward their functional implications. In particular, it has been claimed that the breakdown patterns reflect the selective impairment of components of the reading process and hence that the study of these disorders can contribute to the understanding of normal reading (Shallice, 1981; Patterson, 1981; Coltheart, 1981). Data collection in this area of neuropsychology has, in fact, been closely associated with efforts to construct models of the reading process that incorporate the distinctions implied by the pathological data. We will focus on these model-building efforts in this article, which reviews research on four varieties of acquired dyslexia.

A brief methodological comment is in order before we begin. The data base for this article is an unusual one for cognitive psychology, in that it is drawn largely from studies of individual cases. Given the rarity with which brain lesions give rise to selective reading impairments, it is seldom possible to assemble homogeneous groups of patients. Patterns of impairment are usually identified on the basis of single case studies and later validated and further characterized in additional patients. While strong claims cannot be made on the basis of individual data, corroborating evidence can be sought in the consistency of deficit patterns across patients, in the complementarity of patterns across syndromes, and ultimately in the compatibility between deficit patterns and models derived from normative data (see Patterson, 1981, and Shallice, 1979, for further discussion).

It should also be pointed out that most of the evidence gathered thus far has been derived from oral reading tasks, oral reading of single words at that. Data on other tasks, such as lexical decision and word comprehension, are generally more limited. In most of the cases to be discussed below, then, "inability to read" should be taken to mean "inability to read aloud," and not necessarily to imply failure of word recognition or understanding.

II. DEEP AND SURFACE DYSLEXIA: THE BASIC DISSOCIATION

A framework for the cognitive analysis of the acquired dyslexias was provided in a seminal paper by Marshall and Newcombe that appeared in 1973. On the basis of the oral reading errors that predominated in individual patients, these authors were able to differentiate three types of dyslexic disturbances which appeared to reflect disruption at particular stages of the reading process.

Two of these error types will concern us here: (1) those in which there is a *phonological* relationship between target word and error, as in *recent* → "rikunt" and *gauge* → "jug"; and (2) those in which the relationship is *semantic* in nature, as in *berry* → "grapes" and *nephew* → "cousin." The syndrome in which phonological errors predominated was termed *surface dyslexia,* reflecting the assumption that the errors arise in the phonological recoding of the graphemic information and hence at a fairly early stage in the reading process. The syndrome characterized by semantic errors was designated *deep dyslexia,* on the grounds that the errors must arise subsequent to lexical access and therefore at a fairly late stage in the reading process. These deficit patterns have by now been confirmed in many other cases [~ 25 for deep dyslexia (Coltheart, Patterson, & Marshall, 1980) and ~ 12 for surface dyslexia (Coltheart, Patterson, & Marshall, 1984)].

Marshall and Newcombe (1973) offered an account of these deficit patterns in terms of a "two-route" or "dual access" model of the reading process, similar to the one outlined in Fig. 1.

The model stipulates two distinct mechanisms for word recognition, both of which are assumed to be available to the normal reader. Printed words can be identified by matching their orthographic[1] properties to stored lex-

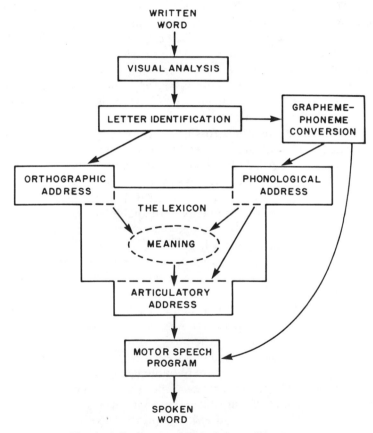

Fig. 1. A dual-access model of the reading process.

---

[1]It seems fairly clear that this mode of lexical access involves the use of letter information, rather than reliance on configurational properties of words. For evidence from normative studies, see McClelland (1977); relevant neuropsychological data may be found in Saffran (1980).

ical entries, as on the left side of Fig. 1; or graphemic input can be translated into a phonological code, which can be matched to lexical entries that are specified phonologically, as on the right side of the figure. If the *orthographic* route is disrupted, the reader is forced to rely entirely on the *phonological* route, and vice versa. The consequences for reading performance of these two types of impairments are outlined below.

1. Reliance on orthographic reading. The model in Fig. 1 stipulates that print-to-sound translation via the orthographic route requires semantic mediation. The articulatory address is accessed via a semantic description of the printed word, presumably in the same way that output is generated in spontaneous speech production. The performance of an individual who is relying exclusively on this route would be expected to have the following characteristics: (1) the ability to read aloud should be limited to letter strings for which there are orthographic addresses, that is, to real words which are in the individual's reading vocabulary; and (2) errors that occur should be semantically rather than phonologically related to the target.

These are, in fact, two of the cardinal features of deep dyslexia. The tendency to produce semantic errors has already been mentioned; these account for about 25% of the oral reading errors (not counting omissions) of deep dyslexics (see Appendix; also, Table 5.2 in Shallice & Warrington, 1980). The fact that reading in deep dyslexia is limited to known words was demonstrated by Patterson and Marcel (1977) and Saffran and Marin (1977), who showed that these patients were unable to read nonsense words aloud, or even to match written to spoken nonwords or to recognize real words in the guise of phonetic spellings (e.g., *bote, foan*). On the model in Fig. 1, these are tasks that require grapheme–phoneme translation. It can reasonably be argued, moreover, that semantic paralexias like *ancient* → "historic" would be unlikely to occur if the reader were able to generate some phonological information from the letter string. This information would presumably lead to the rejection of candidate responses that depart radically from the phonology of the target word.

But while the phonological reading deficit may help to account for the failure to suppress responses that are phonologically unrelated to the target, it does not explain why the lexical/semantic system is generating off-target responses. Substitutions that are nearly synonymous with the target—errors such as *bough* → "branch" and *gift* → "present" (from Coltheart *et al.,* 1980, Appendix 2)—might be expected to occur in cases where reading aloud is based on semantic description. However, the majority of the semantic errors produced by deep dyslexics are not so closely related to the target (see examples in the Appendix); in many cases, as in *turtle* → "crocodile" and *genealogist* → "babies" (Coltheart *et al.,* 1980, Appendix 2), the relationship is in fact rather remote. Errors like these suggest that the lexical/

semantic operations that underlie oral reading in deep dyslexia are not entirely normal.

There are other features of deep dyslexic performance that point to impaired lexical processing as a component of this syndrome. Deep dyslexics' ability to read aloud is consistently found to vary both as a function of abstractness (or imageability) and part-of-speech.[2] Concrete nouns are read better than abstract nouns, and nouns, as a class, tend to be read better than verbs or adjectives (e.g., Shallice & Warrington, 1975; Colthart, 1980a). Deep dyslexics have most difficulty reading function words, such as auxiliaries and prepositions, despite the fact that these are among the most frequent words in the language. The level of accuracy of function word reading is typically in the range of 10–20%, with most of the errors consisting of failures to respond ["Little words—No!" was the apt title that Morton and Patterson (1980b) gave to a paper on this topic] or within-category substitutions (e.g., *for* → "with"). The pattern of performance across word classes is highly consistent across patients (see the review of cases in Coltheart, 1980a).

Oral reading in deep dyslexia is therefore limited to a vocabulary of known words that is restricted along the lines of the word class parameters noted above. Other salient features of deep dyslexic performance include (1) derivational[3] errors, such as *directing* → "directions" (see Patterson, 1980, for a study of these errors), and (2) visual errors, such as *soul* → "soup" and *prosper* → "proper" (see Patterson, 1978, and Coltheart, 1980b, for discussions of this error type). Further examples of errors produced by deep dyslexics can be found in the Appendix. In general, oral reading performance on standard lists which sample across word classes is in the order of 50% correct.

Other measures of reading performance suggest, however, that oral reading tests may seriously underestimate the reading capabilities of at least some deep dyslexics. Using a comprehension measure, the reading vocabulary of one deep dyslexic patient (V.S.) was estimated to be in excess of 16,500 words (Saffran & Marin, 1977). One of Patterson's patients (P.W.), who showed the usual advantage for concrete words in reading aloud, performed equally well with abstract and concrete words in a comprehension task (Patterson, 1981); the same patient performed at the level of normal controls in a lexical decision task involving abstract words (Patterson, 1979). Furthermore, though deep dyslexics read function words aloud with only

[2]Imageability and part-of-speech are to some extent confounded (Allport & Funnell, 1981).

[3]The term "derivational" is only descriptive. These errors could just as well be designated visual or semantic. Whether they do, in fact, reflect a mechanism that has something to do with derivational or inflectional processes is not yet clear.

10 to 20% accuracy, they readily identify functors as words on lexical decision tasks (Patterson, 1979; Saffran, Bogyo, Schwartz, & Marin, 1980; Nolan & Caramazza, 1982) and may also be able to comprehend their meanings (Morton & Patterson, 1980b). Such observations would seem to suggest that the lexical limitations in deep dyslexia are primarily at the level of output from the lexicon (i.e., at the level designated in Fig. 1 as the articulatory address). The problem with this as a general account of deep dyslexic performance is that the comprehension abilities of some patients are more limited than those of V.S. and P.W. (e.g., Shallice & Coughlan, 1980; Patterson, 1981). In such cases, levels of performance on comprehension and oral reading tasks are not so discrepant.

We will return to the problem of lexical limitations in deep dyslexics in Section III. For the present, it is sufficient to note that there are such limitations, and that the reading pattern in deep dyslexia is therefore the product of two underlying disturbances, one involving lexical capacities and the other involving grapheme–phoneme conversion.

2. Reliance on phonological recoding. Now consider what reading performance might look like if the orthographic route was blocked and access to the lexicon depended on a phonological translation of the letter string. The translation process is generally thought to involve the application of a set of grapheme–phoneme correspondence rules (e.g., $d \rightarrow$ /d/; $oo \rightarrow$ /u/), along with a set of rules that govern contextual dependencies, such as vowel lengthening in the environment *VCe* (e.g., Coltheart, 1978). Reading via this phonological route would not pose much of a problem if the orthography were entirely regular, but English contains many "exception" words which cannot be read correctly by means of grapheme–phoneme translation (*pint,* for example, would be read as /pInt/). Orthographic regularity is the dimension along which performance breaks down in surface dyslexia. These patients show a significant advantage for regular words in reading aloud (Coltheart, Masterson, Byng, Prior, & Riddoch, 1983). They also have difficulty comprehending irregular words, which should occur if they are accessing the lexicon on the basis of grapheme–phoneme translation. Thus, for example, one of the patients of Coltheart *et al.* (1983) read *bear* as /bir/ and gave as the definition for this word, "a drink."

Orthographic irregularity is not, however, the only dimension of reading difficulty in surface dyslexia. These patients make many errors, like *recent* $\rightarrow$ /rikənt/ and *gauge* $\rightarrow$ "jug" which clearly represent violations of grapheme–phoneme correspondence rules. While single letters that have consistent phonological realizations present few problems, surface dyslexics tend to have "difficulty with the context-sensitive nature of grapheme–phoneme mappings," in particular with "ambiguous consonants (whose phonetic value depends upon the graphemic context in which they are placed) and markers (such as terminal *e*) which have themselves no phonetic value but rather specify the realization of some other part of the word" (Marshall & Newcombe, 1973, p. 191). These effects suggest that while impairment of an orthographic access route may be the primary cause of reading dysfunction in surface dyslexia, the phonological translation process has also been partially affected.

The two syndromes of deep and surface dyslexia provide evidence for a distinction between two pathways in reading, one involving direct access to the lexicon via orthography and the other requiring translation into a phonological code. These syndromes do not represent a complete dissociation between the two pathways, since in neither case can the residual mechanism be said to be entirely unaffected; the lexical system seems to be partially impaired in deep dyslexia, while in surface dyslexia the capacity for phonological recoding is to some degree limited. Nevertheless, the contrasting deficit patterns offer strong support for a dual access model of the reading process, as outlined in Fig. 1. The performance pattern in deep dyslexia provides particularly compelling evidence that lexical access can occur in the absence of phonological recoding, a possibility that was seriously questioned at the time these studies of acquired dyslexia began to appear (see, e.g., Rubenstein, Lewis, & Rubenstein, 1971).

At an empirical level, the basic distinctions raised by Marshall and Newcombe's (1973) work have not been contested. The contrasting patterns of performance that define deep and surface dyslexia have been confirmed in many other patients (cf. Coltheart *et al.,*1980, 1985). Subsequent work has been concerned with clarifying the nature of the deficits in these syndromes and with the description of additional varieties of acquired dyslexia (Sections III and IV). In the domain of theory, the dual access approach has been highly influential (see, e.g., papers in Coltheart *et al.,* 1980; Patterson, 1981). However, the original model has required modification (Section IV) and has been challenged in fundamental respects by some investigators (Section V).

III. DEEP VS PHONOLOGICAL DYSLEXIA

At a behavioral level, deep dyslexia is certainly the most intriguing of the dyslexic syndromes that have been described thus far. That someone could read *tulip* as "crocus" and read *chrysanthemum* correctly but not *do* or *if* (Saffran & Marin, 1977) does not cease to astonish even the seasoned observer. There is, however, some question as to the relevance of this syndrome for normal reading.

Ideally, assuming that the two-route model in Fig. 1 captures the essential componential structure of the normal reading process, and that Marshall and Newcombe's (1973) interpretation of deep dyslexia on this model is correct, the reading performance of deep dyslexics should reveal the characteristics of reading via the orthographic route to the lexicon. The limitations discussed in the previous section—the abstractness effect, the part-of-speech effects, the semantic paralexias—give one pause, however. It is difficult to believe that these limitations on lexically based reading could represent "normal reading minus phonology."

As suggested earlier (Section II), the limitations on word reading in deep dyslexia indicate that the lexical processes which subserve reading performance in these patients are in some way deficient. In most cases, there would seem to be an obvious explanation for these deficiencies. Virtually all of the deep dyslexics that have been described thus far have been at least moderately aphasic (cf. Coltheart, 1980a). Assuming that these patients are reading via the same set of lexical procedures that they use in spontaneous speech, the reading impairment should mirror the language impairment. By and large, this does seem to be the case. The language profiles of most deep dyslexics are characteristic of Broca's aphasia, a syndrome in which speech is "agrammatic" (i.e., lacking in inflectional morphemes and function words) and its content biased toward concrete words (e.g., Saffran, 1982). In such cases, there do seem to be striking parallels between speaking and reading. In addition to the difficulty with function words and the concreteness effect, these patients are likely to produce semantic errors in production tasks as well as in reading (e.g., Friedman & Perlman, 1982). However, as Coltheart (1980b) has noted, deep dyslexia has been observed in several patients who show either little language impairment, or patterns of impairment that do not parallel their deficits in reading. While the similarities between the reading deficits and language disturbances of dyslexic patients clearly require further investigation (cf. Nolan & Caramazza, 1982; Friedman & Perlman, 1982), it does not seem, on the basis of the data presently available, that the lexical limitations on deep dyslexic reading are entirely explained by the aphasic impairments of these patients.

An alternative to the view that deep dyslexia is the result of impairment to two separate systems, one involving phonological recoding and the other lexical/semantic processes (see Morton & Patterson, 1980a; Shallice & Warrington, 1980; Nolan & Caramazza, 1982, for statements of this position), is that these patients are relying on an auxiliary mechanism that may have little to do with normal reading. Similarities between deep dyslexia and the pattern of reading performance demonstrated by the isolated right hemisphere in split brain and hemispherectomy patients have suggested that deep dyslexics are utilizing right hemisphere mechanisms for reading (Coltheart, 1980; Saffran *et al.,* 1980). Thus there is evidence that while the right hemisphere may be capable of sustaining a large reading vocabulary (Zaidel, 1978), it is unable to encode print phonologically (Zaidel & Peters, 1981), and its vocabulary, like that of the deep dyslexic, is biased toward concrete nouns (Zaidel, 1978). Evidence that deep dyslexics have extensive left hemisphere lesions involving most of the area thought to be committed to speech and language (see Coltheart *et al.,* 1980, Appendix 1) provides further support for the right hemisphere view. One piece of evidence against this view is that lesions restricted to the left hemisphere can result in total reading disability, or *alexia* (e.g., Hecaen & Kremin, 1976). This should not occur if there is auxiliary reading capacity in the right hemisphere. It may reasonably be argued[4] however, that there is variability within the population with respect to right hemisphere language representation, and that deep dyslexics lie at one end of this distribution and alexics at other (Saffran *et al.,* 1980). Attempts to test the right hemisphere hypothesis directly, by means of split field studies in deep dyslexics, have provided data that are consistent with this hypothesis, though they are by no means conclusive (Saffran *et al.,* 1980).

Whether one views the performance patterns of deep dyslexics as reflecting the limitations of a right hemisphere language system, or those of an impaired left hemisphere lexicon serving, in the absence of a grapheme-phoneme conversion mechanism, as the sole basis for reading, there is reason to question whether the performance patterns of deep dyslexics have any bearing on reading in the normal state. There are, however, several recent reports of cases in which a severe phonological recoding deficit occurs in the absence of the limitations on word reading that are characteristic of deep dyslexia. These patients, first identified by Beauvois and Desrouesne (1979; Desrouesne & Beauvois, 1979; see also Shallice & Warrington, 1980; Patterson, 1982; Funnell, 1983) who termed them *phonological dyslexics,* fare little better than deep dyslexics in reading nonwords aloud (their success rate with monosyllabic nonsense words is typically in the range of 10 to 20%, while that of deep dyslexics approaches zero). But phonological dyslexics are much better than deep dyslexics at reading real words; on standard word lists, their performance is 80–100% correct, compared with the typical deep dyslexic's 50%. They do not make semantic errors (see Appendix), and factors such as abstractness and part-of-speech have little influence on their performance. The only significant word class effects involve grammatical morphemes: some phonological dyslexics have difficulty reading function words, though they are considerably less impaired than deep dyslexics; they also tend to make derivational errors (but see Funnell, 1983, for a report of a patient who had neither of these problems).

---

[4]Though with some sacrifice of the testability of the model.

Thus we have two syndromes, deep dyslexia and phonological dyslexia, in which print-to-sound translation is critically dependent on lexically stored information. The two classes of patients differ in degree of reading impairment, a difference which might be attributed to the relative preservation of lexical capacities in phonological as compared with deep dyslexics (this view is tenable on both the multiple deficit and right hemisphere accounts of deep dyslexia). The implication to be drawn from these cases of phonological dyslexia is that it is possible to read tolerably well, at least at a single word level and within the boundaries of an established vocabulary, in the absence of a functional mechanism for grapheme–phoneme conversion. The existence of such a syndrome is predictable on the view, put forth by Coltheart (1980c), that prelexical phonological recoding plays a minimal role in normal skilled reading. The evidence from phonological dyslexia does not, of course, exclude the possibility that normal readers engage the phonological translation mechanism in reading words aloud. It does suggest, however, that the store of orthographic input addresses can be extensive enough to support fairly adequate reading performance at the single word level.

As noted above, some phonological dyslexics have difficulty reading function words and affixes, but this does not appear to be a consistent feature of the syndrome (Funnell, 1983; Shallice & Warrington, 1980). The lack of consistency suggests that the association between impaired phonological recoding and difficulty in reading grammatical morphemes in phonological dyslexia may reflect proximity of the anatomical subsystems that subserve these functions, and hence their common susceptibility to focal brain disease, rather than functional interdependence. In general, it should be noted that arguments based on the *association* of deficits in pathological cases are necessarily weaker than arguments based on *dissociations*. If two symptoms occur independently, it is possible to conclude that they depend on different mechanisms. In cases where symptoms co-occur, it is necessary to consider the possibility that their association has an anatomical rather than a functional basis (Saffran, 1982).

To summarize: while the relevance of deep dyslexia to normal reading is currently in some doubt, the performance pattern in phonological dyslexia permits a stronger claim than could be made for deep dyslexia: that it is possible to read nearly normally at the single word level in the absence of a functional system for a grapheme–phoneme conversion.

IV. SURFACE VS SEMANTIC DYSLEXIA

The reading disorders that have been discussed thus far result from focal lesions that are usually of acute onset, resulting in most cases from stroke or traumatic injury to the brain. Recently, investigators have begun to look at reading performance in cases of progressive, degenerative brain disease, or dementia.

Some dementia patients exhibit selective deterioration of the semantic aspects of language at a time when other language functions (phonology and syntax) remain relatively intact (Warrington, 1975; Schwartz, Marin, & Saffran, 1979). Word retrieval and comprehension become severely impaired, as a result of a progressive loss of word meanings. It is therefore appropriate to describe the residual reading performance of these patients as "reading without semantics" (Shallice, Warrington, & McCarthy, 1983).

Several interesting findings have emerged thus far from studies of reading in semantically impaired patients. The first bears on the issue of semantic mediation in word reading. On the two-route model in Fig. 1, either the orthographic or the phonological mechanism will serve for the pronunciation of orthographically regular words; but the phonological encoding of exception words such as *pint* and *broad* can be accomplished only via the orthographic route. Since the model stipulates that this process is semantically mediated, the ability to read exception words aloud should be closely linked to the ability to understand them. This prediction was not borne out in a case study of a patient (W.L.P.) with a profound semantic impairment (Schwartz, Saffran, & Marin, 1980). W.L.P. was able to read exception words (*leopard* and *tortoise,* for example) which she failed to understand, as indicated by her inability to match these words to pictures or to category labels. These observations led to the suggestion that a pathway involving "word-specific print-to-sound associations" be incorporated into the dual access model (Schwartz *et al.,* 1980; Morton & Patterson, 1980a). The revised model, which is outlined in Fig. 2, therefore provides *three* ways of deriving a pronunciation for a letter string: one involves grapheme–phoneme translation; a second, which involves orthographic access to the lexicon, locates an articulatory address by semantic description; the third, which is also orthographically based, maps the orthographic address directly onto the articulatory address.

The second finding that is of interest concerns the existence of a regularity effect in semantically impaired patients. While W.L.P. was able to read most irregular words aloud despite her severely impaired comprehension, she did, nevertheless, make more errors in reading exception words than regular words. This pattern was first reported in a semantically impaired patient (E.M.) studied by Warrington (1975). The discrepancy between regular and irregular words was more dramatic in E.M. than in W.L.P., though W.L.P., too, began to have more difficulty with exception words as her dementia progressed (Schwartz *et al.,* 1980).

The characteristics of reading in a semantically impaired patient at a stage when a significant regularity effect was demonstrable have been analyzed in a recent study by Shallice *et al.* (1983). Their patient, H.T.R., read 86%

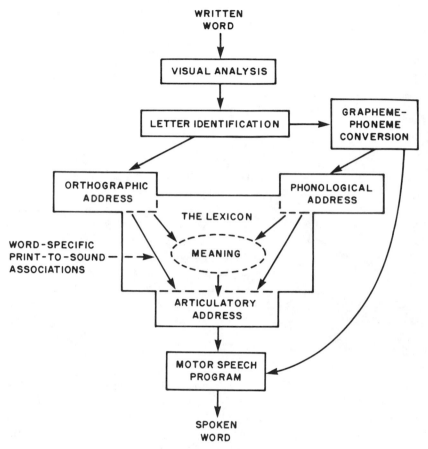

Fig. 2. A revised dual-access model of the reading process.

of regular words correctly, as compared with 33% of frequency-matched irregular words. Errors on the latter were typically nonlexical regularizations (e.g., prove → /prauv/). These observations, along with H.T.R.'s very good performance (88% correct) on nonsense words, suggested that this patient was performing print-to-sound translation by rule rather than by means of word-specific associations.

The reader may already have noted similarities between these semantically impaired patients and surface dyslexics, who also show a regularity effect in oral reading. In other respects, however, there are differences between the two groups of patients. The *semantic dyslexics,* as we will provisionally call them (after Shallice *et al.,* 1983), seem to have better control over spelling–sound rules than surface dyslexics. Thus, 46% of H.R.T.'s errors could be regarded as regularization errors (that is, as pronunciations consistent with grapheme–phoneme conversion rules), while the proportion of regularization errors in five surface dyslexics studied by Coltheart, Masterson, and Byng (1984) ranged from .12 to .23 (see Appendix). Furthermore, while surface dyslexics tend to read very slowly and often seem to be engaged in conscious assembly of the word in the fashion of beginning readers, H.T.R.'s reading rate was approximately normal (Shallice *et al.*, 1983).

Surface dyslexics also differ from semantic dyslexics in their tendency to "lexicalize" letter strings—that is, to pronounce them as words. It has been pointed out that the proportion of surface dyslexics' errors that are nonwords is lower than one might expect, if it is the case that they are relying solely on grapheme–phoneme correspondence rules and, moreover, often applying them incorrectly (Marcel, 1980). Thus Patterson (1981) notes, "The reading error *incense* → 'increase', for instance, can be considered an example of difficulty with the ambiguous consonant *c*; but if that were the only factor, the patient should have produced the neologism 'inkense'." The lexicalization effect was the focus of a recent case study (Saffran, 1985), in which it was demonstrated that a surface dyslexic's pronunciation of CVCe nonwords (e.g., *dipe, vide*) was influenced by the lexical status of the incorrect (i.e., short vowel) pronunciation (e.g., *dip, vid*). If the short vowel pronunciation yielded a word, the probability of error was higher ($p = .58$) than if it yielded a nonword ($p = .32$); thus, for example, the patient would be more likely to pronounce *dipe* as "dip" than *vide* as "vid." While comparable data are not available for semantic dyslexia, H.T.R.'s low error rate on nonwords (.12) suggests that lexicalization is not as important a factor as it appears to be in surface dyslexia.

The lexicalization effect considerably complicates the interpretation of reading performance in surface dyslexia. Real-word responses would seem to be of doubtful utility, insofar as the assessment of surface dyslexics' ability to utilize grapheme–phoneme correspondence rules is concerned, since the extent to which any particular response reflects lexicalization as opposed to rule application (or misapplication) will be difficult to determine. It seems likely, moreover, that many of the surface dyslexic errors previously characterized as "visual" (e.g., *scare* → "scarf"; *spend* → "speed") might be explained in terms of lexicalization on the basis of partial—and in many cases faulty—phonological translation, as opposed to failure at some level of orthographic analysis.

In light of all of these problems, the relevance of surface dyslexia for phonological processing in normal reading is questionable. As Henderson (1981) has put it, "it does not seem that a normal reader who reads aloud pseudowords that lack a lexical entry performs at all like a surface dyslexic." The performance patterns of surface dyslexics are, however, quite similar to those of beginning readers: both groups demonstrate a tendency toward lexicalization, and both tend to be insensitive to contextual dependencies in grapheme–phoneme translation (Marcel, 1980). Presumably, the underlying mechanisms are similar as well: like the surface dyslexic, the beginning reader has a limited store of orthographic addresses, and is therefore forced to rely on phonological recoding mechanisms which are as yet quite limited. Surface dyslexia might therefore provide a useful model for beginning reading, and possibly for certain forms of developmental dyslexia in which the deficit patterns appear similar to those of acquired dyslexics (e.g., Holmes, 1978; Temple, 1984). We have to look to semantic dyslexia to find a disorder in which phonological translation procedures that are operative in skilled readers appear to be well preserved, relative to other mechanisms for pronouncing printed words.

In terms of the model in Fig. 2, then, semantic dyslexia represents a progressive disorder in which (1) the ability to read words aloud by semantic description is the first mechanism to be affected, as indicated by the loss of word comprehension that occurs relatively early in the patient's course; (2) the ability to read by direct print-to-sound associations is gradually lost, as indicated by the increasing effect of orthographic regularity; (3) the nonlexical print-to-sound conversion mechanism is most resistant to the dementing illness and gradually comes to provide the sole basis for oral reading.

The nature of these phonological translation procedures, currently a matter of debate, will be our next topic of discussion.

V. FROM PRINT TO SOUND: WHAT IS THE MECHANISM OF TRANSLATION?

The revised dual access model in Fig. 2 postulates three mechanisms for the translation of print into phonology. Two of these mechanisms utilize lexically stored information: one proceeds via a semantic description of the printed word, while the other maps directly from the orthographic address onto the corresponding phonological unit. Neither of these mechanisms is suitable for the reading of nonwords. On the dual access model, this is accomplished by a translation process separate from the lexicon, which operates on submorphemic units. The standard view is that this process is based on a limited set of grapheme–phoneme correspondence rules (e.g., Coltheart, 1978). Two alternative formulations have recently been proposed which have two characteristics in common: (1) they postulate a larger variety of translation units and (2) they combine word-level and submorphemic print-to-sound mapping processes within a single system.

Shallice and his colleagues (Shallice & Warrington, 1980; Shallice *et al.*, 1983) have proposed a model in which the mapping from print to phonology is based on a stored set of correspondences that vary in size from single letters to whole morphemes. This model, diagrammed in Fig. 3, incorporates an orthographic parsing device, the Visual Word Form System, which registers the occurrence of familiar orthographic units. These units range in size from single letters through submorphemic letter groups to whole morphemes. Output from the Visual Word Form System interfaces directly with the lexicon at the level previously referred to in this article as the orthographic address. Word forms recognized by the lexicon can be interpreted semantically (understood) without phonological translation. The

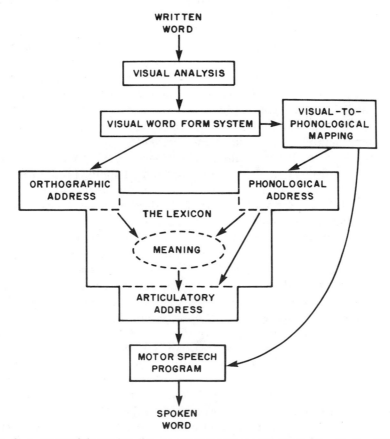

Fig. 3. A model of the reading process adapted, with modifications, from Shallice (1981).

orthographic mechanism is essentially identical to the direct route of the dual access models we considered earlier. Output from the Visual Word Form System also accesses corresponding phonological units, which include phonemes, consonant clusters, and syllable-sized segments as well as morphemes. Thus, for a given letter string, units of various sizes may be activated, a feature that could in some cases give rise to conflicting pronunciations (consider, for example, the possible outcomes for an exception word such as *colonel*). The model handles this problem by means of some additional assumptions: (1) correspondences are weighted in terms of frequency of occurrence, so that, for example, *-ave* is more likely to be realized as /eɪv/ than as /æv/; (2) a mapping which must be assembled from a series of small units will take longer to achieve than a mapping based on a single, larger unit. The effect of (2) is that morphemic realizations will predominate, i.e., *colonel* will, in the normal course of events, be pronounced as /kɜ˞nəl/ rather than as /kalənəl/.

Critical data that favor the multiple-level model over the standard grapheme–phoneme approach come from the study of Shallice *et al.* of the semantic dyslexic, H.T.R. In addition to showing a superiority effect for regular over exception words, H.T.R. was found to be sensitive to the *degree of irregularity* of irregular words. Words containing a single grapheme–phoneme correspondence that was not the most common one for English (e.g., *crow, remind*) were more often read correctly than words containing multiple irregularities (e.g., *colonel, yacht*) or correspondences that occur very rarely (e.g., *gauge, busy*). On the assumption that a patient like H.T.R. is using a nonlexical print-to-sound mapping procedure (an assumption which is required to explain the relative difficulty of irregular words), it follows that the mapping procedure must incorporate a wider range of mapping possibilities than the standard grapheme–phoneme theory would allow; on the standard theory, *crow* is as deviant as *busy,* since neither respects the standard set of correspondence rules. Data from experimental studies of normal subjects also provide support for this notion. Glushko (1979) has shown that the pronunciation of nonwords is affected by the consistency with which segments are pronounced in real word contexts. Thus, it takes longer to pronounce nonwords (e.g., *tave*) generated from "inconsistent" words (like *gave* and *have*) than it does to pronounce nonwords (e.g., *taze*) that are generated from "consistent" words. On the grapheme–phoneme correspondence rule theory, *ave* in a nonword context should always be pronounced /eɪv/. Glushko's results, like the behavior of the patient of Shallice *et al.,* can be taken to indicate that the phonological translation mechanism must incorporate a wide range of mapping possibilities. The earlier characterization of this process in terms of a restricted set of grapheme–phoneme correspondence rules is clearly inadequate.

Shallice *et al.* (1983) account for the reading patterns in semantic dyslexia and in surface dyslexia in terms of two deficits: (1) the inability to read via the direct, or semantic, route, which is common to the two syndromes; and (2) varying degrees of impairment of the phonological route, in which the size, frequency, and/or age of acquisition of the mapping units are the critical parameters. Smaller, high frequency units acquired relatively early are presumably the most robust. The two extremes on a continuum of phonological route impairment are represented by the mildest form of semantic dyslexia, as seen in W.L.P. (Schwartz *et al.*), on the one hand, and by surface dyslexia on the other. W.L.P.'s set of correspondence units appeared to be nearly intact, while only the smallest and most frequent units are available to surface dyslexics. H.T.R., the semantic dyslexic studied by Shallice *et al.* (1983), would seem to represent an intermediate stage of impairment.

A different approach to the mapping problem has been proposed by Marcel (1980; Kay & Marcel, 1981). Like the multiple level process just discussed, Marcel's model allows the print-to-sound conversion procedure to utilize correspondences of various sizes and degree of generality. However, this model differs from both the dual access and multiple-level approaches in locating the mapping process *within* the lexicon. As in the procedure of Shallice *et al.*, the letter string is segmented "in all possible ways," but instead of accessing corresponding phonological segments directly, as in Shallice's model, these orthographic units activate "matching segments in the orthographic lexical input addresses of all words which contain these segments in equivalent positions." (Thus, *tave* would access *wave, save, gave, have,* etc.) "This in turn activates the pronunciations of those segments as they occur in each of these words." Words and nonwords differ only in that for known words, the segmentation equivalent to the whole letter string will already be represented, while for nonwords the phonology will have to be assembled from the activated segments. "For an orthographic segment with more than one pronunciation (e.g., AVE), that pronunciation which occurs in more lexical exemplars will predominate and, in the case of non-words, be produced. In the case of words, the pronunciation produced by the complete letter string will override any competing pronunciations produced by subsequent segments" (Kay & Marcel, 1981, p. 401). Since the pronunciation of nonwords is based explicitly on real-word pronunciations, this has been referred to as a "lexical analogy" model.

Surface dyslexia is viewed as the result of impairment to the store of orthographic addresses, which on the lexical analogy model will have consequences for word and nonword reading as well. One result of the paucity of orthographic addresses is that "letter segmentations early in the string are not overridden by letters later in the string," i.e., that contextual dependencies are ignored in word reading. Thus these patients produce errors such as *niece* → "nice" and *unite* → "*unit.*" A second result is that segments are given their most frequent pronunciations, as in *recent* → /rikənt/ and *disease* → /dIsiz/. While Marcel does not address the pattern of impairment in semantic dyslexia [his papers predate the report of Shallice *et al.* (1983) on H.T.R.], he would presumably view this disorder as a milder form of the deficit in surface dyslexia, i.e., as involving a less radical depletion of the orthographic store. The "level of irregularity" effect found in H.T.R. could easily be accommodated by the lexical analogy model.

This model, like the multiple-level mapping model proposed by Shallice and co-workers, is therefore capable of handling the phenomena in acquired dyslexia that bear most directly on the nature of the nonword print-to-sound translation process. There are, however, some problems with the lexical analogy approach. The model stipulates that orthographic segments within the lexical input addresses activate the corresponding phonological segments within the phonological addresses for those words. It is not made clear, however, how these correspondences are recognized. One possibility is that the reader refers to a stored table of correspondences.[5] But if such a table exists, why not use it *directly* to generate pronunciations for orthographic units, as in the model of Shallice *et al.,* rather than indirectly, by activating and segmenting what in many cases will be scores of orthographic and articulatory addresses? An alternative possibility is that the match is generated by a "maximum overlap" procedure. To pronounce *aze,* for example, the reader would generate the phonology for all the words that contain that sequence of letters and select the phonological segment that they have in common. This procedure not only seems cumbersome, it also flies in the face of some very pervasive tendencies in human cognition (but see Rumelhart & McClelland, 1982, for arguments in favor of such a mechanism). It seems highly unlikely that a normal reader could regularly be exposed to sets of words such as *gaze, maze, daze,* and fail to deduce, and to encode in memory, the relationship between *aze* and /eIz/. If such correspondences are encoded, it seems likely that they would be put to use. Of these two approaches to multilevel mapping, then, the one proposed by Shallice and co-workers seems preferable.

VI. A CRUCIAL ISSUE: THE INTERPRETATION
OF WORD READING IN PHONOLOGICAL DYSLEXIA

A model of the reading process that could account for the patterns of impairment in the dyslexic syndromes discussed in this article would have to incorporate for the following components: (1) a procedure for mapping submorphemic orthographic segments of various sizes onto phonological

---

[5]A similar point has been made by Shallice and McCarthy (1985).

segments; (2) a procedure for mapping written words directly onto their phonological representations; and (3) a procedure for pronouncing written words via their semantic representations. Accepting, provisionally, the need for these three types of operations, it remains to decide how to organize them into a model of the reading system.

The model in Fig. 3, based on proposals by Shallice and co-workers (Shallice & Warrington, 1980; Shallice *et al.,* 1983) that incorporate these three processes, will provide the starting point for our discussion. This model, like the original dual access model in Fig. 1, distinguishes between a semantically mediated reading process on the one hand and a process involving direct mapping between orthographic and phonological units on the other. The direct mapping system incorporates word-level as well as submorphemic correspondences; in other words, procedures (1) and (2) above are part of the same system (the box labeled Visual-to-Phonological mapping in Fig. 3). Morphemic units within this system have none of the properties that accrue from lexical status; for example, it should not be possible to perform lexical decision on the basis of the information available in this system, which simply registers correspondences between orthographic units of various sizes and their possible phonological realizations.

The modified two-route model in Fig. 2 suggests an alternative form of organization. Here all mapping procedures involving known words are contained within the lexicon, whether these procedures are based on semantic description or on word-specific print-to-sound associations. Mapping processes involving submorphemic units comprise a separate, nonlexical system. In the model in Fig. 2, this nonlexical translation process is based on grapheme–phoneme correspondences. In light of the level-of-irregularity effect in semantic dyslexia (Shallice *et al.,* 1983), and of the effect of inconsistency on normal readers' pronunciation of nonwords (Glushko, 1979; Kay & Marcel, 1981), it would seem reasonable to extend the range of correspondences in this nonlexical system to include higher order units; a suggestion of this nature may be found in Morton and Patterson (1985), who designate this as the "Modified Standard Model." This model is, in essential respects, the same as the model in Fig. 2 except that a multilevel mapping process is substituted for the arrow labeled "grapheme–phoneme conversion."[6] The principal difference between the Modified Standard Model and that of Shallice and co-workers does not reside in the nature of the operations that are performed, but in the way they are distributed between lexical and nonlexical processes.

While this may seem a minor point, it is of considerable importance when

---

[6]There are in fact, some differences between Morton and Patterson's (1980a,b) "Standard" model and the one outlined here in Fig. 2. They are not, however, substantial and they need not concern us here.

it comes to interpreting the patterns of reading impairment in acquired dyslexia. The critical syndrome for the purpose of this discussion is phonological dyslexia, where words are read at near-normal levels (with the possible exception of grammatical morphemes) despite the fact that nonword reading is extremely impaired. That this syndrome involves preservation of a lexical reading process and disruption of a nonlexical phonological encoding process seems fairly clear. However, the two models we have just discussed (Shallice's and the Modified Standard Model) would have to account for the preservation of word reading somewhat differently. On the Modified Standard model, the phonological dyslexic should be able to use either the semantically mediated route or word-specific print-to-sound associations for reading words aloud. On Shallice's model, the phonological dyslexic would seem to be limited to the route that requires semantic mediation. Though this model also provides for word-level print-to-sound correspondences, these units belong to the nonlexical multilevel mapping system that is presumably the locus of impairment in phonological dyslexia. There would seem to be no principled argument for the retention of word-level units in this system at the same time that submorphemic units are lost; in fact, Shallice *et al.* (1983) argue that just the opposite (preservation of smaller units) results from impairment to this system in semantic dyslexia.

A choice between these two models might be based, then, on one's judgment of how reasonable it is to account for the oral reading performance of phonological dyslexics in terms of reading by semantic description.[7] Judging from studies which have compared latencies for word-naming (i.e., reading a word aloud) vs picture-naming (e.g., Potter & Faulconer, 1975) one might expect reading via semantic description to be slow relative to reading by direct print-to-sound associations.[8] One might also expect the semantic procedure to be somewhat lacking in precision, particularly in the case of words that have synonyms (consider the difficulty of specifying *car,* as distinct from *automobile,* on the basis of semantic description) or words that the reader does not entirely understand. The production of semantic errors in which the response is synonymous with the target word would certainly be expected. These errors do not occur in phonological dyslexia, unless derivational errors, which generally involve minimal semantic dis-

---

[7]Further specification of what is meant by "semantic description" would entail a lengthy, and probably unproductive, excursion into semantic theory. However, if we take deep dyslexia to exemplify the process of reading by semantic description, it would appear that this process involves the activation of a broad semantic representation of the word.

[8]It might be argued that this latency difference reflects additional time needed to process pictorial stimuli as compared with words. However, if we take speed of performance on a categorization task as an indication of the time it takes to access semantic information from a stimulus array, pictures appear to have an advantage over words (Potter & Faulconer, 1975).

tinctions between target and response (see Appendix), are to be considered semantic errors. These, along with the phonological dyslexics' difficulty in reading function words, might be taken to indicate the limits of reading by semantic description. It could be argued, for example, that functors such as *that* would be difficult to recover on the basis of their semantic descriptions. However, it would still be necessary to account for the fact that these difficulties do not occur in all phonological dyslexics (Funnell, 1983).

The issue cannot be resolved at this writing. However, there is some evidence from studies of normal subjects that would tend to support the notion of distinct systems for word and nonword (or subword) reading. Frederiksen and Kroll (1976) reported that words were read aloud faster in lists that consisted solely of real words than conditions in which words were mixed with nonwords. This effect could be explained, on the Modified Standard Model, by the necessity to distribute resources between the lexical (word-specific print-to-sound associations) route and the nonlexical (segmental translation) process in the mixed-list condition; words would be read more efficiently in the words-only condition, where resources could be devoted to a single process. It is more difficult to account for this result on Shallice's model, in which print-to-sound correspondences for words and nonwords are represented in a single system.

VII. CONCLUDING REMARKS

We have seen, then, that brain lesions can in some cases give rise to deficits that appear to be specific to particular aspects of the reading process. On the assumption that the residual reading capabilities of such patients are based on mechanisms that were spared by the lesion rather than on mechanisms acquired *de novo*,[9] the performance patterns of these acquired dyslexics can help to reveal the componential structure of the reading system.

The fractionation of cognitive systems in cases of brain damage can be particularly useful in delineating components that may be difficult to isolate in studies of normal subjects. But while neuropsychological evidence can help to identify the components of a complex system, it is unlikely to reveal how these components work together. Split brain research is a case in point: these studies have identified operations that only one cerebral hemisphere can perform, but in doing so have opened up difficult and as yet largely

---

[9]See Patterson (1981), Caramazza and Martin (1982), and Saffran (1982) for further discussion.

unresolved questions with respect to the integration of these operations under normal conditions.

A similar point can be made for the study of acquired dyslexia. It is reasonable to conclude, on the basis of current evidence, that the normal reading system includes components for orthographically based word identification and pronunciation and for the conversion of orthography to phonology at submorphemic levels. But evidence as to how output is determined on the basis of the (possibly conflicting) contributions of these components is not available in the pathological data. Nor can one expect that it will be forthcoming. Such evidence is best obtained by manipulating aspects of reading performance in the intact reading systems of normal subjects.

One should be cautious, furthermore, in generalizing from patterns of breakdown that occur in skilled readers to the organization of reading processes during acquisition. Processes that may be capable of operating independently once reading skills have been well established may critically depend on other processes in the course of their development. As Henderson (1984) has pointed out in a recent discussion of the acquired dyslexias in relation to normal reading, there appears to be a relationship, during acquisition, between the growth of sight vocabulary (which presumably reflects the cumulation of orthographic addresses) and the ability to use phonological translation procedures: children who fail to develop adequate phonic skills also have limited sight vocabularies. The ability to derive a phonological representation for the letter string presumably helps the child to associate the orthographic information with the phonological and semantic information about the word that is already stored in his lexicon. If phonological recoding skills are absent, it is necessary to provide the child with an alternative means of identifying the word—a picture, for example. The child would also have no means of checking the adequacy of candidate whole-word translations. The utility of phonic skills in establishing a sight word vocabulary is well illustrated by educational practices in Japan, where entirely different scripts are used for phonic and for whole word reading. While it is possible to transcribe all words using kana, a syllabic script, content words are typically written in kanji, a logographic script originally borrowed from Chinese.[10] Japanese school children are initially instructed in kana, which they learn fairly easily; the acquisition of kanji, which is more difficult, comes later. In texts used to teach kanji, the kana repre-

[10]A discussion of reading disturbances in languages with writing systems that are substantially different from English has not been included in this review. The interested reader should consult papers by Marshall (1976), Sasanuma (1980), and Coltheart (1982).

sentation of the word appears alongside the corresponding kanji symbol (Gibson & Levin, 1975). There is a functional equivalence, insofar as the acquisition of a sight vocabulary is concerned, between providing the Japanese child with an explicit means of deriving a phonological representation for a logogram and teaching phonic skills to a child who is learning to read English.

The acquisition of orthographic addresses, then, is clearly facilitated by the ability to encode words phonologically. Once a sight vocabulary has been acquired, the evidence from phonological dyslexia indicates that the orthographic route is capable of operating autonomously. But it is likely that some interaction occurs even in skilled readers. Thus, for example, phonological information could help to specify the lexical location of a word that is difficult (by virtue of low frequency, perhaps) to identify on the basis of orthography.

Knowledge of how reading breaks down in cases of brain damage is clearly not going to tell us all that we need to know about reading in the normal state. But to the extent that evidence from patterns of reading breakdown can help to isolate and to characterize components of the reading process, studies of acquired dyslexics should prove to be a useful adjunct to experimental investigations of normal readers.

VIII. APPENDIX

This appendix (Table I) provides examples of errors produced in the various forms of acquired dyslexia discussed in this article, along with data on the frequency of occurrence of these error types, where such data are available. Some caveats should be noted in interpreting these data: (1) Classification of errors is often difficult. Thus, for example, derivational errors could be considered visual or semantic errors. (2) The frequency with which error types occur is a function of parameters such as imageability, part of speech, word frequency, regularity, etc. Furthermore, different lists have been used across patient groups, and, except in the case of surface dyslexia, across patients belonging to the same diagnostic category.

ACKNOWLEDGMENTS

I am grateful to Max Coltheart, Nadine Martin, Debra Pate, Tim Shallice, and an anonymous reviewer for helpful comments on the manuscript, and to Floretta McMillon for skilled

TABLE I
Error Types[a]

Syndrome	Semantic	Visual	Visual + semantic	Derivational	Regularization	Phonological translation
Deep dyslexia						
Occurrence	+	+	+	+	−	−
Estimated frequency[b]	.27 (.04–.54)	.37 (.13–.61)	?	.15 (.04–.32)	...	...
Examples[c]	vice → "wicked" zebra → "giraffe" found → "lost" sepulchre → "tomb" robin → "bird"	life → "wife" liver → "live" deep → "deer" charm → "chair" soul → "soup"	sympathy → "orchestra" earl → "deaf" overturn → "music" pivot → "airplane"	fleeing → "flee" beg → "beggar" sits → "sitting" knew → "know" baker → "bakery"		
Surface dyslexia						
Occurrence	−	+	−	−	+	+
Estimated frequency[d]	...	.36 (.21–.59)	...	...	.19 (.12–.23)	.33 (.15–.49)
Examples[e]	...	free → "tree" trout → "touch" sew → "jew" cult → /klæt/	...	...	broad → /brod/ sew → /su/ shove → /ʃov/ break → /brik/	gang → /dʒændz/ hedge → /hɛdzi/ kept → /kipt/ brake → /bræk/
Phonological dyslexia						

Occurrence[f]	−[g]	+	−	−
Examples[f]	...	sip → "sup" violate → "velocity" bibliography → "bi- ography" contemplate → "compensate"	applaud → "applause" disposal → "dispose" fail → "failure" solve → "absolve"	...	...
Semantic dyslexia				
Occurrence[h]	−	?	−	+
Examples[h]	...	...	...	sew → /su/ bury → /bʌri/ gauge → /gɔdʒ/ steak → /stik/	meld → /mɪld/ breed → /breɪd/ vouch → /vɒdʒ/ radish → /reɪdəʃ/

[a] The data summarized here are based on responses to real words only; nonword errors have not been included. Errors that appear to reflect lexicalization have also been omitted, since these errors are likely to involve a visual error, or an error in grapheme–phoneme translation, as well as lexicalization. For example, *incense* → "increase" probably reflects lexicalization of an incorrect translation of the segment *ince* (→ /Ink/ instead of /Ins/).

[b] These figures are excerpted from Table 5.3 in Shallice and Warrington (1980), which summarizes error frequency data from seven deep dyslexics. The occurrence of each error type is reported as a proportion of the total number of errors of commission produced by the patients; omissions did not enter into the computation. Different word lists were used across patients.

[c] These examples were taken from Table 2.6 in Coltheart (1980a), in which errors from 15 deep dyslexics are represented.

[d] These data are taken from Coltheart et al. (1985), who summarize evidence from five cases of acquired surface dyslexia.

[e] These examples are taken from Coltheart et al. (1985) and from Saffran (1985).

[f] Frequency data are not yet available for this group of patients.

[g] While semantic errors do not occur in content word reading, within-category substitutions do occur in reading functors (e.g., *their* → "they"; *this* → "these"; *which* → "what"). In most cases, these could also be classified as "visual" errors. See Patterson (1982) for further examples.

[h] As yet, only one case has been reported in detail (Shallice et al., 1983). These data are from that study.

255

and patient secretarial assistance. Preparation of this manuscript was aided by Grant NS18429–01 from NINCDS.

REFERENCES

Allport, D. A., & Funnell, E. Components of the mental lexicon. *Philosophical Transactions of the Royal Society of London, Series B* 1981, **295**, 397–410.

Beauvois, M. F., & Desrouesne, J. Phonological alexia: Three dissociations. *Journal of Neurology, Neurosurgery and Psychiatry,* 1979, **43**, 1115–1124.

Benson, D. F. Alexia and the neuroanatomical basis of reading. in F. Pirozzolo & B. Whitrock, (Eds.), *Neuropsychological and cognitive processes in reading.* New York: Academic Press, 1981.

Caramazza, A., & Martin, R. C. Theoretical and methodological issues in the study of aphasia. In J. B. Hellige (Ed.), *Cerebral hemisphere asymmetry.* New York: Praeger, 1982.

Coltheart, M. Lexical access in simple reading tasks. In G. Underwood (Ed.), *Strategies of information processing.* New York: Academic Press, 1978.

Coltheart, M. Deep dyslexia: A review of the syndrome. In M. Coltheart, K. Patterson, & J. Marshall (Eds.), *Deep dyslexia.* London: Routledge & Kegan Paul, 1980. (a)

Coltheart, M. Deep dyslexia: A right-hemisphere hypothesis. In M. Coltheart, K. Patterson, & J. Marshall (Eds.), *Deep dyslexia.* London: Routledge and Kegan Paul, 1980. (b)

Coltheart, M. Reading, phonological reading, and deep dyslexia. In M. Coltheart, K. Patterson, & J. Marshall (Eds.), *Deep dyslexia.* London: Routledge & Kegan Paul, 1980. (c)

Coltheart, M. Disorders of reading and their implications for models of normal reading. *Visible Language,* 1981, **15**, 245–286.

Coltheart, M. The psycholinguistic analysis of acquired dyslexias: Some illustrations. *Philosophical Transactions of the Royal Society of London Series B* 1982, 151–164.

Coltheart, M., Masterson, J., & Byng, S. Types of error in surface dyslexic reading. In K. Patterson, J. Marshall, and M. Coltheart (Eds.), *Surface Dyslexia.* London: Erlbaum, 1985.

Coltheart, M., Masterson, J., Byng, S., Prior, M., & Riddoch, J. Surface dyslexia. *Quarterly Journal of Experimental Psychology,* 1983, **35A**, 469–496.

Colthert, M., Patterson, K. E., & Marshall, J. C. (Eds.), *Deep dyslexia.* London: Routledge & Kegan Paul, 1980.

Desrouesne, J., & Beauvois, M. F. Phonological processing in reading: Data from alexia. *Journal of Neurology, Neurosurgery and Psychiatry,* 1979, **42**, 1125–1132.

Frederiksen, J. R., & Kroll, J. F. Spelling and sound: Approaches to the internal lexicon. *Journal of Experimental Psychology: Human Perception and Performance,* 1976, **2**, 361–379.

Friedman, R. B., & Perlman, M. B. On the underlying causes of semantic paralexias in a patient with deep dyslexia. *Neuropsychologia,* 1982, **20**, 559–568.

Funnell, E. Phonological processes in reading: New evidence from acquired dyslexia. *British Journal of Psychology,* 1983, **74**, 159–180.

Gibson, E., & Levin, H. *The psychology of reading.* Cambridge Massachusetts: MIT Press, 1975.

Glushko, R. J. The organization and activation of orthographic knowledge in reading aloud. *Journal of Experimental Psychology: Human Perception and Performance,* 1979, **5**, 674–691.

Hecaen, H., & Kremin, H. Neurolinguistic research on reading disorders resulting from left hemisphere lesions: Aphasic and 'pure' alexia. In H. Whitaker & H. A. Whitaker (Eds.), *Studies in neurolinguistics* (Vol. 2). New York: Academic Press, 1976.

Henderson, L. Information processing approaches to acquired dyslexia. A critical notice of M. Coltheart, K. Patterson and J. Marshall (Eds.) *Deep Dyslexia. Quarterly Journal of Experimental Psychology,* 1981, **33A**, 507–522.

Henderson, L. Models of pronunciation assembly in normal reading. In K. Patterson, J. Marshall, and M. Coltheart (Eds.), *Surface Dyslexia.* London: Erlbaum, 1985.

Holmes, J. M. "Regression" and reading breakdown. In A. Caramazza & E. B. Zurif (Eds.), *Language acquisition and language breakdown: Parallels and divergencies.* Baltimore: John Hopkins Press, 1978.

Kay, J., & Marcel, A. One process, not two, in reading aloud: Lexical analogies do the work of non-lexical rules. *Quarterly Journal of Experimental Psychology,* 1981, **33A**, 397–413.

McClelland, J. Letter and configuration information in word identification. *Journal of Verbal Learning and Verbal Behavior,* 1977, **16**, 137–150.

Marcel, A. J. Surface dyslexia and beginning reading: A revised hypothesis of the pronunciation of print and its impairments. In M. Coltheart, K. Patterson, & J. Marshall. (Eds.), *Deep dyslexia.* London: Routledge & Kegan Paul, 1980.

Marshall, J. C. Neuropsychological aspects of orthographic representation. In R. J. Wales & E. Walker (Eds.), *New approaches to language mechanisms.* Amsterdam: North Holland Publ., 1976.

Marshall, J. C., & Newcombe, F. Patterns of paralexia: A psycholinguistic approach. *Journal of Psycholinguistic Research,* 1973, **2**, 175–199.

Morton, J., & Patterson, K. E. A new attempt at an interpretation, or, an attempt at a new interpretation. In M. Coltheart, K.E. Patterson, & J. C. Marshall (Eds.), *Deep dyslexia.* London: Routledge & Kegan Paul, 1980. (a)

Morton, J., & Patterson, K. "Little Words-No!." In M. Coltheart, K. E. Patterson, & J. C. Marshall (Eds.), *Deep dyslexia.* London: Routledge & Kegan Paul, 1980. (b)

Morton, J., & Patterson, K. An attempt at an old interpretation. In K. Patterson, J. Marshall, and M. Coltheart (Eds.), *Surface Dyslexia.* London: Erlbaum, 1985.

Nolan, K. A., & Caramazza, A. Modality-independent impairments in word processing in a deep dyslexic patient. *Brain and Language,* 1982, **16**, 237–264.

Patterson, K. Errors of meaning and the meaning of errors. *Quarterly Journal of Experimental Psychology,* 1978, **30**, 587–607.

Patterson, K. E. What is right with "deep" dyslexic patients? *Brain and Language,* 1979, **8**, 111–129.

Patterson, K. E. Derivational errors. In M. Coltheart, K. Patterson, & J. Marshall (Eds.), *Deep dyslexia.* London: Routledge & Kegan Paul, 1980.

Patterson, K. E. Neuropsychological approaches to the study of reading. *British Journal of Psychology,* 1981, **72**, 151–174.

Patterson, K. E. The relation between reading and phonological coding: Further neuropsychological observations. In A. W. Ellis (Ed.), *Normality and pathology in cognitive function.* New York: Academic Press, 1982.

Patterson, K. E., & Marcel, A. J. Aphasia, dyslexia and the phonological coding of written words. *Quarterly Journal of Experimental Psychology,* 1977, **29**, 307–318.

Patterson, K., Marshall, J., and Coltheart, M. (Eds.) *Surface Dyslexia.* London: Erlbaum, 1985.

Potter, M. C., & Faulconer, B. A. Time to understand pictures and words. *Nature (London),* 1975, **253**, 437–438.

Rubenstein, H., Lewis, S. S., & Rubenstein, M. A. Evidence for phonemic recoding in visual word recognition. *Journal of Verbal Learning and Verbal Behavior,* 1971, **10**, 645–657.

Rumelhart, D. E., & McClelland, J. L. An interactive activation model of context effects in letter perception: Part 2. The contextual enhancement effect and some tests and extensions of the model. *Psychological Review,* 1982, **89**, 60–94.

Saffran, E. M. Reading in deep dyslexia is not ideographic. *Neuropsychologia,* 1980, **18**, 219–223.

Saffran, E. M. Neuropsychological approaches to the study of language. *British Journal of Psychology,* 1982, **73**, 317–337.

Saffran, E. M. Does lexicalization affect reading performance in surface dyslexia? In K. Patterson, J. Marshall, and M. Coltheart (Eds.), *Surface Dyslexia.* London: Erlbaum, 1985.

Saffran, E. M., Bogyo, L. C., Schwartz, M. F., and Marin, O. S. M. Does deep dyslexia reflect right hemisphere reading? In M. Coltheart, K. E. Patterson, & J. C. Marshall (Eds.), *Deep dyslexia.* London: Routledge & Kegan Paul, 1980.

Saffran, E. M., & Marin, O. S. M. Reading without phonology: Evidence from aphasia. *Quarterly Journal of Experimental Psychology,* 1977, **29**, 515–525.

Sasanuma, S. Acquired dyslexia in Japanese: Clinical features and underlying mechanisms. In M. Coltheart, K. Patterson, & J. Marshall (Eds.), *Deep dyslexia.* London: Routledge & Kegan Paul, 1980.

Schwartz, M. F., Marin, D. S. M., & Saffran, E. M. Dissociations of language function in dementia: A case study. *Brain and Language,* 1979, **7**, 277–306.

Schwartz, M. F., Saffran, E. M., & Marin, O. S. M. Fractionating the reading process in dementia: Evidence for word-specific print-to-sound associations. In M. Coltheart, K. Patterson, & J. C. Marshall (Eds.), *Deep dyslexia.* London: Routledge & Kegan Paul, 1980.

Shallice, T. Case study approach in neuropsychological research. *Journal of Clinical Neuropsychology,* 1979, **1**, 1–29.

Shallice, T. Neurological impairment of cognitive processes. *British Medical Bulletin,* 1981, **37**, 187–192.

Shallice, T., & Coughlan, A. K. Modality specific word comprehension deficits in deep dyslexia. *Journal of Neurology, Neurosurgery and Psychiatry,* 1980, **43**, 866–872.

Shallice, T., & McCarthy, R. The operation of the phonological route: Evidence from 'phonologic reading' in acquired dyslexic patients. In K. Patterson, J. Marshall, and M. Coltheart (Eds.), *Surface Dyslexia.* London: Erlbaum, 1985.

Shallice, T., & Warrington, E. K. Single and multiple component central dyslexic syndromes. In M. Coltheart, K. E. Patterson, & J. C. Marshall (Eds.), *Deep dyslexia.* London: Routledge & Kegan Paul, 1980.

Shallice, T., Warrington, E. K., & McCarthy, R. Reading without semantics. *Quarterly Journal of Experimental Psychology,* 1983, **35A**, 111–138.

Temple, C. M. Surface dyslexia and surface dysgraphia in children and adults: A comparison of case studies and a classificatory framework. In M. K. Patterson, J. Marshall, and M. Coltheart (Eds.), *Surface Dyslexia.* London: Erlbaum, 1985.

Warrington, E. K. The selective impairment of semantic memory. *Quarterly Journal of Experimental Psychology,* 1975, **27**, 635–657.

Zaidel, E. Lexical organization in the right hemisphere. In P. Buser & A. Rougeul-Buser (Eds.), *Cerebral correlates of conscious experience.* Amsterdam: Elsevier, 1978.

Zaidel, E., & Peters, A. M. Phonological encoding and ideographic reading by the disconnected right hemisphere: Two case studies. *Brain and Language,* 1981, **14**, 205–234.

INDEX

A

Abstractness, 235, 238, 239
Age differences, 30–35, 39–44
AID analysis, 72–75
Alexia, 238
Ambiguity, 156, 161
Attention, 156, 169–170
Automatization, 98, 111–112, 149–172
  development of, 115–138
  and text understanding, 113–138

B

Broca's aphasia, 238

C

Calling patterns, 148–149, 155
Case alternation, 145–146, 163
Chinese readers, 24–25, 28
CLC, see Closed-loop control
Closed-loop control (CLC), 148–149
Code-centered (phonics) approaches, 109–110
Coding skills, 34–35, 39–42
Color naming, 150–152
Comprehension
  efficiency, 194–196, 207–209
  rate limitations, 198–200
  of sentences, 168–169
Conceptual selectivity, 203–207, 220–221
Conceptually driven processes, 184–186, 224
Condition-action rules, 149, 156
Context, 145, 152, 157, 163, 185
Contextual predictors, 141

D

Data driven processes, 184–186, 224
Decision making, 149
Derivational errors, 235

Dyslexia

Dyslexia, 231–258
  acquired, 231–258
  audio-visual, 90
  auditive, 90
  deep, 232–240
  developmental, 231, 244
  phonological, 237–240, 253
  vs poor readers, 47–49
  semantic, 240–244
  subtypes, 90, 100–101
  surface, 232–237, 240–244, 247
  visual, 90

E

Effective reading rate, 221
Episodic memory, 141
Exception words, 19–23
  difficult, 21–23
  easy, 19–21
Expectancy, 161–163
Eye movement
  and coding skills, 38–42
  and comprehension, 220–224
  limitations, 198
  nonfixated words, 174–175
  in nonreading task, 45–46
  patterns, 187, 199, 219–224
  plodder-explorer dimension, 6, 36–39
  reading style, 35–46
  during speed reading, 219
  visual-spatial subtype, 45–46

F

Facilitation, 153–154, 162
Feature extraction, 144
Feedback, 148
Flexibility, 197–198
FRUMP, 209–210, 215